AN INTRODUCTION
TO SOME ETHICAL PROBLEMS
OF MODERN AMERICAN ADVERTISING

STUDIA SOCIALIA

Series published by the Institute of Social Sciences
of the Gregorian University

1. LEONI, ALDO: *Sociologia e Geografia religiosa di una Diocesi.*
(out of print)

2. BELTRÃO, PEDRO, S.J.: *Vers une politique de bien-être familial*
1957.

3. PELLEGRINI, VINCENTE S.J.: *Algunos Aspectos del Mercado Co-
mun Europeo,* 1960.

4. CARRIER, HERVÉ S.J.: *Psycho-Sociologie de l'appartenance re-
ligieuse* 1960.

5. GREMILLION, JOSEPH B.: *The Catholic Movement of Employers
and Managers,* 1961.

6. GARRET, THOMAS M. S.J.: *An Introduction to some Ethical Problems of Modern American Advertising,* 1961.

Thomas M. GARRETT, S. J.

Instructor in Philosophy at The University of Scranton

AN INTRODUCTION
TO SOME ETHICAL PROBLEMS
OF MODERN AMERICAN ADVERTISING

THE GREGORIAN UNIVERSITY PRESS

ROME

1961

IMPRIMI POTEST

Romae, die 4 aprilis 1961.

R. P. Paulus Muñoz Vega, S. I.
Rector Universitatis

IMPRIMATUR

E Vicariatu Urbis, die 7 aprilis 1961.

† Aloysius *Card. Provicarius*

TYPIS PONTIFICIAE UNIVERSITATIS GREGORIANAE - ROMAE

ACKNOWLEDGEMENTS

The author wishes to acknowledge his debt to all those whose interest and advice have in one way or another contributed to the present study. Particular thanks are due to the Reverend Philip Land, S. J. of the Pontifical Gregorian University who gave long hours to a detailed criticism of the entire study. Without his help this work would not have been possible. The author is also indebted to the Reverend Edward Jacklin of Georgetown University and to Prof. E. Bongras of the University of Fribourg, (Switzerland), who read and criticized substantial portions of the preliminary drafts of this study. Though the final formulations are the responsibility of the author, the help of these friendly critics was invaluable.

The Stiftung « Im Grüene » (Zuerich-Rüschlicon) was kind enough to make a small grant to cover the expenses of preparing the manuscript for publication. My thanks, then, go to its founder, Herr G. Duttweiler, and to its Secretary, Herr H. Böckli.

Finally, the author wishes to thank all those members of the advertising profession both in Europe and the United States who supplied him with every possible facility during the course of the research. It is hoped that this study will aid them in answering at least a few of the difficult ethical problems which they must solve in the course of their work.

The publishers have been most generous in granting special permission to use the numerous citations scattered throughout this work. Though I have made the usual acknowledgements in the appropriate places, special note should be taken of the following. The Printers' Ink Publishing Company now controls the copyright of the various articles which we have cited from *Tide*. Permission to quote *The Challenge to America: Its Economic and Social Aspects*, copyrighted by Rockefeller Brothers Fund, Inc. has been granted by Doubleday and Company. Holt, Rinehart and Winston now hold the copyright to *Public Opinion and Propaganda*, edited by Daniel Katz *et al.* which was originally published by the Dryden Press. Permission to use the booklet *Facts You Should Know About Advertising*, has been granted by the Better Business Bureau of Metropolitan Boston. Though we have cited from the Anchor Book Edition of *The Organization Man* by William H. Whyte, Jr. the quotations are by permission of Simon and Schuster, Inc., New York the original publishers in 1956 on behalf of the author who holds the copyright. Alderson Associates, marketing and management counsels of Philadelphia have been kind enough to allow us to use material from their private news letter, *Cost and Profit Outlook*. All other citations are by special permission of the publishers mentioned in the footnotes. To them we extend our thanks.

TABLE OF CONTENTS

CHAPTER I

INTRODUCTION

AIM OF THE THESIS

The present thesis is intended to be a modest introduction to selected ethical problems of modern American
advertising, and of consumer advertising in particular [1]. It
is in no sense either a complete or a definitive treatment
of the ethics of advertising. In the first place, the ethical
problems of advertising are at once too numerous and too
complex to be treated in a single work. In the second place,
the subject is, as we shall see, too undeveloped to permit
of anything but a preliminary attempt to clarify problems
and to develop some of the principles necessary for their
solution.   Consequently, this thesis is largely exploratory,
that is, an attempt to stake out certain areas and to locate
them with reference to the norms of sound ethics.

We have chosen to study the ethical problems of American advertising for three reasons. First, advertising has
had its greatest development in that country. Secondly, the
literature bearing on the ethical and social implications of

---

[1] Though there is no agreement about the definition of advertising,
the following is accurate enough for the purposes of this study. « Advertising includes those activities by which visual or oral messages are addressed to the public for the purposes of informing them and influencing
them either to buy merchandise or services or to act or to be inclined
favorably towards ideas, institutions or persons featured ». Neil H. Borden,
The Economic Effects of Advertising, (Chicago: Irwin, 1942), p. 16.

The first half of the above definition, (up to and including the words
« or services ») is a definition of consumer advertising.

For other definitions of advertising *cf.* Mark Abrams, « The Function
of Advertising in the Economy », *Advertising: A Financial Times Survey*,
April, 1957, p. 5; Nicolas Kaldor and Rodney Silverman, *A Statistical
Analysis of Advertising and the Revenue of the Press*, (Cambridge, England:
University Press, 1948), p. 2; Bernard de Plas and Henri Verdier, *La Pu-
blicité*, (Paris: Presses Universitaires de France, 1957), p. 5.

1

advertising, though not particularly abundant, gives more attention to the American problems than to those of other nations. Thirdly, the present work is intended to be a guide for those members of the American advertising profession who encouraged this undertaking.

Though we have considered the ethical problem of advertising in a concrete situation, the principles developed will, it is believed, be generally useful. Furthermore, and despite the limitations of this study, it is hoped that the general approach will be a useful guide to future students of the questions we have treated.

NEED FOR AN ETHICAL STUDY OF ADVERTISING

The need for even an introductory study of the ethical problem of advertising in the United States rests on two facts: the economic and social importance of advertising in that country and a general lack of systematic efforts to evaluate advertising in the light of ethical principles. A few rather brief remarks will serve to demonstrate the validity of these two contentions.

Three factors, among others, help to explain the importance of advertising in America: the size of the expenditure involved; the results which some attribute to it; first in the economic and, then, in the social sphere. Though, as we shall see, the results of advertising have been somewhat exaggerated, these alleged effects do call for study.

In 1957 American businessmen spent $ 10.4 billion on advertising[2]. A sum this large is equal to the national budget of some smaller countries, and represented 2.7% of American personal consumption expenditures in that year[3]. Though this percentage varies from year to year, it has over the past twenty years remained fairly constant[4]. Present indications, however, are that it will rise and assu-

---

[2] *Printers' Ink*, January 31, 1958.

[3] cf. *The Economic Report of the President*, January, 1958, (Washington, D. C.: The Government Printing Office), p. 117.

[4] Stanley Resor, « We Can Sell $ 600 Billion of Output », *U. S. News and World Report*, January 4, 1957, p. 72.

me even a greater importance [5]. In any event, advertising expenditures represent a significant part of the national income.

Statistics, however, give no real idea of the importance of advertising in the United States. The real meaning is to be found rather in the causes of its growth, the uses to which it is put and in the wonderful results it is supposed to produce. The following citation summarizes many of these points.

> The unique importance and complexity of American advertising plainly stem from a large number of factors which, though not individually restricted to the United States, have been combined possibly more favorably in the United States than elsewhere. The industrialization which accompanied and followed the Civil War required manufacturers to seek ever larger markets in which to dispose of their expanding production, and nationwide advertising proved to be an unusually efficient technique in gaining such markets. The successful absorption of throngs of immigrant peoples soon swelled the demand for goods, while advertising soon became cheaper than other means of selling in an economy where labor costs remained high and distances great. Simultaneously mass media also expanded on a scale made possible by the cheapness of newsprint, by new techniques in periodical publishing, by a mobile population, and by the generally powerful political influence of publishers who were able to obtain legislation favorable to wide circulation of periodicals at low cost to themselves [6].

From the above citation it is clear that advertising was an important factor in an expanding economy based on mass production for mass markets. In a society characterized by rapid economic expansion and social change, and in which consumption was a crucial factor, selling and advertising became important, even essential tools [7]. Where other institutions in society worked against change in many cases, advertising became a means of changing consumption

---

[5] *loc. cit.*

[6] Otis Pease, *The Responsibilities of American Advertising*, (New Haven, Connecticut: Yale U. Press, 1958), p. 3.

[7] Ralph M. Hower, *The History of an Advertising Agency*, (revised edition, Cambridge, Mass.: Harvard U. Press, 1949), p. 126.

habits rapidly in accord with the needs of the producer who wanted to stabilize his demand [8].

While the producer may have adopted advertising in an attempt to control consumption, it must be admitted that society itself was in search of a guide for consumption since in the midst of rapid change there is always a certain confusion in what concerns dress, taste and the use of free time [9]. One writer puts it as follows.

> Consumer advertising is the first rough effort of a society becoming prosperous to teach itself the use of the relatively great wealth of new resources, new techniques and a reorganized production method. Whatever eventually becomes of advertising, society must provide some device for this task [10].

To some extent, however, advertising was more than a tutor in consumption. It was in the eyes of some professionals a guide to the good life, a crusader « for the liberation of a middle-class people from the tyranny of Puritanism, parsimoniousness, and material asceticism » [11]. From this point of view, advertising obviously has an importance far greater than that of mere salesmanship. It is, in a certain sense, a moral guide.

In contemporary American society, then, advertising is not merely another big business, but a part of the economic machinery which has repercussions on the life of society and of the individual. It is not merely a tutor in consumption, but to a certain extent, a tutor in the « good life » [12]. The full extent of the effects attributed to advertising will be considered more carefully in the following chapter. Here, it is enough to observe that we are dealing with an important economic and social phenomenon.

Despite the importance attributed to advertising, and despite the controversy which has raged about its utility

---

[8] Daniel Bell. « La publicité, son impact sur la société », *Rond Point de la Publicité dans le Monde,* 2 (1958), mars, no. 9, p. 35, and Hower, *loc. cit.*

[9] Bell, *loc. cit.*

[10] Leverett S. Lyon, « Advertising », in *Encyclopedia of the Social Sciences,* ed., Edwin R. A. Seligman, (N. Y.: Macmillan, 1930), Vol. I, p. 470.

[11] Pease, *op. cit.,* p. 41.

[12] Pease, *op. cit.,* pp. 20ff.

and legitimacy, its ethical aspects have not been carefully studied. To the best of this author's knowledge there is no study of any scope written by a professional moralist or ethician. There are, of course, occasional articles and passing remarks in books on social ethics, but there has been no systematic attempt on the part of an ethician to explore the ethical, social and economic implications of modern advertising.

Although the writings of professional moralists and ethicians have given only passing attention to the problems of advertising, sociologists, economists, historians and members of the advertising profession have produced some work on the subject. Again, however, most of the work is found in occasional remarks or in short articles many of which are only indirectly concerned with ethical considerations. Four works, however, must be singled out not only because they represent attempts at a systematic study of pertinent aspects of advertising, but also because their limitations explain the need for the present study.

Borden's work, *The Economic Effects of Advertising,* is the only extensive factual study of the economic significance of advertising. Invaluable as a source book, it suffers from two limitations from the ethician's point of view [13]. First, it explicitly prescinds from questions of ideology and of basic ethical issues [14]. Secondly, its explicit treatment of the so-called, « Ethical Aspects of Advertising », is confined to an attempt to find out if advertisers have transgressed the moral sentiments of the public and to trace the growth of those ethical attitudes which have determined the codes of business ethics [15].

In addition, the Borden study, though scholarly, accepts too readily the beneficent effects of advertising on economic growth as an excuse for certain losses resulting from

---

[13] Though the reviews of this book were in general laudatory, the critics have also picked out certain defects in its economic treatment. *cf.* C. Chisholm, *Economic Function of Advertising,* (London: Business Publications, 1943), 20 p.

[14] Borden, *op. cit.,* pp. 1-8.

[15] *ibid.,* Part VII.

less desirable aspects of advertising [16]. Since this point will be the object of a large part of the present study, its development is postponed to the chapters on the psychological and economic assumptions of advertising.

If Borden's work is the only extensive factual treatment of the economics of advertising, F.P. Bishop's *The Ethics of Advertising*, is the only book of any sort devoted exclusively to the ethical problem [17]. This is, on the whole, an excellent book filled with good sense and balanced judgments based on a personal knowledge of advertising, publishing and government [18]. Mr. Bishop, however, is not an ethician and so avoids coming to grips with what, we may call, the ultimates. Thus, in writing of the ends of life he betrays a relativistic bias,

> They (the ends of life) are for each individual to decide for himself with the aid of such light as he can gain, not from « sales talk », but from the great systems of religion and ethical philosophy. From Buddhism, with its doctrine of emancipation from desire, to the more extreme forms of Hedonism, which teach that pleasure is the sole end of life, these systems offer men a wide choice of the ideals of the « good life » at which to aim [19].

Again in writing of the morality of consumption, he seems to embrace a sort of subjective norm of morality.

> The consumer decides, for while free competition remains there is no appeal from his decision. Nor is there any standard by which his decisions can be judged to be wrong; for no man, be he never so wise, can judge the satisfactions of another [20].

This failure to take a stand on basic moral issues needs to be remedied, and the present study attempts to give at

---

[16] *ibid.*, p. XXV.

[17] (London: Robert Hale, 1949).

[18] Mr. Bishop at present a member of parliament was formerly editor of *The Times* (London) and for many years active in advertising.

[19] Bishop, *op. cit.*, p. 34. In all fairness it must be admitted that Mr. Bishop is arguing principally against the right of the state to decide what the ends of life shall be. He himself informed me in an interview that he considers his work in need of revision since at the time of its composition he had been too preoccupied with the menace of certain extreme socialist elements in England.

[20] *op. cit.*, p. 49.

least the beginnings of a fundamental ethic of advertising. In this respect it constitutes an advance on Bishop's work.

The third book which is deserving of mention is the work of a historian. Though Pease's *The Responsibilities of American Advertising* is not a work of ethics nor of political economy, it provides a useful study of the background and the disputes over the ethics of advertising [21]. For the ethician it is a source book of problems and a key to the complexity of these problems in a given society.

In the last place must be mentioned the excellent, but little known *Werbung und Wohlstand* by Dr. Kurt Steuber [22]. This book is a penetrating analysis of the relation between advertising and the public weal. In many ways our own study is a supplement to Steuber. There are, however, three important differences. First, *Werbung und Wohlstand* is confined largely to a consideration of the economic aspect of advertising while the present work seeks to deepen the understanding of the ethical issues involved [23]. Secondly, where Steuber devoted only about five pages to advertising as a factor in economic growth, we have made this the key question in our study [24]. Thirdly, *Werbung und Wohlstand* uses a generalized analytic approach, whereas this thesis considers a concrete economy at a given instant. The two works, however, complement each other and taken together should provide a starting point for more profound studies.

These few pages on the importance of advertising and on the paucity and limitation of previous studies offer proof that a study of the ethical problems of advertising is a necessity.

---

[21] This book was written under the direction of Prof. David Potter whose work *People of Plenty* includes a chapter on advertising as an institution of abundance. The two works taken together provide an excellent introduction to the significance of advertising as a social phenomenon.

[22] Kurt Steuber, *Werbung und Wohlstand: Die volkswirtschaftliche Untersuchung der Werbung*, (Zürich: Polygraphischer Verlag, 1958).

[23] Steuber has one short chapter on the ethical aspect. *cf. ibid.*, pp. 201-208.

[24] *ibid.*, pp. 121-125.

METHOD

The method followed in this thesis is based on two
assumptions. First it is important to know the *intentions*
of advertisers as well as the *effects* of advertising. Second,
the effects of advertising should not be assumed as given,
but must be carefully investigated in order to establish the
real reasonsibility of advertisers and their agents[25].

In view of these assumptions, Chapters II and III have
been devoted to a study of the intentions of advertisers
and their agents. Chapter II gives a general view of these
intentions and by comparing them with the charges of
the critics of advertising attempts to set up the state of the
question. Chapter III then takes a particular proposal of the
advertising profession and presents it in greater detail
with an eye to a study of the morality of the intentions
and of the effects of such a proposal. Chapters IV and V,
then study the ethical assumptions and principles which
have bearing on the liceity and utility of the proposal.
Chapters VI and VII in their turn consider some of the
basic factual issues which must be settled before a judgment can be passed· Chapter VIII concludes with a summary and with a statement of some tasks which still face
the ethician before he can give a final and definitive evaluation of the intentions of the advertiser and the effects
of advertising.

---

[25] Special ethics and in particular social ethics are not pure ontological sciences, and the content of the commands they give can be determined only after both a factual and ontological analysis. *cf.* Arthur-Fridolin Utz, *Sozial Ethik, I. Teil: Die Prinzipien der Gesellschaftslehre,*
(Heidelberg: F. H. Kerle, 1958), p. 71. In achieving this factual analysis
the ethician and social philosopher require the aid of the economist and
the sociologist. *cf.* Oswald von Nell-Breuning, *Wirtschaft und Gesellschaft,
I. Grundfragen,* (Freiburg im Breisgau: Herder, 1956), p. 203. The necessity
of such factual investigation complicates the task of the social ethician,
but without it, it is impossible to discover what order is possible and
obligatory. *cf.* Johannes Messner, *Das Naturrecht,* (3rd ed. Innsbruck):
Tyrolia Verlag, 1958), p. 1020.

Chapter II

CLAIMS AND COUNTERCLAIMS

Introduction and Definitions

The present chapter has a twofold purpose. Its first part contains a general presentation of the intentions of advertisers and their agents as these are contained in their claims as to what benefits they bestow on business, the individual, the economy and society as a whole. In the second place we will present the opposing claims of the critics of advertising. The confrontation of these two sets of opinions will enable us to attain an overall view of the ethical problem of advertising and to situate the aspect which has been chosen for further investigation.

Before proceeding to outline the claims and the counterclaims, a few remarks will help to orientate the reader. The claims of the advertising profession are to a large extent defensive, that is to say, answers to the various charges which have been made against advertising. They are further based on literature which is part of a propaganda campaign in favour of advertising [1]. Consequently, they are, generally speaking, intended *as a defense of all advertising except that part which is false, misleading or offensive to public decency* [2]. In the concrete, this means that the arguments of the advertising profession seek to justify not only consumer advertising, but institutional advertising as well; and even more important, persuasive, suggestive or competitive advertising in addition to informative advertising.

---

[1] For an analysis of the techniques of this propaganda, *cf.* Leonard I. Pearlin and Morris Rosenberg, « Propaganda Techniques in Institutional Advertising », in Daniel Katz, *Public Opinion and Propaganda*, (N. Y.: Dryden, 1954), pp. 478-490.

[2] *cf.* any of the codes listed in the bibliography and especially the papers from the conventions of the Association of American Advertising Agencies.

The critics, on the other hand, admit the utility of a certain amount of informative advertising, and attack what is variously called persuasive, suggestive or competitive advertising[3]. Since these terms will appear frequently in the present study, a few definitions will be useful. These definitions, however, must be prefaced with two remarks. First, *an actual advertisement* may at one and the same time have elements proper to more than one definition. Thus, as Kaldor has noted, all advertising is informative in content and persuasive in intent[4]. Second, there being no accepted definitions, our formulations are intended only to indicate the general ideas more or less common to the critics[5].

Informative advertising is that advertising which seeks to inform the consumer of the *objective* qualities of a product; of its specifications, functions, price and availability. This advertising is rational, directed to the intellect and allows the consumer to make a conscious choice[6].

Persuasive advertising does not merely inform the consumer about the objective qualities of a product, but aims at creating a need for the product. As Steuber puts it, where informative advertising shows the consumer how he may satisfy a need, persuasive advertising seeks to create the need itself[7]. This advertising tends to be emotional, irrational and is directed to the feelings and even to the unconscious[8].

Competitive advertising includes persuasive advertising and such informative advertising as exceeds the consumer's need for information[9]. Often, the term is used as a

---

[3] E. A. Lever, *Advertising and Economic Theory*, (London: Oxford U. Press, 1947), p. 47. The author also notes that it is sometimes called manipulative or combative advertising.

[4] Nicolas Kaldor, « The Economic Aspects of Advertising », *Review of Economic Studies*, 18 (1950-51), p. 4.

[5] For other definitions *cf.* Dorothea Braithwaite, « The Economic Effects of Advertisement », *Economic Journal*, 38 (1928), p. 17 and Edward H. Chamberlin, *The Theory of Monopolistic Competition*, (6th ed. Cambridge, Mass.: Harvard U. Press, 1948), p. 120 and Kurt Steuber, *Werbung und Wohlstand*, (Zürich: Polygraphischer Verlag, 1958) pp. 17 and 75 ff.

[6] Steuber, *op. cit.*, p. 16.

[7] *loc. cit.*

[8] *loc. cit.* In chapter IV we shall draw an important distinction between persuasive activity in general and irrational advertising.

[9] *ibid.*, pp. 209-210. For other opinions *cf.* Kaldor, *op. cit.* p. 22 and Chamberlin, *op. cit.*, pp. 120 ff.

catch-all for advertising which does not seek to serve the consumer, but merely to protect or better the competitive position of the advertiser [10].

THE CASE IN FAVOR OF ADVERTISING

The advertising profession claims to benefit not only individual companies, but the consumer, the economy as a whole, and the society of which this economy is a part. Though advertising is essentially a tool used by the businessman, its effects are such that the whole society benefits so that advertising has a valid social justification.

The services of advertising to the individual company are manifold. First and most important advertising enables the company to sell more and to sell it more effectively so that profits are maximized [11]. In addition, advertising can help a company to improve both its public and its industrial relations [12]. Often, advertising enables a company to protect itself against infringers, to stabilize its own demand, or to strengthen its competitive position in the market [13]. The list can be extended, of course, but these few points show that advertising can be used to serve the firm in many ways.

In the present study, however, we are not interested in the services of advertising to the firm, but to the public. Among other things, advertising is supposed to aid the consumer in buying more easily and efficiently [14]. More-

---

[10] This seems to be the idea of Braithwaite, *op. cit.*, p. 17.

[11] The Editors of Printers' Ink, *What Advertising is ... What it has Done ... What it Can Do Now*, (N.Y.: Printers' Ink Publishing Company, 1953, no pagination), Reprinted from *Printers' Ink*, May 15, 1953. For explanations of how this is effected *cf.* Lloyd E. Partain, « How Advertising Affects Your Job », *Address to the Philadelphia Foreman's Club*, December 7, 1955, (Typescript); Better Business Bureaus, *Facts You Should Know About Advertising*, (N. Y.: 1953), p. 3.

[12] Bruce Barton, « Advertising, Its Contribution to the American Way of Life », *Reader's Digest*, April 1955 (Reprint) and « The Advertising Business », *The Royal Bank of Canada Monthly Letter*, July, 1948; The Editors of Printers' Ink, *op. cit.*

[13] The Editors of Printers-Ink, *op. cit.*; Bayard F. Pope, « What Good is Advertising », *Advertising Agency and Advertising and Selling*, May, 1952 (reprint).

[14] Otto Kleppner, *Where Does Advertising Fit In?* (N. Y.: Association

over, by educating him to a higher standard of living it increases his enjoyment of life [15]. In addition, advertising is supposed to encourage product improvement [16] and to lower costs by enabling the manufacturer to attain his optimum production [17].

These benefits to the consumer as an individual are accompanied by even greater contributions to the economy as a whole. By raising the standard of living, advertising acts as a dynamic factor which encourages growth [18], research [19], production and employment. In addition, by stabilizing demand in the economy as a whole, advertising helps to mitigate the cyclic fluctuations which are so destructive in modern economies [20]. In short, advertising is not merely a means of spreading information about products but of powering the economy and stabilizing its swings.

Finally, advertising makes important contributions to society in other spheres. In the American society it is advertising which, by paying the bill for the mass media, makes them less subject to outside control and more reliable [21]. In addition, advertising itself is used to combat harmful propaganda and to promote national causes [22]. It is, in short, a public servant used in the public interest.

---

of National Advertisers, 1953), p. 16; Elon G. Borton, *Some Questions and Answers about Advertising* (N. Y. Advertising Federation of America, n. d.), p. 3.

[15] Bruce Barton, *op. cit.*; J. Chalmers O'Brien, « Advertising Job: To Get People to 'Live it Up.' » *Eight Addresses Delivered at the Fifth Annual Chicago Tribune Distribution Forum on Advertising to Raise the Standard of Living*, May 18, 1954, p. 11; Better Business Bureaus, *op. cit.*, p. 9.

[16] Otto Kleppner, « Is There Too Much Advertising? » *Harper's* February, 1951 (Reprint, n. p.); Barton, *op. cit.*, Pope, *op. cit.*

[17] The Editors of Printers' Ink, *op. cit.*; Partain, *op. cit.*; Thomas D'Arcy Brophy, *Address to the Advertising Association of the West*, cited in *Advertising Age*, July 5, 1954, p. 1.

[18] Frederic R. Gamble, « The Role of Advertising in Economic Development », *Address to XVth Congress of the International Chamber of Commerce*, Tokyo, Japan, May 13, 1955, (Reprint, American Association of Advertising Agencies, 1955, n. p.).

[19] *cf.* note 16 *supra*.

[20] *cf.* Robert Mc Intyre, « Advertising Called Depression Medicine », *Editor and Publisher*, April 12, 1958, p. 16.

[21] Pope, *op. cit.*; The Editors of Printers' Ink, *op. cit.*, Better Business Bureau, *op. cit.*, pp. 4-5.

[22] Charles G. Mortimer, « Advertising: An Integral Function of Business », *Printers' Ink*, February 15, 1957, (reprint).

There are, of course, other claims which might be listed, but in general they reduce to the main headings given above. In any event, the alleged services of advertising to the company, the consumer, the economy and society are sufficient to indicate the general nature of the claims used to justify advertising and non-informative advertising in particular. The full meaning of these claims, however, becomes clear only when confronted with the charges against advertising.

THE CASE AGAINST ADVERTISING.

The critics of advertising will, as already noted, admit the utility, and indeed, the absolute necessity of informative advertising in a free economy. They object strongly, however, to persuasive, suggestive and competitive advertising on the grounds that they harm the individual, the economy and society.

Persuasive or suggestive advertising injures the individual in many ways. The critics see much of this advertising as an insult to the basic dignity of man [23] which seeks to create an unhealthy conformism [24] and to cripple the capacity for critical thinking [25]. At the same time, by its constant appeals to lower motives, it tends to strengthen hedonism and materialism [26]. In addition, it frequently aims at producing effects which may lead to tensions and unhappiness [27].

These undesirable effects on the individual's psychic life have additional harmful results in his economic life as well. Unreflective buying motivated by a false set of values can lead men to spend on luxury products what should go

---

[23] Vance Packard, « The Mass Manipulation of Human Behavior », *America*, December 14, 1957, p. 343.

[24] Frank Sheed, *Society and Sanity*, (London: Sheed and Ward, 1953), p. 197.

[25] Leonard W. Doob, *Public Opinion and Propaganda*, (London, The Cresset Press, 1949), p. 242.

[26] Alberto J. Villaverde, « Publicidad y la Moral », *Razon y Fe*, 151 (1955), p. 403.

[27] Two critics are especially explicit with regard to the effect of advertising on children. *cf*. H. Lauterbach, *Man, Motives and Money: Psychological Frontiers of Economics*, (Ithica, N. Y.: Cornell U. Press, 1954), p. 86. Harold Ernest Burtt, *Psychology of Advertising*, (Boston: Houghton Mifflin, 1938), pp. 9-10.

for subsistence [28], and to pay higher prices even for necessities [29]. It is, moreover, often associated with a victimization of the consumer [30].

The criticisms go, however, much further; competitive suggestive and persuasive advertising are attacked as being to a large extent mere waste. The most serious criticism is that much, if not most, consumer advertising merely diverts demand from one producer to another without any real benefit to either the consumer or the economy as a whole [31]. In addition, because a great deal of advertising is concentrated on goods of little or no utility, it causes further waste by diverting resources to the consumption and production of frivolous goods [32].

In practice, moreover, advertising becomes a substitute for real price competition [33], and may even reduce competition in general by favoring the formation of monopolies [34]. This is to say that it can lead to the formation of imperfect markets which do not tend to maximize economic welfare.

Finally, advertising which encourages psychological obsolescence and leads to price rigidity not only encourages waste but may be a cause of instability in the economy [35]. Advertising may even tend to accentuate cyclic fluctuations in so far as it is generally increased during the upswing and cut on the downturn [36].

---

[28] Marius Gonin, « L'aspect moral du problème de la publicité », in 23ᵉ *Semaine Sociale de France: La morale chrétienne et les affaires*, (Lyon: Gabalda, 1931), p. 491.

[29] For an analysis of a whole series of arguments against advertising *cf.*, Leland J. Gorden, *Economics for Consumers*, (2nd ed., N. Y.: American Book Company, 1944), pp. 168 ff.

[30] Leo C. Brown *et al.*, *Social Orientations*, (Chicago: Loyola University Press, 1954), p. 148.

[31] K. William Kapp, *The Social Costs of Private Enterprise*, (Cambridge, Mass.: Harvard U. Press, 1950), pp. 190-195; Willard W. Cochrane and Carolyn Shaw Bell, *The Economics of Consumption*, (N. Y.: Mc Graw-Hill, 1956), p. 386.

[32] Gorden, *op. cit.*, p. 148 and p. 169; A. S. J. Baster, *Advertising Reconsidered*, (London: P. S. King and Son, 1935), pp. 96-97.

[33] Mary Jean Bowman and George Leland Bach, *Economic Analysis and Public Policy*, (N. Y.: Prentice-Hall, 1943), pp 316 ff especially p. 320.

[34] Kapp, *op. cit.*, p. 186.

[35] Ronald S. Vaile, *et al.*, *Marketing in the American Economy*, (N. Y.: Ronald Press, 1952), p. 101; Charles S. Wyand, *The Economics of Consumption*, (N. Y.: Macmillan, 1937), p. 435.

[36] *cf.* Neil H. Borden, *The Economic Effects of Advertising*, (Chicago: Richard D. Irwin, 1942), p. XXXVI.

To complete the catalogue of advertising's sins, mention must be made of its effects on social institutions. More than one serious author has viewed with alarm the effects of advertising on language and on the whole communication structure of a nation. The « venal » or commercialized poetry of advertising is accused of having caused the common man to distrust words at the same time that it has debased the common value symbols such as courage, beauty, domesticity, patriotism and even religion [37]. This debasing of language, however, is part of a larger problem which arises from the commercialization of the media of mass communication.

Advertising is one of the forces which has led to the commercialization of the media which in its turn has led to a situation where one's right to diffuse ideas is seriously limited by one's ability to pay for the diffusion [38]. Thus, it is contended that advertising is partially responsible for a serious threat to the freedom of communication. It is not, however, merely the fact that one's ability to pay limits the freedom, (this, after all has always been true to some extent), but also that the media are so sensitive to economic boycott that fresh, original and provocative ideas may be blocked lest they offend someone [39]. Commercialization, then, chokes the communication system and threatens to give the public only what it thinks the public wants [40].

---

[37] S. I. Hayakawa, « Poetry and Advertising », in Lyman Bryson, ed. *Approaches to Group Understanding, Sixth Symposium of the Conference on Science, Philosophy and Religion*, (N. Y.: Harper and Brothers, 1947), p. 373, and Margaret Mead, « Some Cultural Approaches to Communications Problems », in Lyman Bryson, ed., *The Communication of Ideas*, (N. Y.: Institute for Religious and Social Studies, 1948), pp. 19ff.

[38] David M. Potter, *People of Plenty; Economic Abundance and the American Character*, (Chicago, University of Chicago, 1954), p. 183 and David Riesman *et al.*, *The Lonely Crowd: A Study of the Changing American Character*, (New Haven, Connecticut: Yale U. Press, 1950), pp. 211 and 217.

[39] Elmer Rice, «« The Supreme Freedom: Three Hundred Years after Milton », in R. M. MacIver, ed. *Great Expressions of Human Rights*, (N. Y.: Harper and Brothers, 1950), p. 121.

[40] Reinhold Neihbuhr, writing the introduction to Wilbur Schramm, *Responsibility in Mass Communication*, (N. Y.: Harper and Brothers, 1957), p. XIX, put it this way. « The community becomes the tyrant through the conception of itself protected by the images of the mass media ». The question of the content of the mass media and the influence of advertising upon it, is of utmost importance and deserves further study.

Summary and State of the Question

Though the foregoing pages do not contain all the arguments either for or against advertising, they are sufficient to indicate the multiplicity, complexity and debatable nature of the issues involved. If we prescind from the benefits which advertising is supposed to contribute to the individual firm, the following broad conflicts emerge. On the one hand, advertising is supposed to make life easier, more pleasant, less expensive and better served by improved products, while on the other hand it is accused of degrading man, his reflective processes and his values, without making any real contribution to his material welfare. In the second place advertising's claim to be of service in stimulating growth and assuring stability is directly countered by those critics who see it as a cause of waste, of instability and of less perfect competition. Finally, the contribution of advertising revenue to the freedom of the press is offset by its indirect influence on the free expression of ideas, just as its utily as a weapon of counterpropaganda is rendered dubious by its debasement of language and of the common cultural symbols.

The present study is centered on the claim that advertising contributes to economic growth and stability for several reasons. First, in examining the liceity of the methods by which growth and stability are to be obtained, it will be possible to examine some of the basic ethical issues involved in the use of persuasive and suggestive advertising. Second, if advertising can help growth and stability by ethically acceptable means, much of the waste attributed to it can be written off as the price society pays for these benefits. Third, the investigation of the ethical, psychological and economic issues involved in this claim will shed much light on other problems in the ethics of advertising.

Before giving a more exact formulation of the questions to be answered, it is first necessary to examine the claim itself in greater detail with an eye to determining the precise benefits bestowed and the methods by which these are to be realized.

The chapter on the ethics of persuasion indicates some of the issues in greater detail.

CHAPTER III

ADVERTISING AND ECONOMIC GROWTH

The previous chapter gave a short introduction to the various problems, economic and ethical, which are connected with modern advertising. In the present chapter we wish to give careful consideration to the claim that American advertising, by raising the standard of living, makes an important contribution to that economic growth which is necessary for the health of American society. In the chapters which follow, we shall then discuss the assumptions which underlie this claim.

In so far as possible, the advertising profession is allowed to speak for itself so that further discussion can be focused on their intentions as well as on the effects of advertising. The material cited was supplied or recommended by the American Association of Advertising Agencies or its members [1] and it may be taken as presenting a representative, if not the best possible case in favor of advertising.

The following statement by Arno H. Johnson of the J. Walter Thompson Agency contains most of the elements which will be studied in this chapter.

> The aggressive and intelligent advertising of a worthy product or service, while serving the self-interest of the producer through profitable sales, does — at the same time — contribute importantly to our national economy in educating many people to a higher standard of living and to the higher levels of consumption that our productivity and resources justify [2].

---

[1] *Bibliography of Material Discussing the Contribution of Advertising to Our Economy and Way of Life, (Mimeographed,* 1958, 4 pp.).

[2] Arno H. Johnson, « The Job for Advertising in the Continued Expansion of Our National Economy », *Papers from the 37th Annual Meeting of the A. A. A. A.,* Group II, (N. Y.: American Association of Advertising Agencies, 1955), p. 2.

An understanding of this claim demands that at least five basic questions be answered. First, what is meant by the standard of living? Second, how does the advertising profession propose to raise the standard of living? Third, how does raising the standard of living lead to economic growth? Fourth, why does the advertising profession believe this growth is necessary in the United States? Fifth, why does it believe this growth must take place through the increased production of consumer goods?

THE STANDARD OF LIVING

The phrase « standard of living » is more than a little vague, because, like that other common expression, « the American way of life », it can mean whatever one wishes. In practice it is used to designate the standard of living as such, the level of living, the standard of consumption and the level of consumption.

By the *standard of living as such is meant all those goods, both material and spiritual which are desired by an individual or a group.* It is a standard because it is *also a norm* by which groups and individuals judge the relative importance of these goods. The advertising profession refers to this standard when it speaks of the « habits and desires » of people [2a] « the concept of how to live » [3], « the concepts of the mass of our population » [4].

These concepts and desires include among their objects gratifications « of a spiritual, intellectual and artistic nature » [5], as well as purely material goods and services [6]. The standard of living as such is not purely material, but includes, the whole range of goods which men can desire.

The *level or plane of living is the sum total of* SPIRITUAL *and* MATERIAL GOODS *which groups and individuals*

[2a] Johnson, *op. cit.*, p. 3.
[3] *ibid.*, p. 5.
[4] *ibid.*, p. 12.
[5]. Paul Mazur, *The Standards We Raise*, (N. Y.: Harper and Brothers, 1953), p. 38.
[6] *cf*. Melvin Brorby, *We Ask Ourselves Four Questions*, (N. Y.: American Association of Advertising Agencies, 1958), p. 8; and *Who has the Ultimate Weapon*, (N. Y.: McCann-Erickson, 1958), p. 7.

ACTUALLY ENJOY. The advertising profession seems to refer to this when it speaks not merely of raising the standard of living, but of helping people to secure or attain it [7].

The *standard of consumption is the sum total of* MA-TERIAL *goods and services which groups and individuals desire*. It may also be considered as a norm by which people judge the relative value of these goods and services. The term is used in both these senses when one speaks of changing the level of demand for the « infinite variety of goods and services that measure a standard of living » [8].

Finally there is the *level of consumption or the sum total of all goods and services* ACTUALLY *consumed by groups and individuals* [9]. This is mentioned frequently when the advertising profession speaks of the concrete objects it sells [10]. Clearly, when there is talk of teaching people to « live it up », the idea is to raise the standard of consumption in order to raise the actual level of consumption [11].

These standards and levels are, of course, interrelated. The sum of all things desired and the relative importance given to them determines what material objects will be desired and the material things sought after and the relative importance given to them will have much to do with what people actually consume. In the following pages we will see that the advertising profession wishes to change the standard of living in order to change the standard of consumption [12]. The change in the standard of consumption is, however, ordered to a change in the level of consumption which then enables people to have

---

[7] The Editors of Printers' Ink. « What Advertising Is ... What it Has Done ... What it Can Do Now », Reprint from *Printers' Ink*, May 15, 1953, p. 1 (no printed pagination).

[8] Johnson, *op. cit.*, p. 2.

[9] William C. McKeehan, « If we as a People ... The Challenge to American Enterprise », *Papers from the 37th Annual Meeting of the A. A. A. A.* Group II, (N. Y.: American Association of Advertising Agencies, 1954), p. 36 and *cf.*, Johnson, *op. cit.*, p. 2.

[10] For an example *cf.*, Elon G. Borton, *Some Questions and Answers about Advertising*, (N. Y.: Advertising Federation of America, no date), no. 14.

[11] J. Chalmers O'Brien, « Advertising's Job: To Get People to ' Live it Up ' », *Fifth Annual Chicago Tribune Distribution and Advertising Forum, Area III, Advertising to Raise the Standard of Living*, (1954), p. 11.

[12] *cf. infra,* Chapter III.

a higher level of living. In general, however, the emphasis
is on raising the standard of consumption, or on changing
the standard of living in such a way as to give more
importance to material goods and services.

RAISING THE STANDARD OF LIVING

With the definitions of the last section in mind, we
can now turn to our second basic question: how does advertising propose to change the standard of living? More
precisely put, the question should read, how does advertising propose to increase the importance given to material goods and services? To put it yet in another way:
how does the advertising profession propose to increase
the importance given to the standard of consumption which
is only one part of the standard of living?

Our purpose here is not to give a treatise on the
techniques of advertising, but merely to discover the general approach which the advertising profession proposes
to follow. In later chapters, however, more will be said
of the techniques and methods which are actually used
or approved of by the advertising profession.

In the first instance we shall give typical statements
of the advertising men themselves, and then attempt to
reduce these statements to their basic elements. It should
be noted beforehand that many of the following statements consider advertising not only in so far as it affects
the standard, but also in so far as it influences the actual
level of living.

> It is my feeling that the greatest secret behind using
> advertising to help build a better world is the ability to differ-
> entiate between advertising as news and advertising as pro-
> paganda. If the product is right — if the price is right — if
> the distribution is adequate — then newsworthy advertising
> can play its part in helping to raise the standard of living [13].

Advertising's first tool is, then, the distribution of
information about goods and services which people need

---

[13] Glenn Gundell, « Advertising Must be Believable », *Fifth Annual Chicago Tribune Distribution and Advertising Forum*, Area III, *Advertising to
Raise the Standard of Living*, (1954) p. 6.

or want. By giving information advertising then increases the public's knowledge of possible ways of satisfying needs and desires and so expands their outlook.

Advertising does more than give information about products which the public needs or wants. « What advertising does, and does well, is to increase what might be called the "wantability" of goods » [14]. « By constantly stimulating new wants and by satisfying latent as well as new desires... advertising has widened markets and raised the standards of living generally » [15].

Advertising goes further and breeds discontent of the type described by the Editors of *Printers' Ink* in the following statement of one influenced by advertising.

> Old ways of doing things are no longer good enough for me. I want something better, and here it is. So off with the old, and on with the new, like the guy says in the ad [16].

The second class of means used to change the standard of living is concerned with the desirability of things, with motivation and attitudes. It is to effect the change not merely by informing the intellect but by moving the will and influencing the evaluations which affect choices. These increases in « wantability », in desire and the creation of an attitude favorable to the new, and a general discontant with the old, modify the concept of life by augmenting the importance given to material goods and to services.

The statements cited above do not merely assert the ability of advertising to arouse a desire for a particular product, but claim that it can « stimulate ambition and desire — the craving to possess, which is the strongest incentive to produce » [17]. More commonly, however, the

---

[14] Thomas D'Arcy Brophy, « The Role of Advertising in Our Economy », *An Address Delivered to the Advertising Club of New Orleans* on June 5, 1956. p. 2 of Mimeographed notes supplied by Mr. Brophy.

[15] McKeehan, *op. cit.* p. 44.

[16] Editors of Printers' Ink, *op. cit.* No. 4, For similar ideas *cf. Facts You Should Know About Advertising*, (N. Y. Association of Better Business Bureaus, 1953), p. 2 and p. 8. Loyd E. Partain, « How Advertising Affects Your Job », *Address to the Philadelphia Foreman's Club*, December 7, 1955, page 4 of mimeographed manuscript.

[17] Bruce Barton, « Advertising: Its Contribution to the American Way of Life », *The Reader's Digest*, April, 1955, p. 104.

advertising profession insists not so much on its power
to create a desire for material things in general, but on
its ability to create new wants and new desires for particular products and services.

> Second, by stimulating new wants and new desires — and
> for cultural services as well as commodities — advertising is
> one of the most powerful agents in raising the standard of
> living [18].
> It is a principle of faith of the advertising profession
> that while most people desire an advancing standard of living
> the specific items which make it up must be sold [19].

By making people desire a given product, by making
that product a part of the life a person wants to lead,
advertising modifies the standard of living. If it succeeds
in making people want a large number of new goods and
services, the cumulative effect may be a significant increase in the importance given to material things, and so
the equivalent of a general strengthening of the desire to
possess.

In summary, then, advertising changes the standard
of living by increasing the desirability of both particular
products and for material goods in general. This is ac-
complished by giving information about goods and services, and by the presentation of motives and values which
stimulate desires.

ADVERTISING, THE STANDARD OF LIVING AND ECONOMIC GROWTH

How does raising the standard of living lead to economic growth? This is the third of the basic questions
which must be answered before we can understand the
claim advanced by the advertising profession. The follow-

---

[18] Frederic R. Gamble, « The Role of Advertising in Economic Development », *address given at the XVth Congress of the International Chamber of Congress*, Tokyo, May 18, 1955, (N. Y.: American Association of
Advertising Agencies), no pagination.

[19] « Advertising and the Pursuit of Happiness », *Cost and Profit Outlook*, 9 (1956) no. 6, June, p. 1. (This is the news letter of Alderson and
Sessions, Marketing and Management Counsel) *cf.* any of the literature
cited previously for other examples of this expression of the way in which
advertising raises the standard of living.

ing citations present some of the answers given to this question. First, the raising of the standard of living causes growth by increasing consumption. Thus Paul Mazur writes:

> The standard of living is the great catalyst which converts the potential of demand into actual consumption — the force of purchasing power into actual purchases. *And it is only the advancement of the American standard of living which can contribute to the economy the essential growth it requires, if production is to have continuity, real wages progressive increases, and employment the expansion necessary to absorb a growing population of workers*[20].

However, if this increase in consumption is to be a real cause of growth it must be large. Here advertising has a role to play in assuring a mass increase.

> Advertising is a sparkplug in our economy. It helps make mass distribution possible; that in turn calls for mass production. Mass production and distribution together employ most of us. And they generate the prosperity on which all of us depend[21].

The argument continues to note that mass consumption encourages mass production which in its turn creates jobs.

> It all adds up to the fact that mass consumption makes mass production possible and mass production means more jobs. Advertising because of its ability to accelerate the regular acceptance of new products, and by lifting the level of acceptability of established products, unleashes a tremendous flood of new demand — and new employment[22].

Finally the argument points out that the alternative to increased consumption and production is idle resources and unemployment.

> Our tremendously productive economy is capable of producing goods and services at a rate never before achieved... But unless it is possible to increase the wantability of products this total potential productive capacity will not be

---

[20] Paul Mazur, *The Standards We Raise, The Dynamics of Consumtion,* (N. Y.: Harper and Brothers, 1953), p. 83. Italics in the original.

[21] Borton, *op. cit.,* no. 20, C.

[22] Brophy, *op. cit.,* p. 4.

fully used. And if it is not fully used, it will mean the existence
of idle resources. And idle resources mean idle people [23].

The basic process described in all these citations may
be summarized briefly as follows. When you raise the
living standards of people who have purchasing power
this causes an increase of effective demand and of consumption. This demand then causes an increase of production and of productive facilities which in their turn
involve an increase of the number of people employed.
Increased employment means that the end result of this
process is an increase in income and national wealth,
which makes it possible to satisfy the needs and aspirations of the citizens [24].

In order to understand the full significance of this
process, it is necessary to consider the concrete factors
which make the defenders of advertising consider a rising
standard of living as « the sociological catalyst of the
American economy ». In particular, we may ask: why
does the advertising profession place the emphasis on
increasing the desire for goods rather than on increasing
purchasing power as a method of increasing the demand
necessary to move the economy forward [26]?

In attempting to answer this question, the first point
which must be made is that the United States has the
productive capacity necessary for economic growth. This
means that it is not the inability to produce which will
inhibit expansion, but rather the lack of demand. Here
are typical expressions of this point of view.

> American history reveals few instances in peacetime of
> inadequate production to satisfy the then existing active de-
> mand for products. But there is emphatic evidence of critical
> times, even crises, when the demand necessary to absorb the
> production has simply evaporated [27].
>
> The President in his Economic Report to Congress on
> January 20, 1955, gave a measure of the opportunity and the
> selling job in the next 10 years by pointing out that 'our

---

[23] *ibid.*, p. 13.

[24] Mazur, *op. cit.*, p. 28. McKeehan, *op. cit.*, p. 46.

[25] Mazur, *op. cit.*, p. X.

[26] There is, of course, an underconsumption theory of stagnation or of
the cycle hidden here. This will be discussed in chapter VII.

[27] Mazur, *op. cit.*, p. 22.

country can within a decade, increase its production from the
current annual level of about $ 360 billion to $ 500 billion, or
more, expressed in dollars of the same buying power' [28].

To support that level of over $ 500 billion of production
by 1965 will require a major increase in our standard of
living. We will have to increase sales of goods and services
to consumers by at least 50%, to a minimum level of $ 350
billion compared with $ 234 billion in 1954 [29].

Granted that the productive capacity exists, growth
will depend on the sales and demand which will justify
the actualization of this capacity. Now, effective demand,
that is demand which will result in sales, depends on two
factors: purchasing power and a desire which makes people willing to spend their money for products and services [30]. Just as the argument of the advertising profession
assumed that productive capacity was present, so it assumes that of the two factors in effective demand, the first,
purchasing power is already given.

> The increased productivity of our population between 1940
> and 1954, for example, has resulted in an increase of 74% in
> real purchasing power — even after adjustment for inflation,
> higher taxes, and heavy defense needs. The production level
> of over $ 500 billion possible by 1965 could yield disposable
> income to individuals, after taxes, sufficient for a further 50%
> increase — to over $ 350 billion of consumer purchases, plus
> a high level of over $ 20 billion annually in personal savings [31].

It is not merely a question of purchasing power already being present and of growing, but of its being pos-
sessed by more and more family units [32]. This new distribution of purchasing power, which has also involved an
increase in the discretionary income of large numbers of
families, could represent a substantially increased demand
« if only they (the families with new income), were to

---

[28] Johnson, *op. cit.*, p. 1.
[29] *ibid.*, p. 2. The same argument can be found in Brophy, *op. cit.*,
p. 13 and in Stanley Resor, « We Can Sell $ 600 Billion of Output », *U. S.
News and World Report*, 42 (1957), January 4, pp. 72-80.
[30] E. A. Lever, *Advertising and Economic Theory*, (London: Oxford
U. Press, 1947), p. 49.
[31] Johnson, *op. cit.*, p. 2. It should also be noted that Johnson foresees a great expansion in consumer credit. *ibid.* p. 7 and p. 20.
[32] *ibid.* p. 4.

take on the habits and desires of the income group into which they move » [33].

America has the productive capacity necessary for growth, and Americans have in ever increasing numbers the purchasing power necessary to create effective demand, so that the missing element which will turn potential into effective demand is the desire for goods and services and the willingness to spend on them. In short, it is the standard of living which will bring about effective demand which, in its turn, will justify the increased production of which the nation is capable.

People, however, do not automatically adjust their standard of living to an increase of income. This is a key premise in the argument being studied.

> We are learning from experience that people do not adjust quickly, of themselves, to better possibilities of living. In the United States, as people move into higher income groups, we know that they have a tendency to carry over their former living patterns. Their sights need to be raised to new and better modes of living, to cultural services as well as physical products [34].

There are, of course, trends in American society which are operating to change the standard of living. The trend toward family life and toward larger families as well as a mass move to the suburbs and a rising educational level are all factors which exert an influence on the acceptance of, or desire for a better standard of living [35], but because these operate slowly, there is still a major job for advertising in changing the concept of how to live so as to bring it into line with changes in income [36].

The preceding paragraphs indicate that the precise task assigned to advertising is the *speeding up* of changes in the standard of living so that purchasing power is turned into purchases *at a rate* which matches the increases in potential production. « Advertising is the great *accelerating force* in distribution » [37]. Advertising has the task

---

[33] *ibid*. p. 5.
[34] Gamble, *op. cit.*, (no pagination).
[35] Johnson, *op. cit.*, pp. 8-10.
[36] *ibid.*, p. 5.
[37] Gamble, *op. cit.*, (no pagination).

of « keeping consumption *abreast of* ever-increasing production » [38]. « It must play a vital note in the basic task of expanding our standard of living *fast enough* to keep up with our productive ability » [39].

With these facts clearly in mind it is now possible to give a fuller answer to the question: how does advertising's effect on the standard of living lead to economic growth? In the American economy, as described by the advertising profession, there is a great productive capacity which will remain idle unless there is an effective demand for the products it can produce. There is, moreover, purchasing power sufficient to activate this productive capacity if and when the desire to possess turns it into actual purchases. Although more basic forces than advertising are changing the standard of living and increasing this desire to possess, the increase is not rapid enough to guarantee an effective demand sufficient to activate all the productive capacity of the American society. Advertising by accelerating changes in the standard of living, and in consumption helps to create that effective demand which calls for an increase of production and production facilities with a consequent growth of the number of men employed.

THE NEED FOR ECONOMIC GROWTH

Economic growth is not an end in itself, so that the significance of this growth depends on the answer to the fourth question posed at the beginning of this chapter. Why does the advertising profession believe that economic growth is necessary in the United States? In particular, why does the United States need a growth based on increased production of consumer goods and services?

Though the United States is the richest nation in the world, it still has enormous economic needs. In 1955 William C. McKeehan, chairman of the Joint Committee of the Association of National Advertisers and of the Ame-

---

[38] Brophy, *op. cit.*, p. 15.
[39] Johnson, *op. cit.*, p. 12.

rican Association of Advertising Agencies on Understanding Our Economic System, gave the following list of
needs [40].

> NEW JOBS. We must provide 10 million additional jobs in the
> next 10 years (with new people coming into our labor
> market at the rate of about a million a year).
> EXISTING JOBS. We must provide, even better working condi-
> tions, better returns, for our 63 million existing jobs.
> OLDER PEOPLE. We must provide, in practical ways, for the
> more than 17 million older people we will have by 1965.
> SOCIAL GAINS. We must preserve — and advance — our social,
> health and educational gains.
> We have a lot of further requirements too; schools, hospi-
> tals, homes, better highways, etc.   The list is extensive.

According to the American Association of Advertising
Agencies and the Association of National Advertisers, the
United States has $ 500 billion of needs in the following
sectors: $ 40 billion for schools and hospitals, $ 60 billion
for highways, $ 100 billion for housing and $ 300 billion
for equipment and construction [41].

America's needs do not stop here, for its position in
the modern world demands that it spend huge sums both
on defense and in aiding other nations to meet their economic needs [42]. It is not merely a question of maintaining a
huge arsenal, but of paying for the research and education
needed to develop that arsenal [43]. Because the necessity
for both military and economic defense of the United States
and the free world will continue into the future, it demands
a continued expansion of the economy.

Though the advertising profession puts great emphasis
on these economic needs, they do not fail to note that
this growth is a condition which makes possible the pursuit of other goods.

> Raising our economic level of living not only means greater
> consumption of goods and services in itself, but it creates the

---

[40] McKeehan, *op. cit.*, p. 35. Presented as in the original.
[41] Cited without other indication of source by Royal H. Ray, « Advertising and Economic Support, 1955-57 », *Journalism Quarterly*,   32
(1955), p. 38.
[42] *Who has the Ultimate Weapon*, (N. Y.: McCann-Erikson, 1948),
pp. 11-12.
[43] Meloin Brorby, *We Ask Ourselves Four Questions*, (N. Y.: American
Association of Advertising Agencies), p. 10.

means and the leisure time for raising our non-economic culture too [44].

The increase in wealth is to give the many and not merely the few the possibilities of having more education and time and resources to cultivate an interest in music and literature [45]. The ultimate benefits of this growth are, then, to be found not merely in a higher material level of living, but in the possibilities of a human and cultural development of the citizen.

Growth is necessary if all these needs are to be satisfied, and if people are to have the means not merely of maintaining life, but of developing themselves. The arguments in favor of economic growth can be extended, however, to show that the American economy must go forward in order not to go backwards: Paul Mazur presents his case in the following words.

> There is, in fact, a constant challenge in the very nature of our economy. We must *progress* in our dynamic system in order not to *retrogress*. Men's appetite for goods must be quickened and increased if their standard of living is to be improved sufficiently to absorb increasing quantities of goods, and thereby to maintain private competitive enterprise. The American way of life simply cannot afford a state of stagnation [46].

Mazur's argument is of special interest since it not only shows the need for growth, but also shows why this growth depends on consumption. In its briefest form the argument states that the American economy of mass production and mass consumption requires increases in both fields *merely to maintain* employment at a high level. In an expanded form, the argument goes on to show the relation of this to economic stability and the avoidance of the wastes which are associated with cyclic fluctuations.

> ...American mass production has created a great economic and sociological combination of high wages and low costs.

---

[44] Vergil D. Reed, « We Uncultured Americans », *Address to the 35th Annual Meeting of the American Association of Advertising Agencies*, April 2, 1953, p. 3 of manuscript supplied by J. Walter Thompson Co. of which the author was vice president.

[45] *op. cit.*, p. 46.

[46] Mazur, *op. cit.*, p. 86.

However, to continue to do this, mass production must have available for its needs huge and continuous volume. When volume is static, mass production is a creator of unemployment, for increasing productivity means that fewer and fewer men will produce the same amount of goods. The giant of mass production can be maintained at the peak of his strength only when his voracious appetite can be fully and continuously satisfied. This means that products must be consumed at the same rate they are produced [47].

The sequence of factors is clear: static consumption equals static volume which means static production. Static production, however, when coupled with rising productivity spells out unemployment. If full employment is a goal of economic activity, and if rising productivity is desirable as a means to higher wages and lower prices, it follows that the economy must grow.

Mazur goes on to show the effects of this unemployment on the economic continuity and stability of the country. Unemployment can cause consumer demand to fall [48], which fall then causes a pile up of inventories which in its turn can lead to a lowering of production and a further diminution of employment and purchasing power [49]. Once the continuity has been broken, there is risk of recession or even depression. Unless production continues to grow, increasing productivity per man hour may cause unemployment and unbalance the economy with serious results. From this it follows that the American economy must, because of its nature, progress in order not to retrogress.

GROWTH AND CONSUMER GOODS

Granted that the nature of the American economy and the needs of the American people make growth a necessity, it remains to ask why this growth should be based on an increased production of consumer goods and services. The public needs of the nation, as listed by the advertising men,

---

[47] Paul Mazur, « The Advertising Force — Its Challenge and Potentials in Today's Economy », A reprint from *Printers' Ink* September 18, 1953, (no pagination).

[48] Mazur, *The Standards We Raise*, pp. 134-135.

[49] *ibid.*, p. 33 and *cf.*, pp. 21-22.

are so great that it would seem unnecessary and possibly even harmful to base the needed expansion on consumer goods.

Two main reasons are given for the need of increasing the production of consumer goods and services. First, this is the best way of creating the wealth to pay for the necessary public expenditures and of maintaining a high level of living. Second, this is the best way of protecting the American way of life and the system of private competitive enterprise.

In support of the contention that this is the best way of satisfying both public and private needs, the advertising profession points first to the fact that this system has worked in the past. America met the challenge of the Second World War, and gave billions of dollars of aid to other nations, not by freezing the standard of living at the level of thirty years ago, « but by creating buying power and a standard of living almost double that of 1928 »[50]. This is, however, only secondary to the main argument.

The main argument contends that it is the productive apparatus which produces television sets and washing machines which generates the wealth needed to pay for necessary expenses of government[51]. If the purchase of consumer products collapsed, there would be real unemployment and no way of paying for new military and research ventures except by heavy borrowing and an increase of the national debt[52].

> What will enable us to meet these critical challenges of today and tomorrow? *A healthy and expanding consumer economy, with an even greater era of abundance from the proceeds of which we can pay these new costs and assume on every front of this cold war the full responsibilities of world leadership*[53].

This growth which brings more goods and money to the American people also increases the flow of taxes into the public treasury and so pays the bills for labor and

---

[50] *Who has the Ultimate Weapon*, p. 14.
[51] *ibid.*, p. 15.
[52] Brorby, *op. cit.*, p. 5.
[53] *ibid.*, p. 6.

equipment needed for the public weal [54]. Taxes might be increased, of course, but if the tax level is to be such as to encourage investment and permit that extra margin of consumer spending which spells the difference between prosperity and recession, increased tax revenue should come from increased production [55].

Not only economic, but socio-ethical considerations point to the need for the continued growth of production for consumer needs. Unless private competitive enterprise continues to grow, and to give the necessary employment, there will be a further expansion of government activity in order to create jobs [56]. This movement of the government into the economic sphere raises the specter of a controlled, planned or collectivist economy [57] and with it a threat to the political freedom of Americans [58]. It is this threat of government intervention and the possibility of a planned economy which makes it imperative that the private sector of the economy be kept healthy and vigorous. In the last analysis, it is no longer a question of economic abundance, but of freedom itself [59].

As it stands, this argument only proves that the private competitive system must be kept strong if government intervention and finally collectivism are to be avoided. However, there are three reasons why the strength of the private competitive economy depends on the increased production of consumer goods and services. First, the demand for military goods is not great enough to keep production increasing. Second, consumer goods are the incentives which keep people at work. Third, the rising level of living is a goal of the economy.

Mazur presents the first argument in the following words:

> Capacity for production is growing. In spite of more than 50 billions spent for war preparedness, civilian inventories are increasing. Unless there is a third world war, military expenditures are likely to stabilize at present levels or be reduced.

[54] *Who has the Ultimate Weapon*, p. 16 and Brorby, *op. cit.*, p. 6.
[55] *Who has the Ultimate Weapon*, p. 16.
[56] Mazur, *The Standards We Raise*, p. 78.
[57] Mazur, *The Standards We Raise*, pp. 84-85, and Brorby, *op. cit.*, p. 5
[58] Mazur, *The Standards We Raise*, p. 84.
[59] *ibid.*, p. 80.

> Therefore the requirements for growth must be contributed primarily by the civilian economy and by a rise in the standard of living [60].

Even though government expenditures are high, the danger of a surplus and of an indigestion of inventory remains [61], so that there is danger of a shutting down of productive facilities and of unemployment [62]. Even the huge military needs of the United States are not sufficient to maintain a demand which will activate all the productive facilities necessary for a healthy economy.

These two arguments which stress the importance of individual consumption as the power which drives the economy are well summarized in the following quotation.

> In a free enterprise economy like our own, the everyday needs of individuals and families are the primary sources of incentives behind all economic progress and technological change. We are confronted with an acceleration of progress in the communist world. The philosophy of economic freedom apparently requires that demand for consumer goods be stimulated as a means of creating the economic power that is essential to our survival [63].

In the last analysis, however, the economy does not exist merely to produce, and production does not exist merely to create work. Production and work are « to lend assistence in the pursuit of happiness » [64]. This is the basis of the third argument which asserts the importance of consumer goods in the pursuit of happiness.

Though spiritual and cultural values are important in the search for happiness [65], a high level of material well-being also has its place [66]. It is not merely a question of a minimum level of living, but of a level which will satisfy the demands of American society. Now in the American society, of which the economic system is only a part, great value is given to « social equality in the right of consump-

---

[60] Mazur, « The Advertising Force », (no pagination).

[61] Mazur, *The Standards We Raise*, p. 75.

[62] *ibid.*, pp. 74-75.

[63] « Advertising and the Pursuit of Happiness », p. 1 (no pagination is printed), *cf.* also Brorby, *op. cit.*, pp. 8-9.

[64] *loc. cit.*

[65] Brorby, *op. cit.*, p. 8.

[66] Mazur, *The Standards We Raise*, p. 6.

tion, and the emulation of one's neighbour in creating one's standard of living » [67]. The economy, therefore, will reach its goal only when it supplies the goods and services which enable all citizens to realize this equality of consumption and a high level of living. In addition to this, the members of American society « have taken for granted their right to a steady improvement of their material well-being » [68]. Such an improvement is possible « only if production gives the people shelter, clothing, foods, transportation devices, entertainment, and services of constantly improving quality and quantity » [69].

Growth, then, must take place in the production of consumer goods not only because this is necessary to produce the wealth needed for defense and mutual aid and for the protection of private competitive enterprise, but also because the values accepted by Americans demand a steady improvement of their level of living and the chance to have equality in their consumption. Consequently the American society must not merely grow, but grow in such a way as to satisfy all these exigencies simultaneously.

SUMMARY

Since this presentation has been rather long and involves many points, it will be well to give a tabular summary first in order to give an over-all view of the argument.

The proposition: Advertising by raising the standard of living can make an important contribution to the growth of the American economy.

I What is meant by the standard of living?

1. The standard of living *as such*.
2. The standard of living as the *level of living*.
3. The standard of consumption.
4. The level of consumption.

II. How does advertising propose to raise the standard of living as such?

---

[67] *ibid.*, p. 99 and p. 125.
[68] *ibid.*, p. 37.
[69] *loc. cit.*

   1. By increasing the importance given to material goods in general.
     A. By giving information.
     B. By changing attitudes and motives and desires.
   2. By increasing the importance given to particular goods.
     A. By giving information.
     B. By arousing a desire for these goods·

III. How does raising the standard of living lead to economic growth?

   1. In General
     A. By generating increased demand which
     B. Activates production which
     C. Increases employment which
     D. Increases income and wealth.
   2. In Particular
     A. There is a great potential productive capacity.
     B. There is idle purchasing power.
     C. So that only increased desire is needed to start the process.
       a. But other factors do not increase this desire fast enough.
       b. Therefore advertising is needed.

IV. Why is economic growth needed?

   1. The United States has enormous economic needs.
   2. The economy must progress in order not to retrogress.
     A. In order to maintain employment levels.
     B. In order to avoid recessions.

V. Why must this growth be in the production of consumer goods?

   1. The production and sales of consumer goods produces the wealth which pays for the expenses of the government.
   2. This increase is necessary to protect the system of private competitive enterprise.
     A. The demand for military goods is not sufficient to keep private competitive enterprise healthy.

3. This increase is needed to satisfy the American
aspirations for
A. Equality in consumption.
B. A continually rising standard of material well-
being.

The argument as it has been presented assumes that
the means at the disposal of the advertising profession are
ethically acceptable in themselves and that an increase in
personal consumption is not only consistent with, but de-
manded by the goals of the economy as a whole Chapters
IV and V will examine these assumptions· In addition the
argument assumes that advertising has the power to increase consumption in an orderly way, and that the situation in the American economy is such as to demand a
stimulation of consumption. These assumptions will be
examined in Chapters VI and VII.

CHAPTER IV

THE ETHICS OF PERSUASION

INTRODUCTION

The present chapter and the following examine the liceity of the means which advertising proposes to use in increasing consumption and the consistency of increased personal consumption with the goals of the American economy as a whole. In the first instance we shall treat of the ethics of persuasion, that is, of the basic norms which must govern all activity which seeks to influence human choice. In the second place we will then outline some of the special ethical problems involved in mass persuasion. In the following chapter we will then treat of the ethics of consumption, both individual and social, in so far as these are involved in the proposal of the advertising profession.

Though our treatment of both the ethics of persuasion and of consumption is admittedly incomplete, the norms developed in the following pages will suffice to judge the proposal of the advertising profession in its broad general outline. The formulation of more particular norms and their application to individual advertisements lies beyond the scope of the present work.

THE ETHICS OF PERSUASION

The argument of the advertising profession assumes that it is ethically licit to influence the conduct of men by giving information, by presenting motives and this either openly or by suggestion [1]. The profession recognizes, of course, that not all means of persuasion are licit and the

---

[1] *cf.* the previous chapter.

various codes of advertising ethics proscribe certain methods [2]. Typical proscriptions are found in the following
very brief copy code of the American Association of Advertising Agencies [3], which bans:

> a. False statements or misleading exaggerations.
> b. Indirect misrepresentation of a product or service,
> through distortion of details, or of their true perspective, either
> editorially or pictorially.
> c. Statements or suggestions offensive to public decency.
> d. Statements which tend to undermine an industry by
> attributing to its products generally, faults and weaknesses
> true of only a few.
> e. Price claims that are misleading.
> f. Pseudoscientific advertising, including claims insufficient-
> ly supported by accepted authority, or that distort the true
> meaning or practicable application of a statement made by
> professional or scientific authority.
> g. Testimonials which do not reflect the real choice of a
> competent witness.

In recent years various advertising associations have
also condemned the use of subliminal advertising [4]. With
this one exception, however, the codes tend to concentrate
on the issue of truthfulness and decency [5]. If the codes
themselves are silent about the overall ethics of persuasion,
the critics of advertising have been unusually vociferous [6].
In particular the critics have attacked advertising for encouraging nonrational and impulsive buying [7], and for attempting to by-pass the consumer's mind [8], avoiding anything which might stimulate intellectual comprehension.

---

[2] *cf.* the bibliography for a list of codes of advertising ethics.

[3] This code is also approved by the Association of National Advertiser and the Advertising Federation of America. Printed by the A. A. A. A.
under the title, *How You as An Individual Can Help Reduce Objection-
able Advertising.*

[4] Institute of Practitioners in Advertising, *Subliminal Communication,*
(London: IPA, 1958), p. 6. Subliminal advertising may be described as
advertising which depends on the sending, reception and effects of physically weak visual or aural messages which people receive in a physiolog-
ical sense, but of which they are not consciously aware.

[5] There are, of course, special provisions relative to certain products
such as patent medicines, strong drink and so on, but these are special
cases which need separate treatment.

[6] *cf.* Chapter II.

[7] *cf.,* Vance Packard, *The Hidden Persuaders,* (London: Longmans,
Green and Co., 1957), p. 258.

[8] *cf.* Otis Pease, *The Responsibilities of American Advertising,* (New
Haven: Yale U. Press, 1958), p. 175.

While the major part of advertising probably does not seek to use nonrational appeals [9], the advertising profession does seem to accept it as legitimate [10], and the large sums of money being devoted to research on the hidden motives of men indicates that the profession is interested in techniques which can influence the unconscious [11]. What, however, is to be said of advertising which appeals to the irrational and attempts to by-pass the mind?

In the last analysis one's attitude toward irrational appeals will depend on one's attitude toward man himself. If man is only a « helpless bundle of suggestibility » [12], a mass of conditioned reflexes, a creature necessarily ruled by his unconscious drives, then appeals to the irrational do not offend against human nature and are ehical. If, on the other hand, man is a rational animal, obliged to act reasonably, that is, on the basis of an enlightened free choice, then, the advertising profession cannot assume that it is morally free to use suggestive advertising and irrational appeals in any and all circumstances. In fact this latter view of human nature gives rise to certain obligations which are relevant not only to advertising but to all persuasive activity.

In an effort to formulate these obligations which are the basis of an ethics of persuasion [13], we shall treat of

---

[9] *ibid.*, p. 195.

[10] For instance an advertisement of the Leo Burnett Co. (*Fortune*, December, 1957, p. 14) stresses the fact that their advertising can influence the modern American who trusts his feelings.

[11] The interest in motivation research is indicated by the fact that the Advertising Research Foundation has published the following studies, *Introductory Bibliography of Motivation Research*, (N. Y., 1953); *Directory of Organizations which Conduct Motivation Research*, (N. Y., 1954) and *Directory of Social Scientists Interested in Motivation Research*, (N. Y., 1954). The Foundation also underwrote George Horsley Smith, *Motivation Research in Advertising and Marketing*, (N. Y., McGraw-Hill, 1954, XIV, 242 pp.).

Motivation research seeks to discover those motives of which a man is not aware, or which he will not admit to having. While not necessarily concerned with the irrational or impulsive, much publicity has been given to its use in working out advertising appeals based on impulse and the unconscious drives. *cf.* Perin Stryker, « Motivation Research », *Fortune*, June, 1956. or any of the works on motivation research mentioned in the bibliography.

[12] For some enlightening remarks on the relation of the ethics of advertising to various psychological theories *cf.* F. P. Bishop, *The Ethics of Advertising*, (London: Robert Hale, 1949), pp. 55, 65, 87 and 93.

[13] Though we shall develop these obligations on a basis of the Chris-

the following points: 1. the obligation to act rationally; 2. man's dependence on others in fulfilling this obligation; 3. the obligation to help others act rationally.

In treating of the obligation to help others act rationally, it will be necessary to say something about the peculiar responsibilities of those who use the mass media and occupy a certain position of power in modern society. Though our treatment of this matter will be brief, it will serve to introduce the problem and to indicate the need for a development of the social ethics of persuasion [14].

THE OBLIGATION TO ACT RATIONALLY

The obligation to act rationally flows immediately from the very nature of man. Because man is a rational being endowed with freedom, the value of the human person depends on those *acts* (and not merely on the results of them), which proceed from the enlightened use of liberty [15]. This is to say that the moral and so the highest values of a man's being, depend on the degree to which he has made

---

tian humanistic tradition, it should be noted that others working within various philosophical frameworks have come to very similar conclusions. The following works are examples of this.

Karl Jaspers, « Wahrheit, Freiheit und Friede », *Frankfurter Allgemeine Zeitung*, Thursday, September 30, 1958, no. 226, p. 6.

Aldous Huxley, « Tyranny over the Mind », *A Special Supplement to Newsday*, (Garden City, N. Y.), pp. 8, 13, 22.

Harold Brown, « Advertising and Propaganda », *International Journal of Ethics* (later published simply as *Ethics*), 40 (1929), October, no. 1, pp. 39-55.

Charles A. Siepman, *Radio, Television and Society*, (N. Y., Oxford, 1950), pp. 197-199.

E. A. Lever, « The Application of First Principles », *Journal of the Advertising Association*, 5 (1950), December, no. 11. p. 9.

Robert K. Merton, *Mass Persuasion: The Social Psychology of a War Bond Drive*, (N. Y.:Harper and Brothers, 1946), pp. 186ff.

Bishop, *op. cit.*, p. 95.

Paul F. Lazarsfeld, « Why is so Little Known about the Effects of Television on Children and What can be Done » *Public Opinion Quarterly*, 19 (1955), no. 3, p. 249.

[14] Wilbur Schram, *Responsibility in Mass Communication*, (N. Y.: Harper and Brothers, 1957), has given a fine introduction to the problem, but has not developed any satisfactory principles to be used in solving the problem.

[15] Josephus de Finance, *Ethica Generalis*, (Romae, Pontificia Universitas Gregoriana, 1956, ad usum privatum), p. 32.

his activity specifically human [16], that is free, conscious, reflective and deliberate in accord with the demands of right reason. Man becomes more truly human, then, in proportion as his activity becomes more conscious and reflective [17].

For a man to be man it is not sufficient that his external acts be accidentally in accord with right reason. Truly human activity is actively dominated by reason, and man is not free to remain passive in all circumstances. Frequently man is obliged to use his reason and to show himself master of his activities [18]. Of course, man can abandon himself to mere chance or to the manipulation of others, but in doing so he refuses to be a man and to realize his specifically human perfection [19].

Men are obliged to act with reflection and deliberation, but because they are men and not angels, it is impossible for them to place every act with full deliberation and reflection. The limitations of space and time are such that in point of fact very few acts are perfectly human [20]. The ethician recognizes these limitations, and though he requires man to inquire and to reflect on the morality of his acts [21], he qualifies the obligation. In practice, then, a man's effort to control his actions and to discover their morality is proportionate to the importance of the matter at hand and to the responsibilities of the individual as these are evaluated by a prudent individual [22].

Even though a man may not be obliged to place every act with full deliberation, he will not succeed in acting morally unless he habitually strives for self-mastery and self-knowledge. The body can sometimes paralyze and even suppress the higher activity of man [23], and without a long

---

[16] Odon Lottin, *Morale Fondamentale*, (Paris: Desclée, 1954, p. 94.

[17] *ibid.*, p. 82.

[18] E. F. Regatillo and M. Zalba, *Theologia Moralis Summa Vol. I. Theologia Moralis Fundamentalis*, (Madrid: Biblioteca de autores christianos, 1942), p. 95.

[19] John Wild, *Introduction to Realistic Philosophy*, (N. Y.: Harper and Brothers, 1948), p. 59.

[20] Lottin, *op. cit.*, p. 94.

[21] Regatillo, *op. cit.*, p. 254.

[22] Irenaeus Gonzales Moral, *Philosophia Moralis*, (4th ed., Santander, Espana: Sal Terrae, 1955), p. 122.

[23] Jean Mouroux, *Sens chrétien de l'homme*, (Paris: Aubier, 1945), p. 59.

education of the body and its passions, it is difficult to think clearly [24]. The person who habitually abandons himself to his feelings and his impulses can only with difficulty establish the rule of reason in his life and exercise the proper amount of reflection. Habitual self-mastery is a necessary condition for moral activity.

In the real order such self-mastery is impossible without self-knowledge. Unless a man is able to account for his activities in terms of his motives, feelings and principles, he will scarcely be able to master himself and to develop his personality in line with the basic exigencies of his rational nature [25]. The need for self-knowledge is particularly acute in the modern world in which so many outside forces are attempting to influence the conduct of the individual [26].

We may summarize the above paragraphs in the following statements. First, man has a basic obligation to act in accord with right reason and under the direction of reason. Second, though full reflection is not mandatory at every moment, man is still obliged to strive for habitual self-mastery and self-knowledge in so far as they are a necessary preparation for the fulfillment of the obligation to act rationally.

MAN'S DEPENDENCE ON OTHERS

In striving to fulfill the obligation to act rationally man is dependent on others. This dependence, of which we shall note only two aspects, gives rise to rights and obligations which are of the utmost importance for the ethics of persuasion. In particular we shall consider the right to information and the obligation to create a healthy spiritual atmosphere.

The right to truthful information appears to be almost self-evident. An individual's time and natural endowment are limited and yet he is called upon to make numerous and often complex choices which involve a knowledge of

---

[24] *ibid.*, p. 44.
[25] Johannes Messner, *Kulturethik*, (Innsbruck: Tyrolia, 1954), p. 319.
[26] *ibid.*, p. 282.

the ends, means and pertinent circumstances. Since the individual needs information, but has neither the time nor the resources needed to gather it, he must turn to others [27]. The need for information gives rise to a right to information [28] which in its turn creates an obligation in others who control the necessary channels of communication.

Though the need for, and right to information seem fairly obvious, the obligation to create a healthy spiritual atmosphere or ethos is often neglected since individuals are not conscious of their dependence on it. Even though space does not permit an adequate discussion of the moral significance of man's dependence on the spiritual atmosphere of a society, the question of ethos is of some importance in developing an ethic of persuasion.

The ethos of a culture, which some would call a sort of collective unconsciousness, but which is better described as an atmosphere of unquestioned values, permeates and influences the activity of the individual [29]. So subtle is the influence of this spiritual atmosphere that the individual is with difficulty aware of the root causes of his own action [30]. This is true because the ethos colors not merely the speculative judgments of a person, but his value judgments, attitudes and, indeed, his whole moral consciousness [31]. So important is the ethos in the moral life of the individual, that Messner believes the future of Western civilization to be more a question of ethos and its power of moral renewal, than of economic, technical and military potentials [32].

The individual's dependence on his surroundings and in particular on the spiritual atmosphere implies a twofold danger. First, the ethos may be dominated by a false scale of values which will distort the person's practical ethical judgment. Second, the individual may be tempted to surrender to the ethos and abandon any attempt at rational

---

[27] Johannes Messner, *Das Naturrecht*, (3rd ed. Innsbruck: Tyrolia, 1958), p. 726 shows the importance of this in political life.
[28] Union internationale d'études sociales, *Code de morale politique*, (Paris: Spes, 1957), p. 99.
[29] Messner, *Kulturethik*, p. 283.
[30] *loc. cit.*
[31] *ibid.*, p. 331.
[32] *ibid.*, p. 364.

self-determination [33]. This latter temptation may, indeed,
be particularly strong in modern societies with their mas-
sive economic and technical organization [34].

The fact that man's dependence on his ethos gives rise
to these dangers imposes two obligations on him. First,
he must strive to develop his own critical faculties in an
effort to attain that self-knowledge of which we have already spoken [35]. Second, both individuals and groups must
seek to form the ethos according to a correct scale of
values [36]. This is to say that the danger of conflict between
the ethos and the obligation to act rationally gives rise to
both individual and collective responsibilities [37]. If individuals and groups neglect this obligation, they run the
risk of exposing both themselves and the whole of society
to the risk of acting irrationally and of weakening their
capacity for human auto-determination.

In the next section we shall see how the facts of man's
need for information and his dependence on the ethos as
well as his basic obligation to act rationally give rise to
certain obligations which bind those who seek to influence
human activity.

THE OBLIGATION TO HELP OTHERS ACT RATIONALLY

Our treatment of the obligation to help others act rationally, falls into two main parts. In the first of these we
treat of those obligations which arise from the virtue of
charity and affect all who seek to influence another. In the
second part, certain special obligations of those who use
the mass media are studied in view of the special relations
which these persuaders have with the public weal.

The first obligation of the persuader arises from the
natural law which obliges all men to love their neighbor

---

[33] *cf.* William Whyte, *The Organization Man*, (Garden City, N. Y.:
Doubleday Anchor Books, 1957), pp. 16-66 for an analysis of this temptation in contemporary America.

[34] Messner, *Kulturethik*, pp. 290 and 293.

[35] Messner, *Kulturethik*, p. 566.

[36] *ibid.*, p. 331.

[37] *ibid.*, pp. 363ff for a development of these obligations and *cf.* Regatillo, *op. cit.*, p. 136-137 as well as Arthur-Friolin Utz, *Sozialethik*, (Heidelberg: F. H. Kerle, 1958), p. 277.

as themselves [39]. This law of charity rests on an esteem
for the person of one's neighbor in so far as he has the
same nature and existential goal as one's self [40]. Consequently
it forbids man to hate or to wish evil to another and obliges one to work for his good in so far as one is able [41].
Because this charity is built on an esteem and reverence
for human nature, it forbids not only acts which directly
injure the other, or which make it hard for him to attain
his goal, but also such attitudes as imply a contempt for
his dignity as a man [42]. Positively, charity demands that
one exhibits and expresses esteem for others and help them
according to the measure of one's possibilities.

The persuader, no matter what his position or his ultimate goal, is bound by these obligations. He may not
deliberately move another to sin, nor may he deliberately
cooperate in the sin of another [43]. Further, the persuader
may not seek to influence another in such a way as to make
him less a man either by attempting to lessen his conscious
activity or by depriving him of information which he needs
for the formation of a proper judgment.

Now, though these precepts must be imposed with care
and with due regard for the distinctions introduced by the
moralist in the consideration of *scandal* and *cooperation*,
it would appear that certain advertising techniques offend
against these rules. Irrational or suggestive advertising in
particular violates charity on three counts. First, it implies
a contempt for the rational nature of man. Second, it disre-
gards the individual's obligation to reflect and so runs the
danger of causing him to sin. Third, it can stunt a man's
whole moral growth by inducing a habitual lack of reflection.

---

[39] Gonzales, *op. cit.*, p. 340, Messner, *Naturrecht*, p. 396.

[40] Messner, *Naturrecht*, p. 397.

[41] Gonzales, *op. cit.*, p. 342.

[42] For some interesting remarks on the obligation to reverence man,
cf. Messner, *Kulturethik*, p. 302.

[43] F. Hürth and P. M. Abellán, *De Principiis, de virtutibus, et praeceptis*, pars 1, (Romae: Pontificia Universitas Gregoriana, ad usum privatum, 1948), p. 197 for the distinction between scandalum and cooperation implied here.

SUGGESTIVE ADVERTISING

Before developing the three points given in the preceding paragraphs, it will be well to make some basic distinctions. When we speak of suggestive or irrational advertising, we are not referring to persuasive advertising as a whole, that is advertising which in addition to informing the consumer, seeks to move him and even to create new needs. Furthermore, suggestive advertising does not refer necessarily to advertising which plays on erotic themes. By suggestive advertising we mean that *advertising which seeks to bypass the reflective powers of man or to render them inoperative to a greater or lesser extent.* It is advertising which according to the theorists can circumvent conscious reasoning and seize hold of the reader's or listener's emotions directly [44]. To put it yet another way, it is advertising which seeks to influence the subject in spite of himself [45], and even when he disbelieves the claims made [46].

Now, the use of such methods as will produce non-reflective actions, implies a basic contempt for human nature, for as one writer has put it:

> The propagandist does not look upon those whom he attempts to influence as human beings with cogent powers of thought. Rather they are mere robots who will follow the course which he marks out [47].
>
> In its efforts to « modify the behaviour of the communicatee », the press has taken refuge in a semipsychology which looks only at part of and not the *whole* of man [48].

---

[44] Pease, *op. cit.,* p. 175.

[45] *ibid.,* p. 168.

[46] *ibid.,* p. 176. We prescind from the various techniques actually used to by-pass the intellect and to grasp the emotions directly. For some treatment of these questions and an application of the principles to be developed in the following pages *cf.* Thomas M. Garrett, « Moral en advertenies », *De Linie,* (Brussel) vrijdag 24 oktober 1958, no. 525, p. 5 on subliminal advertising. « Depth Research and Depth Communication as Ethical Problems », *Address at the Eight International Conference of the Green Meadows Foundation,* (Rüschlikon-Zürich, July 1, 1959), and « Die Ethik der Propaganda », *Orientierung,* 23 (1959) no. 6, März 31, 1959, pp. 65-68.

[47] John Joseph O'Connor, *Philosophical Aspects of Communication,* (Washington, D.C. Catholic University of America Philosophical Studies, no. 145, abstract no. 11), p. 3.

[48] *ibid.,* p. 5.

It is true, of course, that emotion, impulse and drives do have a part to play in human conduct. The educator recognizes this and attempts to harmonize them with the demands of reason. He may even use emotion to heighten awareness and increase the intellectual consideration of relevant facts. At times, he may even use fear and punishment in an effort to restore the reflective equilibrium which may be disturbed by other emotions· The educator, then, uses emotion to form the whole man, that is a person who uses his intellect to direct his actions [49]. Here, there is no contempt of human dignity, and no intention of lessening it, but a desire to perfect and realize the full value of the person.

The above remarks should make it clear that suggestive advertising is *not evil because it uses emotion, but because it makes man less a man* and is an implicit act of contempt for man's dignity. Such an attitude is ethically reprehensible not only because it sins against the reverence due man [50], but because of its consequences.

If the persuader causes a man to neglect his obligation to reflect he exposes man to all the evil consequences of irrational activity. If it is wrong to act in this way, it is wrong to persuade him to act in this way.

Some try to escape from this conclusion by insisting that the individual acts irrationally even in the absence of persuasion, and that consequently suggestive advertising does not really cause him to neglect his obligations [51]. Even if this excuse were true in its factual assertions, it would not be valid since suggestive advertising by definition intends to cause such action, to reinforce such irrationality, and to by-pass the intellect. No matter what the actual effects may be, the intention remains unethical. Though the intention behind suggestive advertising is reprehensible in and of itself, its unethical character is reinforced when it succeeds in by-passing the intellect and causing acts which are not in accord with right reason. Thus, an induced lack of reflection might lead a person to buy

---

[49] *ibid.*, p. 6.

[50] Messner, *Kulturethik*, p. 303.

[51] Pease, *op. cit.*, p. 179 cites several advertising men whose view of the average consumer as « a fourteen-year old animal », is used to justify suggestive advertising.

luxuries before he has basic essentials. Advertising has, of course, been accused of encouraging just such behaviour. To such accusations the defenders of advertising reply as follows:

> Presumably advertising has played its part in stimulating these purchases. But it does not seem reasonable that advertising should be taken to task because some people are improvident. Advertising is not in a position to determine what each of its readers can or cannot afford, and to gauge its message accordingly. Nor does it follow that the improvident person would cease to be improvident just because there was no advertising.
> That some people live beyond their means is no reason that advertising should desist from encouraging the majority of the consuming public to buy things. For through their purchase, the American standard of living has been raised above that of all the rest of the world [52].

This argument is not without a certain amount of validity. The vast amount of advertising which presents information about the qualities of a product and its uses is not a cause of improvidence, but at most a remote occasion or circumstance connected with the improvidence of individuals. Further, as the citation notes, there are proportionate reasons for permitting the continuation of such advertising. In other words, in so far as the relation between *informative* advertising and improvidence is merely accidental, the advertiser has no obligation to omit an action which is legitimate in itself and placed for good reason [53].

The argument given by the Better Business Bureau is not, however, valid in the case of suggestive advertising, as we have defined it. First, suggestive advertising, being wrong in and of itself, cannot be justified by any « proportionate » reason [54]. Secondly, suggestive advertising by its very nature intends to make the internal act improvident, that is, placed without foresight. Suggestive advertising is, then, responsible to some degree for the external act precisely in so far as it has caused the moral defect from which this act proceeds. Third, even if suggestive

---

[52] *Facts you should Know about Advertising*, (N. Y.: Better Business Bureau, 1953), p. 8-9.
[53] *cf.* Hürth-Abellán, *op. cit.*, p. 294 for principles.
[54] Regatillo-Zalba, *op. cit.*, p. 921 for principles.

advertising were not evil, there would appear to be no room for the application of the principle of proportionately grave reason. This principle is applicable only when there is no other way of obtaining the good effect [55]. Since informative advertising is probably equally if not more effective in promoting sales, there can be ordinarily no reason for persuasive advertising which tries to diminish reflection [56].

For these three reasons, it seems that suggestive advertising is doubly wrong when the lack of reflection leads to improvident external acts. This conclusion is reinforced by the fact that suggestive advertising may lead to a *habitual lack of reflection* capable of stunting moral growth and leading to the placing of sinful external acts [57]. This danger has been pointed out by more than one social scientist. Siepman has this to say:

> . . . the pervasiveness of propaganda, our constant exposure to it at different levels and in different forms, tends to undermine belief in our capacity to be ourselves. The widespread abuse of propaganda raises doubts about the integrity of others, induces a fear of manipulation and weakens our moral fiber [58].

Merton makes a very similar point and stresses the ultimate dangers to society which reside in suggestive advertising.

> No single advertising or propaganda campaign may significantly affect the psychological stability of those subjected to it. But a society subjected ceaselessly to a flow of « effective » half-truths and the exploitation of mass anxieties may all the sooner lose the mutuality of confidence and reciprocal trust so essential to a stable social structure [59].

---

55 *loc. cit.*

56 James D. Woolf, « The More You Tell, the More You Sell, », *Advertising Age*, February 10, 1958, p. 66. Woolf reports on the results of a study made by the Graduate School of Retailing at New York University which confirmed the title of his article.

57 Harold Burtt, *Psychology of Advertising*, (Boston: Houghton Mifflin, 1938), p. 7 has noted the dangers which can result from preferences developed by conditioning, adaptation and suggestion.

58 Charles A. Siepmann, *Radio, Television and Society*, (N. Y.: Oxford U. Press, 1950), p. 196.

59 Robert K. Merton, *Mass Persuasion: The Social Psychology of a War Bond Drive*, (N. Y.: Harper and Brothers, 1946), p. 189.

4

It may be objected, of course, that in the absence of sound research which demonstrates the existence of such effects, there is no obligation to cease using suggestive advertising for this reason. The absence of sound research is not, however, an alibi if the prudent judgment of experts and the available evidence indicates the existence of a real danger. To put it another way, a well founded moral certitude is enough to establish an obligation even in the absence of scientific certitude based on the best research. This is the opinion of even the most serious of social scientists [60].

Not only the opinions given above, but common sense indicates that repeated suggestive advertising designed to reduce reflection should, in the normal course of events, lead to the diminution of reflection or to the creation of an air of distrust. Advertising, to be sure, is not the only force working in this direction, and so not solely responsible for the strengthening of the tendency to act without reflection. Nevertheless, suggestive advertising must bear some of the burden of guilt for effects which flow from the very nature of the instrument used.

These considerations indicate that suggestive advertising is not an ethically acceptable means to be used in increasing consumption. Even if increased consumption were a social necessity, it cannot be used to justify the use of a means which in itself implies a contempt for human nature and tends to lead to the performance of acts and the formation of habits which are destructive, socially and individually.

Though the general tendency seems to be to accept suggestive advertising as a useful tool, some advertising men have laid down principles which would seem to condemn it. Melvin Brorby, Chairman of the Board of the American Association of Advertising Agencies has writen:

> And we must do one more thing that is perhaps most important of all: We must give the consumer a break, treat him as we ourselves would like to be treated. That old Golden Rule isn't so bad after all— and it *can* be made to jibe with the stiffest competition.

---

[60] Paul F. Lazarsfeld, « Why is so Little Known about the Effects of Television on Children and What can be Done? » *Public Opinion Quarterly*, 19 (1955), no. 3, p. 249.

Giving the consumer a break means giving him and her credit for good taste and intelligence... We don't need to play down to them. They are not morons nor illiterates [61].

ETHOS AND PERSUASION

The obligation to form the ethos according to a correct scale of values binds all persuaders in so far as they are men and citizens [62]. This obligation may be particularly great in the case of those persuaders who use the mass media since their influence though not necessarily decisive [63], is greater than that of an ordinary citizen.

In the case of advertising designed to raise the standard of living and to change the concept of how to live [64], this obligation is of great importance. Such advertising is not merely selling a product, but is attempting to change a philosophy of life, a way of thinking and judging. In other words, advertising for a higher standard of living is a form of education, that is of intellectual and volitional formation, and not merely a means of informing the public where and how it can buy goods and services [65].

The fact that advertising men have set themselves up as educators poses a problem for society and imposes an obligation on advertising. The problem is well expressed by William Vickrey.

> Informative advertising shades over imperceptibly into propaganda, education and missionary activity in the broad sense. What is the place, in the broad scale of values, of activity designed to change the opinions, preferences and ideals of individuals? We can hardly rest content to leave the decisions as to how much effort is to be devoted to various kinds of educational and propaganda effort, to be determined by the financial support of those who are interested either commercially or emotionally. This would imply that the ability of

---

[61] Melvin Brorby, *We Ask Ourselves Four Questions*, (N. Y.: American Association of Advertising Agencies, 1958), p. 13.

[62] *cf.* Messner, *Kulturethik*, pp. 331; 363; 566.

[63] For confirmation see Chapter VI.

[64] *cf.* Chapter II and Pease, *op. cit.*, pp. 20ff. « National Advertising and the Good Life ».

[65] For an interesting discussion of this educational aspect of advertising *cf.* David M. Potter, *People of Plenty*, (Chicago: Univ. of Chicago, 1954).

an idea or a program to command financial support would be
the prime measure of the importance attached to its propagation [66].

Though this problem cannot be solved without additional study, its very existence indicates that the advertising profession has a serious obligation to consider not only the psychological effectiveness of the motives it employs, but their moral significance for the whole of society. This is merely to say that the advertiser and his agents must accept the obligations of a public educator at the same time as they claim his privileges [67].

In the following chapter we shall consider some of the values which the advertiser must respect in his attempt to raise the standard of living. The larger problem of advertising and its relation to the whole value scale of modern culture must be left to another study [68]. Here we can only indicate that there is a problem and an obligation to study it [69].

ADVERTISING AND INFORMATION

In the previous sections we considered the obligations to respect the rational and reflective nature of man and to form the ethos or spiritual atmosphere which is of such importance in human activity. Man, however, needs not only reflection and sound values, but information if he is to act as man. He needs information about the alternative means which are available, and about those qualities of the means which make them more or less suitable for

---

[66] William Vickrey, « Goals of Economic Life: An Interchange of Questions Between Economics and Philosophy », in A. Dudley Word, (ed.) *Goals of Economic Life*, (N. Y.: Harper and Brothers, 1953), p. 159.

[67] Their obligation is analogous to that of the press and other mass media. *Cf.* Messner, *Kulturethik*, pp. 518-536.

[68] William Lynch, *The Image Industries*, (N. Y.: Sheed and Ward, 1959) has attempted to do this for television and radio, i. e. tried to show the moral significance of their activity in relation to cultural ideals and values.

[69] « Admen Morally Worried », *America* 100 (1959) no. 23, March 14. p. 675 reports that there is some incipient awareness of this problem in the advertising profession.

the attainment of his goals. Because man needs this information he has a right to it [70].

This right to information imposes corresponding obligations on others. There is first of all the obligation not
to impede an individual in his search for necessary information. Secondly, there is some obligation on the part
of those who control information to supply truthful and
adequate reports bearing on the facts which individuals
need for their decision. This latter obligation can bind
professional groups as well as individuals, whether they
be connected with the state or with private interests.

Before going on to consider the basis of these obligations, in greater detail, it will be well to clarify the position of the advertising profession since it is their obligations which are of particular interest in this study. Some
members of the profession insist that advertising is an
advocate who is to present those facts which are most
favorable to his client [71]. While they admit that the advocate must be truthful, they seem to think of their first
obligation as being to the client and not to the public [72].
This attitude, however, is at odds with such official statements as that in the Code of Standards of Advertising
Practice of the International Chamber of Commerce which
states:

> As part of our system of free enterprise and of our system
> of distribution, satisfying consumers' needs and comfort, ad-
> vertising has a social responsibility towards the consumer.
> Advertising is an important and legitimate means for the seller
> to awaken interest in his products and services.
> In this process, some practices of the seller may at times
> be opposed to the rightful interests of the community. Wher-
> ever a conflict of this kind arises, *the interest of the public
> should be protected first and foremost* [73].

As early as 1911 the Advertising Federation of America
made this declaration.

> Advertising is the voice of commerce. . .

---

[70] *Code Politique*, p. 99.
[71] George D. Bryson, « What Advertising can Give the Consumer »,
The International Advertising Conference, Great Britain, 1951, (London:
Advertising Association), p. 24.
[72] Pease, *op. cit.*, p. 149.
[73] p. 3 (revised edition 1955).

But it has a higher responsibility than private trading or individual conduct because it is a public pledge made in a public medium and disseminates to millions of people information and impressions which affect their daily lives [74].

The following quotations, taken from succeeding pages in a pamphlet published by the American Association of Advertising Agencies clarify somewhat the nature of this obligation to the public.

Let's admit that advertising does *not* have an uplift mission.   Its job is to sell goods effectively.   But if it does this with due regard to the client's long-range public relations, with honesty, fairness, and with increasing understanding (provided by research) of customers' real needs, and with an understanding of the country's needs, then in my opinion there *is* an « uplift » that follows [75].

On the very next page the author writes:

Does advertising, should advertising have a « social consciousness »?   Well, of course — it does and must have one increasingly.   As the power of advertising grows, so does its responsibility grow.   What is good for the public must be an ever growing concern.   That is a responsibility of top management, both agency and advertiser, one it cannot escape [76].

Though one hesitates to say that these obligations are admitted by all members of the profession [77], the opinions and declarations given above do indicate that a segment of the advertising profession admits having a social responsibility. This social responsibility obliges them to consider the real needs of consumers and of the nation, as well as the long-range interests of their clients.

Does this responsibility include the obligation not to impede the flow of necessary information, and the positive obligation to supply information in certain circumstances?

---

[74] cited by Pease, *op. cit.*, p. 145 as reported in *Printers' Ink*, July 9, 1936, p. 44.

[75] Brorby, *op. cit.*, p. 10.

[76] *ibid.*, p. 11.

[77] Interviews indicate that these questions are frequently not considered at all since many members of the profession consider themselves as technicians who do a job and not as members of a profession. Further since they are not ethicians, they tend to express themselves in terms of a common sense morality which revolves around truthfulness and decency without touching on the broader areas of social responsibility.

This question cannot be answered without some understanding of what is meant by such terms as « the interests of the public », « the good of the public », and « the real needs of the consumer ». As we have already shown in the opening passages of this chapter, the individual does need information to fulfill his obligation to act rationally. In a free economy this information is also a social necessity since without it the market will not have that transparence necessary for the socially efficient functioning of the price mechanism [78].

From this need arises the first obligation of the advertiser, and indeed of any persuader who has great power; the obligation not to impede the free flow of information necessary for the decisions of the individual and the efficient functioning of the social economy [79]. In the concrete this implies an obligation not to interfere with the legitimate editorial freedom of editors, publishers and owners of the mass media which are the indispensable channels of information in modern society [80]. In addition, there is an obligation not to interfere with other private groups such as consumers' unions which have as their legitimate and useful function the supplying of information [81].

The obligations stated above are clear enough in so far as they apply to direct interference with the flow of information [82]. What, however, is to be said of the obligation of advertising to avoid indirect and indeliberate interference with the flow of information? This question arises only because the actual position of advertising in American society, seems to have led to a diminution of the supply of unbiased and necessary information available to the public. While we cannot hope to solve this problem in the present study, it should be presented since its very existence casts some doubt on the suitability of

[78] *Cf.* Wilhelm Roepke, *Masse und Mitte*, (Zürich: Rentsch 1950), p. 203.
[79] *cf. Naturrecht*, p. 893.
[80] An obligation recognized explicitly in many codes. *cf.* for example, *Rules for Dutch Press Advertising*, (Amsterdam, 1957), pp. 21-22.
[81] *cf.* Pease, *op. cit.*, p. 105 for examples of this interference with the consumers' unions.
[82] For examples of this direct interference *cf. Leonard* W. Doob, *Public Opinion and Propaganda*, (London: Cresset Press, 1949), p. 427. Bishop, *op. cit.*, pp. 167 ff.; Theodore Peterson, *Magazines in the Twentieth Century*, (Urbana, Illinois; U. of Illinois Press, 1956), pp. 37-38.

privately controlled advertising as a means of economic and social progress.

The problem of indirect interference with the normal channels of information is rooted in the financial relationship which exists between advertiser and media owner. In the United States, for example, the radio and television are supported almost entirely by advertising revenue, while the newspapers and magazines depend on advertising for an important part of their income [83]. Advertising is so important that newspapers cannot in general survive without it [84].

The financial support given by advertising has enabled the media to free themselves from much political influence [85], but at the same time has made them subject to the influence of the advertisers [86]. More fundamentally, however, it has led to an identification of interests which makes impartiality difficult. One does not bite the hand that feeds him.

Students of this question believe that this relationship explains the silence of the media on many questions which affect the welfare of the consumer and the citizen. Thus, Pease in writing about the attacks of advertising on the consumer movement during the thirties notes that many commercial media refused to publish useful information provided by the testing agencies [87]. Another author points out that the releases of the Federal Trade Commission on misrepresentation in advertising are not given very wide circulation in the press even though they are of interest to the public [88]. The most serious danger, as Taylor has pointed out, is not that the media will unduly praise the products of their advertisers, but that they will omit anything which is unfavorable [89].

---

[83] Potter, *op. cit.*, pp. 179 ff.; Peterson, *op. cit.*, p. 22.

[84] Norman John Powell, *Anatomy of Public Opinion*, (N. Y.: Prentice Hall, 1951), p. 231.

[85] Powell, *op. cit.*, pp. 231-232.

[86] Ralph M. Hower, *The History of an Advertising Agency* (revised ed. Cambridge Mass., Harvard U. Press, 1949), p. 430.

[87] Pease, *op. cit.*, p. 105.

[88] Blake Clark, *The Advertising Smokescreen*, (N. Y.: Harper and Brothers, 1944), pp. 19-20.

[89] F. W. Taylor, *The Economics of Advertising*, (London: Allen and Unwin, 1934), p. 152 and p. 153.

This indirect supression of information is not limited to news which bears on products and services, but can extend to information which affects political and national issues. Thus in the depression of 1957-58 newspapers played down pessimistic news since as some said, they did not want to scare the advertiser to death [90].

Though this question of advertising's indirect influence demands further study, the following points should be stressed. First, the responsibility for this situation is divided between ,the advertisers, the media owners and the public. Second, the fundamental responsibility rests with the public and on those institutions which are responsible for its education [91]. Third, the press is responsible both as a semi-educational institution, and as a factor which may have weakened the critical sense of viewers and readers [92]. Fourth, the professional associations of advertisers and their agents have an obligation to work together with other groups to assure that the media have the necessary freedom and the consumer the necessary information for the making of intelligent choices.

This last obligation of the advertising profession is founded on the following facts. First, advertising itself is at least indirectly responsible for the situation in the press. Second, advertising may have conditioned the consumer not to expect or look for information [93]. Third, an informed public is an asset to honest manufacturers and advertisers themselves [94]. Fourth, without the cooperation of the advertising associations, other groups will find it difficult to fulfill their own obligations [95].

Though the obligation of advertisers to avoid impeding the free flow of necessary information seems clear, there remains the question as to whether advertising is obliged

---

[90] *Time*, (Atlantic Edition), 17 March 1958, pp. 45-46 and « Suburbia Snubs the Recession » *Fortune*, 57 (1958), May, no. 5, p. 116.

[91] Messner, *Naturrecht*, pp. 882-883, *Kulturethik*, p. 526.

[92] Messner, *Kulturethik*, p. 522 and p. 526.

[93] This should be the normal result of effective suggestive advertising.

[94] *cf*. Louis Darms, « Le consommateur a-t-il démissioné? » *Organisation Scientifique*, février 1959. The author a Belgian advertising man and professor of advertising is also president of the Union Belge des Consommateurs.

[95] The whole of Pease's book constitutes a well documented proof of this statement. *cf. The Responsibilities of American Advertising.*

to provide the needed information itself.   The Code of
the Association of Better Business Bureaus clearly states
such a duty in the following points.

> Tell the customers what they want to know—what they
> have a right to know and ought to know about what is offered
> so that they may buy wisely and obtain the maximum satis-
> faction from their purchases [96].
> Reveal material facts, the deceptive concealment of which
> might cause consumers to be mislead [97].

The Chamber of Commerce of the United States also
recognizes that the good of the advertising profession itself
imposes such an obligation.

> The effective future of advertising rests upon constant
> improvements in its techniques, *upon increasing use of fac-
> tual information*, upon the recognition of the great harm that
> a small amount of inferior advertising can do, and upon a
> better understanding of advertising by government, by business
> and by the public [98].

The same group also recognizes that this obligation
is founded on the fact that advertising plays an indispensable part in selling and in educating the American people
about goods and services [99].   In short, advertising is obliged
to give more information if it is to fulfill its educational
task.

The basic ideas behind the above statements may be
summarized as follows [100].   Information is indispensable

---

[96] cited by Verne Burnett, *Self-Regulation of Advertising* (N. Y. American Association of Advertising Agencies, 1950), p. 12.

[97] cited by Burnett, *op. cit.*, p. 13.

[98] *ibid.*, p. 27.

[99] *loc. cit.*

[100] For general background on the obligations of professional groups
cf. Messner, *Naturrecht*, pp. 514-515; *Kulturethik*, p. 472. Utz, *Sozialethik*,
p. 152. Union Internationale d'Etudes Sociales, *Code Social* (Paris: Spes.
1948), pp. 51 ff.

It should be noted that though social justice and social charity oblige
all to work for the common good, certain professions have particular
obligations which arise from the fact that the given profession is by its
nature or *de facto* position in a society in a unique position to provide a
service which is necessary for the proper functioning of society.

The fulfillment of these obligations has an importance which extends
beyond the immediate satisfaction of a social need, for when professional
groups fail to cooperate in the service of the general interest of a nation,
the state is obliged to step in. *cf. Code Social*, p. 53. This, of course,

for the efficient functioning of the economy and for the
intelligent consumption choices of individuals. Advertising,
however, is an indispensable source of the information in
question. Therefore the public weal demands that advertising supply this information. Further, the good of the
advertising profession itself depends on the efficient functioning of the economy. Therefore the common good of
the profession itself demands that it supply this information.

It should be noted that this obligation to give information necessary for intelligent buying is shared by a whole
series of agents in the marketing process: the national
advertiser, the retail advertiser, the salesman. The services
of these agents are complementary so that the national
advertiser often contents himself with announcing the
existence and general availability of a product or service.
The retail advertiser, being closer to the customer, may
specify the qualities of the product and give exact information as to its local price and availability. Finally, the
salesman who is in personal contact with the consumer
can inform about details and characteristics of interest to
the individual.

Now since this division of the information function
seems to be reasonable as well as legitimate, it is difficult
to see how those farthest removed from the consumer
have an obligation to supply *all* the information needed
for an intelligent purchase. The obligation to give adequate and complete information falls first of all on sales
people and retailers, and only secondarily on national
advertisers. When there are no sales people (as is the
case in self-service merchandising), the obligation of the
advertiser increases. However, the amount of information
and its quality need only be adequate relative to the total
information process. This principle should be kept in
mind in judging advertising lest the advertiser be burden-
ed with functions that belong more properly to others
in the total merchandising process.

---

can lead to a diminution of initiative and of self responsibility and ultimately to the danger of other abuses.

The Problem of Application

The conclusions reached in the foregoing pages are concerned with principles and general obligations. They are tools to be used in judging advertising and the proposal of the advertising profession. Though some advertising must be condemned in the light of these principles, our conclusions do not constitute a condemnation of advertising as such. Before a given advertisement can be condemned, the ethician must ascertain if the techniques used are actually of such a nature as to reduce rationality and reflection. He is faced, then, with the problem of application.

The problem of applying principles is complicated by the fact that many techniques can serve either to decrease or to increase reflection. Emotion can be used to arouse the necessary attention as well as to hypnotize and to produce impulsive action. A simplified presentation of the facts may be good pedagogy and an aid to enlightened choice, or it may be a means of obscuring the real point at issue [101].

Finally, it must be recognized that those who use the mass media are not dealing with an homogeneous audience. Consequently a technique or a presentation that would help one reader or listener to make an enlightened choice might only confuse another. Thus, a complete description of the characteristics and performance of an automobile might be of great help to an expert and merely leave the average reader with a confused impression. Indeed, it must be admitted that just such technical presentations have been used in order to flatter the reader and confuse him [102].

---

[101] Packard, *op. cit.*, p. 8 though very critical of those who use depth research, admits that the majority of those in the advertising profession « still do a straight forward job and accept us as rational citizens (whether we are or not) ». Pease, *op. cit.*, p. 195. likewise admits that though there was a growing trend to nonrational advertisements, the majority were still based on rational appeals in 1940.

[102] Pease, *op. cit.*, pp. 177-178.

SUMMARY AND APPLICATION TO THE
PROPOSAL OF THE ADVERTISING PROFESSION

Our examination of the ethical problem of persuasion in general and of mass-media persuasion in particular, has yielded the following conclusions. Persuasion is ethical if it respects the rational nature of man and the obligation of the individual to reflect. Those persuaders who use the mass-media must also see to it that their activity does not lead to the formation of an unhealthy ethos. The peculiar position of American advertising in the overall communication and marketing structure obliges the advertising profession to protect the free flow of necessary information and, in the measure of the public's need and its possibility, to supply this information.

These conclusions are of great importance in evaluating the ethical value of the proposal of the advertising profession. In the first place suggestive advertising, being wrong in and of itself cannot be justified, no matter what its supposed contribution to economic growth and the public weal. The end does not justify the means. So long as the economy is ordered to man, and to his ultimate human perfection, an increase in wealth can never be an excuse for causing a man to neglect his obligation, i. e., to act with that reflection which is the specific perfection of human nature.

In the second place, it should be clear, at least in a general way, that an increase in wealth cannot render acceptable advertising which creates or reinforces an ethos which embodies a set of pseudo-values. Though further study is required before we can formulate precise obligations in this field, it must be recognized that there are real ethical problems involved [103].

In the last place we must consider the mass persuader's obligation to protect and where possible to promote the

---

[103] Dr. Dichter's proposal that the advertising profession encourage a certain hedonism seems clearly unethical. *cf.* citation of Dr. Ernest Dichter in Pachard, *op. cit.*, p. 263. The same is to be said of Dr. Dichter's suggestion that « ... we must reject the image of a heavenly father who rewards and punishes daily conduct the way a father does ». *cf.* Dr. Ernest Dicher, « The Psychology of Prosperity », *Harvard Business Review*, 35 (1957), December no. 6, p. 22.

free flow of necessary information. Advertisers and advertising agents who *deliberately* set out to censor the editorial content of the media [104], or to reduce the amount of product information available to the public are clearly acting against the good of society and cannot be justified by their alleged contribution to economic growth.

Any efforts to slant or distort the news on the actual state of the economy are to be rejected as means of raising the propensity to consume and encouraging economic growth [105].

Such clear cut cases of direct and deliberate interference are, however, more likely to be the exception rather than the rule. More commonly the influence of advertising on media content and on the availability of information will be indirect and unintentional. While such influence may not be desirable, it is to a certain extent counterbalanced by the fact that advertising support does free the media from political control [106]. Further, since the main obligation belongs to the public and the media owners, the advertising profession has limited obligations in this sphere. Consequently, the indirect and unintentional influence on the media can be tolerated and permitted in view of the good effects which flow from honest advertising [107].

---

[104] There may, of course, be occasions when the conscience of the advertiser will oblige him to threaten withdrawal of his support of a given newspaper.

[105] *cf*. note 92 *supra* for examples of such interference.

[106] Some, of course, are not sure that the overall benefits justify all advertising in all media. For an example *cf*. Einar Dessau, « The Responsibility and Ethics of World-Wide Advertising », *Second International Advertising Conference in Europe*, (The Hague: Netherlands Advertising Association, 1957), pp. 38-39.

[107] An application of double effect in the social order seems in place in such questions where the dubious effect is not intended either as an end or a means and where the good effects are of such a magnitude as to outweight the indirect bad effects.

Chapter V

THE ETHICS OF CONSUMPTION

In the previous chapter we considered some of the norms which must govern the use of persuasion and of mass persuasion in particular. Advertising, however, is not persuasion in the abstract, but is directed to changing the consumption of individuals and of society. The present chapter, then, seeks to discover if the proposal of the advertising profession is reconcilable with the ethical obligations of the individual consumer and of society as a whole. As in the previous chapter we shall first consider the obligations of those who are the object of the persuasive activity and, then, those of the persuaders. First, however, it is necessary to recall some basic principles.

At the very start, it will be well to eliminate two false positions which have complicated previous discussions of these questions. The first position contains a hedonistic bias, the second a vague sort of « puritanism ».

The hedonistic approach measures the value of a product by the satisfaction or gratification that it gives to a consumer [1]. It is assumed more or less implicitly that the consumer is free to chose what gives him the greatest satisfaction. Bishop, for example puts it this way.

> The consumer decides, for while free competition remains there is no appeal from his decision. Nor is there any standard by which his decisions can be judged to be wrong; for no man, be he never (sic) so wise, can judge the satisfactions of another [2].
>
> And the moralist who undertakes to define those things undertakes the responsibility of deciding, for other people, what the ends of life should be [3].

---

[1] Otto Kleppner, *Where Does Advertising Fit In?* (N. Y.: Association of National Advertisers, 1952), p. 16.

[2] F. P. Bishop, *The Ethics of Advertising*, (London: Robert Hall, 1949), p. 49.

[3] *ibid.*, p. 51 Bishop does not declare himself a hedonist, but leaves

Granted that the economist sometimes prescinds from the ethical question, and indeed even denies its relevance to economics[4], individuals must consider what the ends of life are, and the relation of « satisfactions », to the attainment of these ends. Some claim that it is the business of advertising to gratify wants and not to determine how much they are needed[5]. However, it should be noted that when advertising sets out to create wants, it is no longer free to pass the responsibility on to the consumer. It must then face the problem of deciding whether its activity will lead to the perfection of man.

The « puritain » mentality lurks beneath the criticisms of those who object to all attempts to stimulate desire[6]. At other times it manifests itself in what appears to be a contempt for all purely earthly values such as money, comfort and progress[7]. Again it may manifest itself in a sort of pessimism founded on men's supposed inability to master material things and to use them for higher purposes[8]. Such attitudes, though not always explicit, oversimplify the problem and to a large extent eliminate the possibility of a solution by posing a dilemma: hedonism or puritanism.

In the following pages both extremes must be avoided. Experience shows us that certain goods and services make no contribution to human development, that others must be used with great caution, and that some, though of varying quality, have in general a real contribution to make. It is further recognized that gratifications are important and supply much of the motive power that drives man to perfect himself[9]. Finally, it is accepted as a fact

---

the individual free to determine the ends of life after having examined the great ethical systems. *cf. ibid.*, p. 34.

[4] *cf.* C. A. Stocking, « Advertising and Economic Theory », *American Economic Review*, 21 (1931), p. 46.

[5] *Facts You Should Know about Advertising*, (N. Y.: Association of Better Business Bureaus, 1953), p. 9.

[6] Colin Clark, « Morals and Economics », in J. M. Todd. (ed.), *The Springs of Morality*, (London: Burns and Oates, 1956), p. 114.

[7] B. Charbonneu, « La Publicité » *Esprit*, 3 (1935), April. no. 31, p. 12.

[8] Lawrence Moran, « The Myth of Machine-Made Leisure », *Social Order*, 6 (1956), p. 438.

[9] Johannes Messner, *Kulturethik*, (Innsbruck: Tyrolia Verlag, 1954), p. 596.

that there is an element of risk which cannot be completely eliminated but only reduced by prudence [10].

Our basic position in the following pages can be stated as follows: Man is to use material goods for the attainment of his existential goal [11]. From this it follows that man must so order his consumption that it contributes to the attainment of this end [12]. Since this goal is common to all men, the individual must also see to it that material goods are used not only for his own personal perfection, but for the perfection of all who share the same goal [13]. Even though it is not necessary that the individual *explicitly* order his economic activity to this goal, he must at least assure its *defacto* harmony with the final end of all human activity [14].

Economic activity is, however, *only one* of the means to the elevation and perfection of man, and must be coordinated not only with the final goal, but with the other means and values which are a part of human life [15]. To put it another way, economic activity must be coordinated with the axiological order of other means, and with the obligatory order in which these means are to be used [16]. Each of these orders must be considered separately before the meaning of these statements can be understood.

By the axiological order is meant the hierarchy of values as determined by the relation of given goods to the perfection of man [17]. At the lowest level are found the infra-human values such as the pleasant or the unpleas-

---

[10] *ibid.*, pp. 545 ff. and expecially, p. 554 and p. 564.

[11] Johannes Messner, *Naturrecht*, (3rd ed. Innsbruck: Tyrolia Verlag, 1958), p. 883.

[12] *cf.* R. P. Laurent, « Progrès technique, progrès économique, progrès humain », *43ᵉ Semaine Sociale de France: Les exigences humaines de l'expansion économique*, (Paris: Gabalda, 1956), p. 106.

[13] Union Internationale d'Etudes Sociales, *Code Social*, (Paris: Spes, 1948), pp. 62 ff.

[14] Oswald von Nell-Breuning, *Wirtschaft und Gesellschaft* (Freiburg i. Br., Herder, 1956), Vol. I, pp. 173 and 203.

[15] André Piettre, « Les fins et les choix d'une politique d'expansion », *43ᵉ Semaine Sociale de France: Les exigences humaines de l'expansion économique*, (Paris: Gabalda, 1956), p. 118.

[16] Messner, *Naturrecht*, pp. 883 and 46 and 118.

[17] Various schemas, all essentially the same can be found in Messner, *op. cit.*, p. 46; Jean Mouroux, *Sens chrétien de l'homme*, (Paris: Aubier, 1945), p. 11 and in Josephus de Finance, *Ethica Generalis*, (Romae: Pontificia Universitas Gregoriana, 1959), pp. 37-38.

ant (sensible values) or as health and sickness (biological
values). After these in ascending order we have economic
values, social values, noetic and esthetic values and finally
the highest of human values which relate to the innermost
perfection of man: the moral and religious values.

This hierarchy of values imposes a certain direction
on all human activity. The lower values are to be realized
in view of the higher so that man must resist the temptation to make lower ones into goals which exclude the
moral and religious values from their primacy [18]. In particular the individual must be on his guard against the
fascination of the pleasure value which can make him
forget the existence and obligatory character of higher
values [19].

Though the lower values must always be ordered to
the higher ones and ultimately to the final perfection of
man, the *temporal order of realization* is determined not
merely by the position of a value, but by the urgency
and necessity of its realization at a given moment [20]. Man
being conditioned by the limitations of space and time
cannot realize all values and satisfy all needs simulta-
niously [21]. The satisfaction of certain needs cannot be
postponed without serious consequences, while other needs,
which are, perhaps, concerned with higher goods, can be
left unsatisfied for the moment without harm to man's
total perfection [22].

In the temporal order the necessary takes precedence
over the merely useful, and the useful over the pleasant.
Often, indeed, the immediately urgent must be cared for
before the higher and the more ultimate values can be
realized. This sort of temporal displacement or postpone-
ment is legitimate and even obligatory, but only on condition that the higher values are not destroyed in the process
and that the lower are still ordered to the higher [23]. Thus
while the urgent need for increased production in the
underdeveloped countries cannot justify the enslavement

---

[18] Mouroux, *op. cit.*, p. 16.
[19] Messner, *Kulturethik*, (Innsbruck: Tyrolia Verlag, 1954), p. 435.
[20] Messner, *Naturrecht*, p. 46.
[21] *ibid.*, p. 188.
[22] *ibid.*, p. 190.
[23] Messner, *Naturrecht*, p. 47.

of the population and the removal of their basic rights [24], fundamental economic development should take precedence over the cultivation of the fine arts.

The temporal element which sometimes makes it obligatory to give precedence to tasks of lesser intrinsic value, can also impose an obligation to forego the present satisfaction of needs in view of a long term maximization of human perfection. The needs of future generations must be considered in determining what goals are to be realized here and now [25]. The economic and cultural needs of the future may often demand that individuals forego what what is merely useful or subjugate the felt need of the present to the unfelt but more important need of the future [26].

When applying these principles to the social economy, it must be remembered that material goods are to be used to satisfy the needs of *all* men [27]. No matter how property is held or administered in a given society, this prime end of all earthly goods must be kept in mind, and safeguarded [28]. This is true even when property is held as a personal possession [29].

This means that society, and the individuals which comprise it, must see to it that the fruits of the economy are used to satisfy the essential needs of all. Society cannot leave this entirely to chance since history has shown that such a method has disastrous results. Thus in the time of *laissez-faire* capitalism there was an enormous economic growth as the result of investment, but the needs of the great mass of the people were left unsatisfied [30]. Similarly, a society which consumes too many luxuries at

---

[24] L.-J. Lebret, « Economie humaine, politique et civilisation », in Lebret *et al., Economie et civilisation: tome 1, Niveaux de vie, besoins et civilisation*, (Paris: Editions ouvrières, 1956), p. 22.

[25] Laurent, *op. cit.*, p, 108.

[26] *cf.*, Messner, *Naturrecht*, p. 887 for remarks on the future as an essential determinate of social policy.

[27] Union Internationale d'Etudes Sociales, *Code Social*, (nouvelle synthèse, Paris: Spes, 1948), p. 63.

[28] *loc. cit.*

[29] V. J. Bourke, « La morale thomiste et la question de la possession matérielle », in Marvin Farber, (ed.) *L'activité philosophique en France et aux Etats Unis*, (Paris: Presses Universitaires de France, 1950), Vol. 1, pp. 310-311.

[30] Messner, *op. cit.*, p. 1065.

the expense of necessary investment can paralyze the
economy to a point where necessary goods and services
are not produced in sufficient quantities [31].

THE CONSUMPTION OF INDIVIDUALS

With the foregoing general principles in mind, we must
now turn to a more detailed discussion of the ethical norms
which should guide the consumption of the individual. In
the following section, we will, then, consider the relevance
of these norms to the proposal of the advertising profession.

The fruits of a man's labor and property [32] are to be
used first to satisfy the needs of the individual and then
the needs of others [33]. The important question is, of course,
what are the needs of the individual? In attempting to
answer this question, it must be remembered that we are
dealing with the needs of a man, of a creature composed
of body and soul and made to live in society. Man, then,
has not only biological needs for food, clothing, housing
and medical care, but psychic needs which require material
goods for their satisfaction. Thus man requires a certain
amount of leisure and freedom from work and drudgery
in order to satisfy his need for beauty and fantasy [34].
Finally man has social needs for communication and union
with his fellows. In realizing this union with others he
can use not merely means of communication and transport,
but even material expressions of that union.

This being so, man may use those things which are
necessary for sustaining life, living it decently and com-

---

[31] *ibid.*, p. 883.

[32] Of course the amount of property a man may own is limited by
his ability to dominate and develop it without detriment to his own personality or to the common good. On this point *cf.* Enrico Di Rovesenda,
« Problemi attuali circa la destinazione dei beni e l'uso del superfluo »,
in *Vita Economica ed Ordine Morale, XXIX Settimana Sociale dei Cattolici
d'Italia*, (Bergamo: Edizione I.C.A.S., 1956), p. 207 and *Code Social*, p. 63.

[33] Di Rovesenda, *op. cit.*, p. 204.

[34] A Piettre, « Besoin et Civilisation », in Lebret *et al*, *Economie et
civilisation, tome 1, Niveaux de vie, besoin et civilisation*, (Paris: Editions
ouvrières, 1956), p. 45).

fortably and for expressing his position in life [35]. These needs, however, are not fixed and static because as man develops and as society affords him the possibility of a fuller expression of himself, it becomes possible to use more things for the development of his personality [36]. Indeed as Messner has pointed out there is a dynamic and reciprocal interrelation between needs and the possibility of satisfying them, so that the mutual development of need and possibility is a basis of both material and spiritual development [37].

The following extensive list of goods which a man may need or may reasonably use indicates that man is not limited once and for all in his consumption· The individual and his family can legitimately use proper nourishment, dress and housing suitable to their state of life and all dimensions of their activity [38]. In addition man may use all those things which are necessary or useful for his work, study, artistic and intellectual development, for travel and necessary recreation [39]. Finally, the individual may retain such property as is necessary for the safety of his person and for the protection of his liberty as well as for the care of his children and heirs [40].

Though this list could be extended, it is sufficient to indicate that there are a great many things which the individual can legitimately use for the development of his personality. Even goods and services which might be considered as luxuries in a given society [41] could in certain cases be lawfully used if they free man from slavery to matter and enable him to devote himself more efficiently to the development of his own personality and the service of others [42]. Quite obviously goods might constitute a dan-

---

[35] Giacchino Azpiazu, *L'uomo d'affari*, (Roma: Edizioni « La Civiltà Cattolica », 1953), p. 234.

[36] Di Rovesenda, *op. cit.*, p. 204.

[37] Messner, *Kulturethik*, p. 443.

[38] Di Rovesenda, *op. cit.*, p. 204.

[39] *loc. cit.*

[40] *loc. cit.*

[41] A luxury is a good or a service which the generality of a society do not consider as necessary for existence or for the decent conduct of life. *cf.* André Arnou, *Eléments d'économie politique* (Paris: Spès, n. d.), p. 176.

[42] *cf.* Messner, *Naturrecht*, p. 883 for a general principle covering consumption.

ger for the individual who lacks balance, perspective and a sound sense of values, but it should be recognized that the danger comes from within the individual rather than from the level of his expenditures [43].

Despite a certain relativity which results from the dynamic nature of man and his needs, there are still limits to be observed and an order to be maintained in consumption. There is first of all the basic obligation to order consumption to the realization of higher values and to the attainment of that harmony and equilibrium which is necessary for the full attainment of human perfection. Further, there is the obligation to see to the satisfaction of essential, non-postponable needs before devoting resources to uses which serve only for the ornamentation of one's life [44]. In the last place there is the obligation to harmonize one's consumption with the demands of the common good and the needs of others.

This last obligation is of extreme importance in the present context since it can limit the right of the individual and of society to increase personal consumption. This obligation can be broken down into three more particular formulations. First, the individual must take care that his own consumption does not render it difficult or impossible for others to fulfill their essential needs. Secondly, the individual must sometimes sacrifice part of his relative surplus for the good of others [45]. Thirdly, the individual must use his absolute surplus in such a way as to help others satisfy their basic needs [46].

In modern economies the first of these particular obligations can be of some weight since the individual consumer is the master of effective demand [47]. Thus, if

---

[43] David Mc Cord Wright, « The Christian Conscience and Economic Growth, VI, Faith is the Lost Factor », *Social Order*, 7 (1957), p. 166.

[44] Messner, *Naturrecht*, pp. 476 and 884.

[45] By a relative surplus is meant that wealth which remains after a man has satisfied the basic needs of his family and before he has made those expenditures necessary or fitting to his state in life. *cf.* E. F. Regatillo and M. Zalba, *Theologia Moralis Summa*, (Madrid: Biblioteca de Autores Cristianos, 1942), Vol. 1, p. 870.

[46] By the absolute surplus is meant the wealth which remains after a man has satisfied not only the basic needs of his family, but has also supplied all that is necessary and fitting for their position. *cf.* Regatillo-Zalba, *loc. cit.*

[47] Messner, *Naturrecht*, p. 882.

consumers use their purchasing power to create a demand
for trivialities or even for goods of lesser utility, they may
divert resources from more urgent tasks. Thus, an effective
demand for luxuries may divert capital from spheres where
it is needed and give rise to an economy poor in essentials
and rich in goods of secondary value [48].

Because the decisions of individual consumers are of
such importance in allocating resources, there is an obligation to consider the effects of consumption on society's
ability to fulfill its obligations to all [49]. It should likewise
be noted that careless consumption which does not look
to the greatest result with the smallest expediture can
have harmful social effects. The consumer who buys without proper information and without regard to price can
encourage non-price competition and cause higher prices
which affect those who have limited incomes [50].

The individual has not only the negative obligation
to avoid consumption which may have an adverse effect
on others, but a positive obligation to help others fulfill
their needs. When one's neighbor is in extreme need, the
obligation requires one to sacrifice even part of those goods
which are necessary for the maintenance of his state in
life [51].

This means that there are cases in which even legitimate consumption must be forsworn in order to help
another. At the base of this obligation is the fact that
material goods are primarily ordered to the satisfaction of
the essential needs of all men and that private ownership
cannot be allowed to frustrate this purpose [52]. The same
principle also founds the obligation to use the absolute
surplus for social ends.

Before going on to consider the ways in which the
absolute surplus must be used, it will be well to give a

[48] Piettre, « Besoin et civilisation », p. 42.

[49] Messner, *Naturrecht*, p. 882-883.

[50] cf. Messner, *Die Soziale Frage*, (6th ed. Wien: Tyrolia Verlag, 1956),
pp. 413-415. For an explanation of this process and of the role of suggestive
advertising cf. Kurt Steuber, *Werbung und Wohlstand*, (Zürich: Polygraphischer Verlag, 1958), pp. 108 ff.

[51] E. F. Regatillo and M. Zalba, *Theologiae Moralis Summa, Vol. 1,
Theologia Moralis Fundamentalis*, (Madrid: Biblioteca de Autores Cristianos, 1942), p. 872.

[52] *loc. cit.*

further clarification of the absolute surplus itself. Generally speaking, the absolute surplus is described as that wealth which remains after a person has the things necessary for life and for the fitting maintenance of his position [53]. However, in a modern society characterized by a rising standard of living, there is a tendency to expand the concept of what is considered fitting to a person's state of life and economic class [54]. In a dynamic economy, then, it is necessary to ask if it is legitimate to expand this concept under all circumstances.

Though the present author is unaware of any fully developed treatment of this question, the following principles seem to be in accord with both right reason and the general tone of what has already been said.

First, it would be socially unjust to expand one's consumption to fit a new concept of what was fitting, if such an increase would interfere with the primary function of material goods: — the satisfaction of the basic needs of all. This might be the case where the expanded luxury consumption of one classe would cut down on the funds needed for necessary investment and philanthropic work [55].

Secondly, it would be wrong to expand the concept of what was fitting in a given class when the expansion was concerned with articles that have little to contribute to human perfection and which might easily retard it. Thus, if the new concept of what was fitting included increased consumption of alcohol and conspicuous consumption it would be illegitimate [56].

It should furthermore be noted that the surplus is not what remains after a man has fulfilled his *desires*, but what is left after he has taken care of his reasonable needs, due consideration being given to the needs of others [57]. In

---

[53] *loc. cit.* and p. 870 and Welty, *Sozial Katechismus*, Vol. 3, *Arbeit und Eigentum*, (Freiburg i. Br.: Herder, 1958), p. 64 and p. 65. on general obligations.

[54] Margaret G. Reid, « Distribution of Income and Consumption », in Elizabeth Hoyt *et al.*, *American Income and its Use*, (N. Y.: Harper and Brothers, 1954), p. 180 notes that in America families always list as things they need items which are consumed by the next highest income class.

[55] Messner, *Naturrecht*, p. 882 ff.

[56] *cf.* Thomas Aquinas, *Summa Theologica*, 2-2, p. 132, a 1 on vain glory.

[57] This view of the surplus underlies all just taxation which strikes at luxury consumption, and which tries to see to it that each makes a

other words, the fact that there is a certain relativity in the norms given does not mean that they are based on mere subjective preferences.

Assuming that some individuals in a society are in possession of a surplus even after having taken care of their needs and paid their taxes, the question to be answered is: how is this surplus to be used for the good of all?

The surplus may be given in alms to the poor or to groups which serve the public good such as churches, hospitals, schools or orphanages. It may also be devoted to the development of the cultural life of the people [58], being invested as it were in the human development of the members of society. Finally, it may be invested in such a way as to create new employment and wealth for society [59]. The individual is free to chose between these various uses, due consideration being given to the needs of society, both present and future [60].

In disposing of this surplus it is just that the individual attend first to the society in which he lives or to the needs of those who are bound to him by some human relations, but it should not be forgotten that the goods of this earth are destined for the use of all men. As economies come to be united in closer and closer unity and modern communications unite all peoples, the needs of other nations may come to have a stronger claim on superfluous wealth by reason of their far greater urgency [61]. This is merely to say that the commonweal of international society must be considered in the use of the surplus [62].

These obligations cannot be reduced to mathematical formulae, but they do indicate the general lines which men must follow in their use of material things. First, an individual may use such goods as are necessary for the satisfaction of his biological and psychic needs, as well

---

suitable contribution to the commonweal. *cf. Code Sociale*, pp. 82 ff. and expecially p. 83.

[58] Di Rovesenda, *op. cit.*, pp. 218-219.

[59] *Code Sociale*, p. 64.

[60] Messner, *Naturrecht*, p. 887.

[61] Bourke, *op. cit.*, p. 314 has pointed out the significance of the shrinking world for the fulfillment of this obligation.

[62] *cf.* Union Internationale d'Etudes Sociales, *Code de Morale Internationale*, (nouvelle édition, Bruxelles: Erasme, 1948), p. 150 for some basic ideas on this point.

as for those social needs connected with his position in society. If after he has satisfied these needs and made his formal contribution to the commonweal by the payment of taxes, there still remains a surplus, this is to be used for the needs of others. This wealth may be applied to investment, charity or cultural development of the society, provided always that the proper order of goals is observed.

It should be obvious that if an individual follows these norms, his activity as a consumer and disposer of material goods should tend to maximize his own welfare and that of society as a whole. These ends, however, will be realized only if men act rationally and with a sense of their responsibility to use material goods to the best advantage of all in a society [63]. That is to say, the best results of free choice are had only when that choice is dictated by reason and founded on knowledge.

ADVERTISING AND THE CONSUMPTION OF THE INDIVIDUAL

For the sake of convenience the present section is divided up into four sections each of which attempts to answer one of the following questions.

1. Does the proposed plan of the advertising profession disregard the hierarchy of values which is to be observed in consumption?
2. Does the proposed plan involve a disregard of the temporal order in which needs are to be satisfied?
3. Does the plan involve an illegitimate expansion of needs?
4. Does the proposal involve a disregard of the social obligations of the individual consumer?

These questions all refer to the *plan proposed* by the advertising profession. They do not refer to the *actual use* which is currently made of advertising but to an *intended use*. Of course, the morality of present day advertising practices poses serious problems, but these are not the precise object of this section. Despite this limitation of

---

[63] Messner, *Naturrecht*, p. 883.

scope, the study of the proposal will provide a starting
point for a future and more extensive treatment of the
whole gamut of current practices.   Where possible, moreover, we have attempted to outline the points to be considered in this more extensive study.

THE HIERARCHY OF VALUES AND THE PROPOSAL OF THE ADVERTISING PROFESSION

The proposal to stimulate needed economic growth by
increasing consumption does not in and of itself offend
against the hierarchy of values.   The increased wealth is
destined to satisfy real needs and is envisaged as provid-
ing a basis for a richer cultural life [64], and with at least
some awareness that spiritual values must be protected [65].

Of course, the proposal necessarilly includes the intention to increase the appreciation of material things and
their utility.   However, material goods are not made the
end of life, nor guarantees of happiness. In short, there is
great emphasis on the material, but no absolute exaltation
of the lower over the higher.

Leaving till a latter section the question of the actual
needs which will be activated, it is necessary to meet a
real objection to the above statements.   The critics will
say that the language of the proposals may be quite in
order and even edifying, but that the *actual practices of
advertising* encourage materialism [66], a loss of detatchment [67]
and an increase of hedonism [68].   In other words the actual
proposal pays merely lip service to the hierarchy of values,
while actions, which speak louder than words, proclaim
a sort of materialism.   Otis Pease in an analysis of one
set of advertisements detected just such a materialistic

---

[64] Brorby, *op. cit.*, p. 10.

[65] *ibid.*, p. 8.

[66] John C. Bennett, « The Theological Conception of Goals for Economic Life », in Dudley A. Ward, (ed.) *Goals of Economic Life*, (N. Y.: Harper
and Brothers, 1953), pp. 417-418.

[67] D. W. « Talking at Random », *The Tablet*, (London), November 16,
1957, p. 441.

[68] Vance Packard, « The Mass Manipulation of Human Behavior »,
America, December 14, 1957, p. 342.

philosophy. Some of his conclusions will illustrate this
philosophy.

> The worries, insecurities, and fears of modern men and
> women stem from failure to be liked, to adjust to one another,
> to find adequate sexual satisfactions, but especially from fail-
> ure to live amid the accoutrements of leisure . . . Harmony
> and happiness in fact depend on the rate of consumption of
> gadgets [69].
>
>   . . . romantic love is desirable in and of itself and is
> bound up with other ends, such as prestige, social success,
> power and wealth. The criteria of romantic love can be
> acquired cheaply by purchase: youth, smoothness of skin, a
> prominent bust, a deodorized body, a daily ritual of body care,
> handsome or alluring clothes, outward manners, and a ready
> affirmative response to these criteria in the other person [70].
>
>   Romantic love is also a function of wealth and the abil-
> ity to consume it [71].
>
>   Leisure to consume and to enjoy material goods was an
> effective guarantee of happiness [72].
>
>   On the one hand, most advertising men continued to
> insist that the principal virtue of high consumption was its
> tendency to stimulate production [73].

If this is the actual philosophy of advertising, it is
obviously to be condemned as representing a radical distortion of the sense of values. This, however, remains
to be established. In all fairness the ethician must ask if
the copy writer actually intends to make such a statement,
or if the normal person would interpret the advertisement
in this sense. It is quite possible for the critic to err and
see appeals to lust, envy, vanity and greed, where there
is really question of an appeal to beauty, emulation, self-
respect, or a legitimate desire for comfort. It is equally
easy to turn other statements into damnable propositions.
Does the copy writer imply that leisure is an aid to human
development, or does he make it a means to pleasure as
a final goal [74]. Does the advertising profession present

---

[69] Pease, *op. cit.*, p. 39.

[70] *loc. cit.*

[71] *ibid.*, p. 40.

[72] *loc. cit.*

[73] *ibid.*, p. 42.

[74] It is one thing to omit mention of the ultimate goal of an activity
and quite another thing to make the activity an end in itself. In certain
cases the omission may be equivalent of an affirmation that the activity

material values as final values or does it, and quite under-
standably, present them as values with no further implication?

If advertising presents temporal things as the goal of
life [75], or so engrosses man in the material that he neglects
spiritual goods [76], it is clearly to be condemned. If the
advertising profession includes such distortions in its
proposal, no contribution to economic growth can justify
it. However, the general goals proposed do not seem to
include such an intention, and so do not directly involve a
disregard of the hierarchy of values. Nevertheless, as we
shall see in a later section, certain details of the proposal
may conceal a possible distortion of the value scale. A
final judgement, then, must await this further consideration.

ADVERTISING AND THE ORDER OF CONSUMPTION

Does the proposal of the advertising profession involve
a disregard for the temporal order in which needs are
to be satisfied? To put it more concretely, does the plan
involve a consumption of « luxuries » before « necessities »,
or a neglect of future needs in favor of present gratifications?

It is extremely difficult to give a clear answer to this
question. On the one hand, the advertising profession
seems to envision increased consumption on the part of
those whose income has increased, but whose consumption
still lags behind that of their class [77]. On the other hand,
the plan includes an increase of consumer credit which
might involve an encouragement of improvidence and a
neglect of future needs.

---

is its own end, but this would hardly seem to be the case in advertising
where no one expects the eternal verities.

[75] S. Thomas Aquinatis, *Summa Theologica* (Romae: Marietti, 1948),
2-2, 56, 6, c. Utrum licitum sit sollicitudinem habere de temporalibus rebus.

[76] *ibid.*, 2-2, 46, 2. Utrum stultitia sit peccatum, and 2-2, 117, to 119
on liberality, avarice and prodigality.

[77] Arno H. Johnson, « The Job for Advertising in the Continuing Expansion of Our National Economy » *Papers from the 37th Annual Meeting
of the A.A.A.A.* Group II, (N.Y.: A.A.A.A., 1955), p. 5.

In so far as the plan only involves changing consumption standards so as to bring them into line with the legitimate usages of an income class, it would seem more or less unobjectionable. The crucial question, of course, concerns the soundness of those standards and of the particular consumption advocated by advertising. In the following section we shall see there is at least some question about the legitimacy of the consumption increases which are advocated.

The advocacy of increased credit and installment buying as a means of encouraging an increase of consumption raises a serious doubt about the soundness of the consumption itself [78]. Installment buying, of course, is not in itself reprehensible, but because it involves a mortgaging of the future in order to pay for a present satisfaction it can be an occasion of improvidence and a cause of uneconomical buying. In a normal buying situation, the necessity of paying cash acts as a break on hasty and irresponsible actions, whereas installment buying makes it all too easy to disregard the needs of the future [79].

Though the evidence is far from complete, there are indications that easy credit terms sometimes lead people to buy without any proper consideration of price or interests rates [80], and that large numbers of middle class people do not save for a rainy day [81]. Whyte describes the situation as follows.

> Most young couples carry life insurance but the actual cash value of their policies is very little. A considerable number make modest accumulations of bonds through pay-roll savings plans, and here and there the venturesome few buy stocks. But that's about it. A check of budgets of a cross section of younger-marrieds in the $ 5,000 - $ 7,500 bracket indicates that the median equity in savings deposits, bonds

---

[78] cf., ibid., p. 20. Johnson was advocating an increase of 68% in consumer credit for the year 1956 over the year 1954, as a part of his plan for increasing consumption.

[79] M. Meerens, « Over benadering en mediakeuze bij de verkoop op afbetaling », Revue Der Reclame, 16 (1956), p. 280.

[80] From The Organization Man copyrighted 1956 by William H. Whyte, Jr. and cited by permission of the original publishers, Simon and Schuster, Inc., New York. Citation from the Anchor Book Edition (1957), pp. 355-364.

[81] ibid., p. 355.

and stocks is about $ 700 to $ 800. The median amount of loan money outstanding: $ 1,000 [82].

The significance of this in reference to a proper attitude towards the future is indicated in the following results of Whyte's studies.

> Even when the suburbanites have not taken out a loan, the knowledge that loans are so readily available today has a pronounced effect on their budget habits. They have a highly inflated idea of the amount they can borrow. When the young couples are asked how much they could raise in an emergency, the median response is usually $ 2,000 to $ 3,000. As a check with bank officers indicated, many of them would be lucky to raise $ 500 [83].

While it is not safe to generalize on the basis of such limited studies [84], the suspicion remains that advertising in favor of increased consumption plus increased credit could, *if successful* lead to a neglect of the proper order of consumption and a neglect of future needs. This suspicion is heightened by the fact that advertising is like a shotgun, which, though aimed at one group hits those who stand on either side. When advertising is coupled with increased credit facilities, the risk of foolish buying is increased since installement buying makes it easier to have luxuries today than to save for tomorrow's necessities [85].

Though the above suspicions do not constitute a condemnation of the advertising proposal, they do indicate that there is a real problem involved in the proposal to increase consumer credit. As Roepke has noted advertising, which encourages installment buying, is likely to be most successful with those who are least capable of a careful judg-

---

[82] *loc. cit.*

[83] *ibid.*, p. 356.

[84] Various studies conducted in Holland lead to contradictory recommendations. One group felt that an overextension of credit was not inherent in installment buying, but was only a result of people's inexperience with this type of buying. Another group (the Dutch Catholic Labor Movement), felt that the dangers of over extended credit made regulation necessary since the danger was an important aspect of installment bying. *Cf.* J. B. Kelholt, « Uit drie afwijkende rapporten over afbetaling », *Revue der Reclame*, 16 (1956), p. 251.

[85] We prescind from the influence of credit buying on inflation and on the economic situation as a whole. For some remarks on this problem *cf.* J. A. H. Delzing, « Economische, sociale en financiële overwegingen », *Revue der Reclame*, 16 (1956), pp. 252-258.

ment, i.e., with the uneducated and the economically inex-
perienced [86]. Statistical studies also show that it is precisely
those in the lower and middle income groups who are
liable to burden themselves with installment payments [87].
This is to say that installment credit is used precisely by
those groups who are most likely to have unfulfilled essential needs.

The advertising profession, of course, has two answers
to these difficulties. First, they may say that advertising
does not cause people to buy improvidently. Secondly,
they may reply that they do not intend to cause even such
improvidence as might be accidently connected with advertising. In other words, the advertising profession is not
responsible for improvidence which is neither intended,
nor necessarily caused by advertising to increase purchases
on credit.

As we shall see in the next chapter, advertising probably has only a limited effectiveness and responsibility
for changes in consumption [88]. Consequently, it is probably
safe to say that advertising in and of itself is not a really
significant cause of improvidence. What, however, is to
be said of the intentions of the advertisers?

In the first place we may repeat what was said in the
previous chapter with regard to the same basic problem.
Suggestive advertising, that is, advertising which seeks to
by-pass the reason is by its very nature ordered to producing improvident acts. Such advertising, then, is wrong
even when it is ineffective· However, when the advertiser
uses informative advertising, or persuasive advertising
which respects rationality, he may be quite sincere in
saying that he does not intend to produce improvident
buying.

Though the preceding analysis does indicate that advertising in general cannot be condemned on the ground
that it causes improvidence, or intends to cause it, some

---

[86] Wilhelm Roepke, *Vorgegessens Brot: Kritische Nachlese zur Diskussion über das Borgkaufwesen*, (Köln: Carl Heymanns, 1955), p. 16.

[87] Delzing, *op. cit.*, p. 254 ff.

[88] The whole of the following chapter will be devoted to an analysis
of the power of advertising. Though the conclusions are only tentative,
they tend to show that the actual responsibility of advertising is smaller
than is commonly supposed.

proposals seem to envisage an increase of debt financed consumption among groups who certainly cannot afford it. This is to say that some do seem to have an implicit intention of causing purchases which would necessarily be improvident. This case may be illustrated by the following example taken from one plan.

Johnson, having noted that consumer credit is closely linked with the market potential for automobiles, foresees a potential market for a second car in from eleven to sixteen million families [89]. The author's breakdown of this market shows that 10% of the families whom he says have a « real need » of a second car have an income of less than $ 1,000 per year, while 53 % have incomes of less than $ 4,000 dollars a year [90]. Since all of these families have incomes below the national average for the year considered [91], it seems clear that the author envisages an increase of debt financed purchases of second cars by those who already have heavy installment debt and who at best enjoy a frugal minimum [92].

Though there is much room for further investigation, the details given by Johnson suggest that he intends to stimulate debt financed consumption even among groups which have not as yet satisfied basic needs. Since such a plan envisages the expansion of consumption without a proper regard for the order in which needs are to be satisfied, it is not ethically acceptable. It must be admitted, however, that such intentions do not appear to be general, and that, on the whole, the proposal of the advertising profession does not necessarily involve a distortion of the proper order of consumption.

---

[89] Johnson, *op. cit.*, p. 7.
[90] *ibid.*, p. 21.
[91] *ibid.*, p. 15.
[92] Samuelson, *op. cit.*, p. 170 notes that in 1955, the year considered by Johnson, the average family needed $ 3,500 to just about break even. Samuelson also notes that only about half the population had enough for the minimum comfort budget, and adds (p. 57) « If we revert to our typical American family of the slick-paper magazine ads, even after stripping them of their station wagon and mink coats, we still find that only 5 % of the population have the $ 10.000 income which we can conservatively estimate was the minimum necessary in 1953 to rough it out at such an existence ». By permission of Mc Graw-Hill Company, Inc. from *Economics* by Paul A. Samuelson, third edition, copyright, 1955.

6

Advertising and the Expansion of Needs

In the present section we turn from a consideration of the advertising proposal in relation to the satisfaction of basic needs and study the ethical significance of the « new » needs it intends to create or activate. To be more concrete, we must ask if the increased consumption of goods advocated by advertising fulfills genuine human needs which can be legitimately stimulated, or if the needs have as their objects mere trivia which contribute nothing to human perfection.

What needs does the advertising profession intends to activate, and what products does it propose to sell as a means of stimulating the economy? In a vague general way, the representatives of advertising speak of raising the sights of the public to a new and better way of living [93]. When they descend to details, however, television sets, washing machines, a second automobile are proposed as objects of increased consumption [94]. Though there is little mention of increased consumption of liquor and cigarettes, at least one writer points to the happy economic effects of increased consumption of cosmetics [95]. Since the arguments advanced are intended to justify advertising as a whole, the proposal of the profession at least implicitly includes all items which are currently advertised.

The list of products sold is not, however, complete since some of the advertising men claim to be selling certain intangibles as well as goods and services. With extreme frankness one author writes.

> The cosmetic manufacturers are not selling lanolin and witch hazel... they are selling *hope*. The perfumers are not selling a pleasant smell... they are selling *allure*: And the reason they are selling these things instead of their products is that women are willing to pay more for hope and allure than for lanolin and witch hazel [96].

---

[93] Frederic R. Gamble, « *The Role of Advertising in Economic Development* », (N. Y.: American Association of Advertising Agencies, 1955), no pagination.

[94] *Who has the Ultimate Weapon?* (N. Y.: Mc Cann-Erikson, 1948), p. 15.

[95] Walter Seiler, « How Advertising and Selling Drive Our Fast-paces Economy », Reprint from *Printer's Ink*, October 21, 1955, (no pagination).

[96] Seiler, *op. cit.* (no pagination).

For the purposes of analysis the products and services mentioned above may be clessified into three groups: first, products, which though they may be considered as luxuries in society, do provide a utility which can help man to realize himself; products which can be used properly, but which have a low utility and can easily be misused; finally, intangibles such as hope, allure, sophistication, swank and glamour.

In the first group of products and services which have a real, though sometimes secondary utility, are included all those which free man from less human activity and toil or are used by man in the cultivation of the higher values. Here we may list such items as a second car for people in the suburbs, a vacuum cleaner, washing machines, and such culturally useful articles as a television set, musical recordings, books, and travel. While social considerations might make increased consumption of such products undesirable, they can contribute to human development.

Products and services of the type mentioned above may be the luxuries of one generation and the necessities of the next precisely because they do contain real utilities. Such items as electric refrigerators, central heating and electric lighting and air transport are all examples of goods and services which have come to be a useful part of everyday modern life [97].

The second class of products have a low utility and can be easily misused. Here we may include that long list of items which have always been considered more or less of a luxury: cosmetics, perfumes, liquor, tabacco and stimulants. It is characteristic of all these items that though they have some utility, their absence does not impede man's perfection. Further, all of these products can be misused and some of them with serious harm to the bodily and spiritual well-being of the individual. Finally, even those moralists who admit the liciety of using these articles insist on the need of moderation and self-control.

----

[97] The medieval moralists would have described such goods and services as contributing to the *bene esse* or the *convenienter esse* cf. Thomas Aquinas, *Summa Theologica*, 2-2, q. 141, a. 6, ad 2m.

Since these objects may be legitimately used, they may be advertized. However, it should be clear that the advertising should not seek to stimulate an immoderate consumption. In particular, those who advertise alcoholic beverages have a serious obligation in a society where both alcoholism and drunkenness are serious social problems [99]. The following remarks of a prominent Catholic moralist who is also an expert on alcoholism are particularly apposite in this context since they indicate that society may have an obligation to curtail such advertising when advertisers avoid their responsibility.

> ... But it is the opinion of many that much of this advertising engenders, especially in young people, false and exaggerated ideas as to the place and prestige of social drinking in our society, and thus reinforces dangerous drinking customs prevalent in the United States. Like others who appeal to sense appetites, the beverage alcohol advertisers have the advantage, in their pursuit of profits, of being able to cater to the lower, pleasure seeking instincts of human beings. Human nature being what it is, these instincts are easily and frequently abused. The advertisers of such products, therefore, have a special social responsibility. When they fail to fulfill it, and when the abuses becomes intolerable, the industry becomes an easy and inevitable mark for further legal restrictions [100].

It may be said, and that, without being too strict, that all religious leaders would condemn advertising which was designed to produce an unlimited and immoderate increase of the consumption of such items. Pope Pius XI seems to have had such activity in mind when he censured « the unscrupulous but well calculated speculations of men who, without seeking to answer any real need, appeal to

---

[98] *ibid.*, 2 - 2, q. 169, a. 1 and a. 2, ad 4m.

[99] John C. Ford and Gerald Kelly, *Contemporary Moral Theology, Vol. 1: Questions in Fundamental Moral Theology*, (Westminster, Maryland: Newman Press, 1958), p. 278 note that there are ten times as many alcoholics in the United States as there are cases of tuberculosis. They refer to alcoholics in a technical sense and not merely to heavy drinkers. For additional remarks *cf.* H. Lauterbach, *Man, Motives and Money*, (Ithica, N. Y.: Cornell U. Press, 1954), p. 120 and The Editors of Fortune, *U.S.A. The Permanent Revolution*, (Garden City, N. Y.: Hanover House, 1951), pp. 147-160.

[100] Ford, *op. cit.*, p. 306.

the lowest of human passions. These are aroused in order to turn their satisfaction into gain » [101].

Though these ideas seem to be more or less self-evident, it should be emphasized that not all advertising for products of the second class is to be condemned. It is only advertising which intends to, or actually causes immoderate consumption, or which uses unethical techniques which must be rejected [102].

The third class of items to be considered includes the intangibles such as hope, allure, glamour, sophistication and swank [103]. These intangibles are not only sold, but sold at a high price. Thus Seiler writes:

> Women pay from 10 to 50 cents for a cake of soap with the intention of making themselves clean, but they pay 50 cents to $ 10 for a jar of cream with the objective of making themselves beautiful. The cost of the actual product is secondary because women are not buying the actual product. They are buying a promise — and the promise is youth and beauty and love [104].

The morality of advertising designed to *increase* the sale and consumption of such intangibles involves many factors. For the present, however, we shall consider only three points: first, the inadvisability of increasing the desire for such intangibles, secondly, the irresponsibility connected with such purchases; thirdly, the dubious nature of the methods used to sell them.

At the very start it must be admitted that within certain limits the desire for allure and glamour is reasonable and licit. Man may within the boundaries of· moder-

---

[101] *Quadragesimo Anno*, (English translation, N. Y.: Paulist Press, n. d.), paragraph no. 148. Several authors have used this text to condemn advertising. *Cf.* Colin Clark, *op. cit.*, p. 114. It should be noted, however, that the condemnation falls only on those whose product answers no real need, and who also appeal to the lowest passions. These two conditions do not seem to be verified in a large number of cases.

[102] It is interesting to remark that despite heavy advertising the per capita consumption of « hard » liquor seems to be declining in the United States. *cf.* The Editors of Fortune, *The Changing American Market*, (Garden City, N. Y.: Hanover House, 1955), pp. 197 ff. Some also see a decline in per capita consumption of beer. *cf.* Martin Mayer, « What is Advertising Good For? » *Harper's*, February, 1958, pp. 25 ff.

[103] These are sometimes called the « extra values » added by advertising, *cf.* Martin Meyer, *op. cit.*, p. 30.

[104] Seiler, *op. cit.*, no pagination.

ation desire to enhance his ego, express his worth and gain the approval of others [105]. This point is not under discussion· Experience, however, shows that these limits are easily transgressed. The legitimate desire for beauty and a reasonable care of one's health can become a sort of idolatry [106]. The desire for recognition on the basis of superficial qualities slips almost imperceptibly over into vainglory [107]. Finally, there is the ever present danger that man can put too much faith in externals, or in the opinion of others, and even come to consider them as ends in themselves [108].

Common sense and everyday observation bear witness to the reality of these dangers [109], and the social scientists have observed the same results. Glamour in sex can easily become a substitute for love [110], and the adoption of the approved patterns of consumption often becomes a means of fleeing from the self [111]. Indeed, when the desire for glamour and allure are motivated by fear of others, there is a danger of frustration and of the development of neurotic tendencies [112].

The moralist, aware of these dangers, advocates a struggle against these desires. It is all too obvious that a preoccupation with pseudo or half values distracts from more important considerations and may distort a man's scale of values [113]. One does not have to be a puritan in

---

[105] cf. St. Thomas Aquinas, Summa Theologica, 2-2, q. 132, a. 1, c For an analysis of the meaning of these intangibles cf. Donald Snygg, « The Psychological Basis of Human Values », in Dudley A. Ward, (ed.) Goals of Economic Life, (N.Y.: Harper and Brothers, 1953), p. 354; and H. Lauterbach, Man, Motives and Money, (Ithica, N.Y.: Cornel U. Press, 1954), pp. 114-115.

[106] Mouroux, op. cit., p. 69.

[107] Summa Theologica, 2-2, q. 132, a. 1, c.

[108] loc. cit. and 2-2, q. 112, a. 1 on boasting; q. 131, a. 1 on ambition and q. 169, a. 1, on modesty in dress.

[109] cf. John Bennett, « The Theological Conception of Goals for Economic Life », in A. Dudley Ward, (ed.) Goals of Economic Life, (N.Y.: Harper and Brothers, 1953), p. 417.

[110] David Riesman et al. The Lonely Crowd, (New Haven, Connecticut, Yale U. Press, 1950), p. 214.

[111] Erich Fromm, The Fear of Freedom. (London: Kegan Paul Trench and Trubner, 1942), p. 160, cf. also Man for Himself, (London: Routledge and Kegan Paul, 1949), p. 149 ff. and the Sane Society (London: Routledge and Kegan Paul, 1956), p. 131.

[112] Karen Horney, The Neurotic Personality of Our Time, (N.Y.: W. Norton, 1937), p. 284 ff, especially p. 288.

[113] Messner, Kulturethik, p. 435

order to see that the development of childish and superficial « needs » can hinder the fulfillment of natural and
higher needs, displace genuine human needs from the
center of preoccupation [114]. In short, the general conclusion is that such desires and needs must be educated and
controlled if man is to perfect himself [115].

In view of these facts advertising designed to increase
the desire for these intangibles must be extremely moderate, and not such as to cause a distortion of the proper
sense of values. Now, though some advertising writers
admit the need of protecting spiritual values [116], the general
tone seems to be expressed in the following citation which
sees the only limit in the « satisfactions » of the consumer.

> The total amount of advertising which is socially desirable
> is limited only by man's enthusiasm and sagacity in supply-
> ing better satisfaction with products to more people [117].

In so far as the advertising profession subscribes to
such a philosophy which permits a practically unlimited
expansion of needs without reference to the *objective* perfection of man, its proposal seems unacceptable. This
conclusion is reinforced by the fact that much of the
advertising for intangibles uses dubious methods and leads
to uneconomical buying. These last two points must now
be considered.

Writing of the methods used to promote the sale of
cosmetics and the intangibles connected with them, Seiler
notes that the demand was created by appeals to fear
and vanity [118]. The use of these appeals is not surprising
since they are at once extremely powerful and connected
with the products which are desired as remedies for insecurity [119]. In the present context the use of such motives
is to be condemned for two reasons. First, they are liable
to cause an excessive emotional involvement with funda-

---

[114] Theodor Haeker, *Was ist der Mensch?* (Frankfurt am M.: Ulstein,
1959), p. 83.

[115] Messner, *Kulturethik*, pp. 439-440.

[116] Melvin Brorby, *op. cit.*, p. 8.

[117] Otto Kleppner, « Is There Too Much Advertising? » reprint from
Harper's February 1951, no pagination, but the above sentence concludes
the article.

[118] Seiler, *op. cit.*, no pagination.

[119] *cf.* Lauterbach, *op. cit.*, p. 85 and pp. 114-115.

mentally superficial values [120].   Second, they are often calculated to create an illusion that the product will help
allay the insecurity, regardless of the actual potencies of
the product [121].   This is merely to say that the methods
used fall under our general condemnation of « suggestive »
advertising.

Now, while the advertising for such products and
intangibles is not always suggestive, nor designed to create
illusions, its constant association with such techniques
and results, creates a presupposition against it.   Further,
since such advertising results in wasteful buying, it can
hardly be said to contribute to the true development of
the individual even when it succeds in giving the impression
and feeling of security.

As already noted, women will pay high price for the
promise of beauty and allure regardless of the physical
properties of the product.   Even though it is difficult to
set a « just price » for a luxury good, such prices are unjust
precisely because they exploit the ignorance, passion and
fickleness of the consumer [122].   This would appear to be
the case almost universally since even a little reflection and
investigation would show that the price bears no relation
either to the value of the product or to its ability to
confer glamour and allure [123].   To encourage such buying
is to encourage the vice of consumption which causes
people to spend more for a thing than it is worth [124].

In addition, it should at least be recalled that such

---

[120] For a general discussion of the problem, *cf.* Riesman, *op. cit.*,
p. 345 and *cf.* the remarks of Marquis W. Childs and Douglas Cater, *Ethics
in a Business Society*, (N. Y.: Harper and Brothers, 1954), p. 168.

[121] For a description of the technique, *cf.* Pease, *op. cit.*, p. 173 « The
practice in each instance was for the advertising industry a popular and
uncomplicated one: having found out what consumers would like to think
the product would do for them, one had only to persuade them, within
the limits of plausability and without reference to the facts that the
product would indeed do it ». *cf.* also Martin Mayer, « What is Advertising Good For? » *Harper's*, February, 1958, p. 30.

[122] A. Muller, *La morale et la vie des affaires*, (Tournai: Casterman,
1951), p. 72.

[123] *cf.*, Warren C. Waite and Ralph Cassady, *The Consumer and the
Economic Order*, (2nd ed. N. Y.: Mc Graw-Hill, 1949), p. 185. The autors
note that the sale of cosmetics is particularly subject to this sort of
price inflation. Thus in one case, a lipstick whose retail cost was 2 cents
sold for $ 1.00, an astringent whose retail cost was 9 cents sold for $ 1.75.

[124] Messner, *Naturrecht*, p. 883.

irrational buying can injure others either by causing them to act in the same way [125], or by raising prices generally [126]. Finally, as we shall see in the following section, such buying may divert resources from more urgent social needs.

Even though we admit the legitimacy of a limited desire for the intangibles connected with personal enhancement, it should be clear that one is not free to seek the strengthening of these desires without the exercise of some moderation. Moreover, if the proposal of the advertising profession includes (as it seems to, in some cases), the intention of exploiting weaknesses and exaggerating fear and vanity, its morality is questionable. Further, the attempt to increase the desire for these intangibles is to be condemned when it involves the use of advertising designed to by-pass the intellect.

Because the judgement of actual cases is more difficult than the formation of principles, the conclusions reached in the present chapter must be used with care. In particular, the following points should be kept in mind. First, one can neither condemn nor praise the effort to activate needs. In each case it is necessary to examine the relationship of the need to the perfection of man. Secondly, even when a need or desire is legitimate in itself, it is still necessary to consider the limits within which the need can be legitimately satisfied and activated. Thirdly, the morality of the techniques must be considered separately since the technique can be unethical even when its object is legitimate.

In the last place, when judging the advertisers' responsibility for unintended results of his promotional activity, one must distinguish carefully between those effects which have an almost natural relation to the advertising and those which are so accidental as to be mere concomitants rather than true effects. As a matter of fact, those advertis-

---

[125] *cf.* Leland Gorden, *Economics for Consumers*, (2nd ed. N. Y.: American Book Company, 1944), p. 145 for the effects which follow from lower classes imitating the wasteful consumption of the wealthier.

[126] *cf.* J. K. Galbraith, « The Unseemly Economics of Opulence », *Harper's*, January 1952, p. 61. He writes as follows. « They (i. e. the poor) bear the higher prices associated with monopoly and higher distribution costs along with those who can afford them, and who as a result of their escape from physical to psychological standards of consumption, actually encourage such expenditures ».

ers who refrain from suggestive advertising, that is from attempts to by-pass the intellect, and who, moreover, maintain a certain moderation, are probably not responsible for the improvidence and folly which are alleged to follow on their advertising.

ADVERTISING AND THE SOCIAL
OBLIGATIONS OF THE INDIVIDUAL

In the first section of this chapter, we investigated the proposal of the advertising profession in relation to the consumer's obligation to himself. Now, we must turn to the obligations of the indivdual to society and to the commonweal. This additional consideration is necessary for the individual is obliged not merely to use material things to satisfy his own needs, but to see to it that they satisfy the needs of all men [127]. As a result of this dual obligation consumption which might be legitimate in itself when considered from a purely individual point of view, might be unethical in a given social context [128]. This means, of course, that the individual must consider the needs of others and must, as both a private person and as a citizen, see that property and wealth are used to satisfy those needs [129].

As a citizen, the individual is obliged to pay such taxes as are needed for the satisfaction of public needs. In addition he must cooperate with the authorities in seeing to it that the economic activity of individuals does not interfer with the realization of the common good [131]. Further, when private institutions fail or are incapable of giving the assistances which the poor and sick need, the

---

[127] Eberhard Welty, *Sozial Katechismus*, (Freiburg im Br.: Herder, 1958), vol. III, p. 64.

[128] In the present chapter we shall not consider the proposal of advertising in relation to the needs of international society, though, of course, there appears to be a growing social obligation to help underdeveloped nations.

[129] Messner, *Soziale Frage*, p. 356.

[130] *Code Social*, p. 82

[131] *ibid.*, p. 64 no. 104 for the right of the state in this matter.

individual citizen should cooperate with the government in making up for these deficiencies [132].

The individual, however, does not exhaust his obligations when he has payed his taxes and cooperated with government efforts to coordinate the activity of individuals with the demands of the common good. The social obligation to use property for the good of all presses upon the consumption of the private citizen, for in modern free economies, the consumer is to a large extent the master of the economy [133]. When the individual buys intelligently with an eye to real values and to the satisfaction of real needs, that is, with an eye to the satisfaction of those needs which increase his human perfection, he fulfills a social obligation [134]. This, however, is only a first step. The individual has additional social obligations with regard to the use of his surplus wealth.

As mentioned above the individual must use his surplus to satisfy the needs of individuals and society [135]. He can do this by charity, by investment, or by philanthropy. Though the individual is free to apply this surplus as he sees fit, he must be guided in his judgement by the same principles that govern his own consumption as an individual. Thus, he must see that essential needs take precedence over accidental needs, or mere desire of comfort. Further, he must see to it that future needs are given a place in his overall calculation [136].

In view of these general principles it is clear that an individual who increases his consumption of luxury goods while many lack necessities, or when society needs vast sums of money for needed investment, is acting contrary to the demands of social justice [137]. Such consumption not only retards the fulfillment of the essential needs whose fulfillment is urgent at the moment, but can also retard the overall development of the economy.

The adverse effects on economic development should

---

[132] *ibid.*, p. 87, no. 176 for a description of the state's rights and duties in such situations.

[133] Messner, *Naturrecht*, p. 882.

[134] *loc. cit.*

[135] *cf.* the opening sections of this chapter General Principles.

[136] Messner, *Naturrecht*, p. 1065, and p. 883.

[137] Messner, *Naturrecht*, pp. 882-883, 1062 ff.

be noted carefully. First, an increase in luxury consumption on the part of those who are in a position to invest may raise the price of capital and make expansion too expensive [138]. Second, even when such consumption does not reduce the supply of capital for private industrial expansion, it may reduce the supply of capital for public and personal investment. This last effect is of extreme importance since long range development depends on investment in health, security and education, on conservation programs and the development of such public services as roads and harbour facilities [139].

While one cannot put a price tag on the fruits of such investment in human development and in public services, they have a real economic utility not only in so far as they satisfy needs, but also in so far as they help to increase productivity. Improved health, better education, a higher standard of honesty all contribute to the wealth of a nation [140]. This should not be forgotten in any consideration of the requirements for economic growth.

The individuals who fail to devote their surplus to social goals not only retard the fulfillment of needs and injure the long-range growth of the economy, but also create a dangerous situation in the political sphere. In general, the needs of society are best cared for by private groups with the state entering in only when these cannot or will not fullfill their duties [141]. However, without extensive private support such institutions as universities, hospitals and charitable organizations cannot fullfill their function. When individuals with a surplus fail to give the support which is needed, they are opening up the road to increased government activity in spheres which should be left to the activity of private groups [142].

---

[138] W. Arthur Lewis, *The Theory of Economic Growth*, (Homewood, Illinois; Richard Irwin, 1955), pp. 216 ff.

[139] Gerhard Colm and Theodore Geiger, *The Economy of the American People*, (Washington, D. C.: National Planning Association, 1958), p. 84 and Rockefeller Brothers Fund, *The Challenge to America*, (Garden City, N. Y.: 1958), p. 25.

[140] Rockefellers Brothers Fund, *op. cit.*, pp. 6, 51, 53, 57.

[141] Messner, *Naturrecht*, p. 260.

[142] Union Internationale d'études sociales, *Code de morale politique*, (Paris: Spes, 1957), p. 147. The code notes that the state is obliged to step in when private individuals and groups do not meet their responsi-

JUDGMENT

Though these principles have an obvious application in underdeveloped countries, it remains to be seen if they have any real pertinence in an advanced economy such as that of the United States. To be more concrete, we must ask if a stimulation of personal consumption would lead to a healthy growth, or whether it would lead to a misallocation of resources. This is the crucial question in the present section.

At first glance, the proposal of the advertising profession might seem a marvelous method of attaining a healthy growth without sacrifice on the part of anyone. A glance at the remarks of the critics, however, brings the problem back into focus and poses the question: of what use is economic growth which stimulates the production of easily advertised goods, of trivia and meaningless objects, while real needs go unsatisfied [143]? Of what use is a growth which provides an opulent supply of consumers' goods and leaves society poverty striken in its public services [144]?

In point of fact, it is impossible to judge either the legitimacy or the usefulness of advertising's proposal in the abstract. To judge its legitimacy and potential utility we must know the concrete state of the economy. In particular we must know if the concrete circumstances permit an increase in consumption without a neglect of urgent needs, of necessary government and private services and of proper provision for investment.

Even if circumstances should be such that an increase in consumption were possible without a disregard of the needs of society, it would not follow that advertising had any contribution to make to sound economic growth. This is merely to say that the attempt to increase consumption

---

bilities. It would seem clear that the increasing encroachement of governments in the field of private welfare has been forced on them by the failure or incompetence of lower social organisms.

[143] *cf.* A. S. J. Baster, *Advertising Reconsidered*, (London: P. S. King and Son, 1935), p. 96 f and Margaret G. Ried, *Consumers and the Market*, (3rd. ed. New Haven Connecticut: Yale U. Press, 1942), p. 355 and Gorden, *op. cit.*, p. 148.

[144] John Kenneth Galbraith, *The Affluent Society*, (Boston: Houghton Mifflin, 1958), pp. 260-261.

might be legitimate in a given society, but not necessarily successful. Before passing judgment on the contribution which advertising claims to make, it will, then, be necessary to examine the general efficacy of advertising as a promotor of increased personal consumption, and then, the possibility of using advertising to promote harmonious and stable growth.

In an attempt to set the stage for a judgement of the liciety of increased consumption and the possibility of using advertising to attain it, we shall examine two sets of assumptions. The following chapter studies the general power of advertising in relation to overall consumption; the subsequent chapter considers the actual economic situation in the United States and the problem of advertising and stable progress. When we are in possession of the results of these investigations, it will be possible to pass a judgment on the social aspect of the proposal of the advertising profession.

CHAPTER VI

THE POWER OF ADVERTISING
PSYCHOLOGICAL ASSUMPTIONS

The present chapter seeks to investigate the basic ability of advertising to change the standard of living and of consumption. This seems necessary for three reasons. First, it will enable us to evaluate the claim of the advertising profession and the *potential utility* of advertising when demand is insufficient to keep the economy moving smoothly ahead. Secondly, it will give us some idea of the general *responsibility* of advertising for certain classes of economic effects. Thirdly, it will also indicate very clearly why the moralist and ethician must be very careful in assigning responsibility to various groups in modern society. This last point seems particularly important since amateur moralists have been too quick to blame advertising for sins which it has not committed.

Since the present section is both long and complicated, it has been divided into five principal parts. The first seeks to determine the point at issue with greater precision, while the second presents a sampling of opinions on the power of advertising. After this introduction the third part then outlines what is known of the power of propaganda and of the mass media in general. In the fourth and fifth sections, these general conclusions about propaganda are then applied to advertising as a means of influencing both the general propensity to consume and the sale of individual products.

The Point at Issue

Since the claim of the advertising profession is advanced in a particular context, it is necessary to reexamine this context in order to determine the precise way in which advertising is to raise the standard of living. The economy described in the argument has a great productive capacity, unemployment and unused purchasing power, that is to say, idle resources. In addition both purchasing power and consumption are increasing and being enjoyed by larger and larger numbers of individuals. However, consumption, especially among middle income and upper class families [1], is not increasing as rapidly as their incomes with the result that the nation is not increasing production as fast as it should, if it it to give employment to all and to meet the demands of its people. Advertising is, then, to accelerate changes in the standard of living in such a way that the middle income groups and the upper classes increase their consumption more rapidly.

To appreciate the nature of this task it must be recalled that though people do increase their consumption as they increase their income, they do not do so at the same rate [2].

In more concrete terms this means that for each additional dollar of income people tend to spend a smaller and smaller percentage on consumption [3]. Advertising, then, is to prevent the percentage of extra income spent on consumption from declining too rapidly [4]. It is not a question of causing people to spend all their extra income

---

[1] Arno Johnson, « The Job for Advertising in the Continuing Expansion of Our National Economy » *Papers from the 37th Annual Meeting of the A. A. A. A.* (N. Y.: A. A. A. A., 1955), p. 5.

[2] Paul A. Samuelson, *Economics*, (3rd ed., N. Y.: Mc Graw-Hill, 1955), p. 170.

[3] *loc. cit.* and p. 217.

[4] We have not pushed the theoretical analysis of these points very far since this would have involved us in a discussion of the definition of savings. Suffice it to note that there can be a great deal of ambiguity. Thus the advertising profession seems to look on everything which is not consumed in the current income period as constituting savings, while the economist insists that « rainy day » savings, being only postponed consumption, do not really add to aggregate savings. *cf.* Kenneth E. Boulding, *Economic Analysis*, (3rd ed., N. Y.: Harper and Brothers, 1941), p. 368.

on consumption, but of getting them to spend enough of it to activate productive capacity and increase employment.

Now, the propensity to consume depends, among other things, on the attitude that people have towards consumption in general and on the number of things they need and want. In other words the importance given to various consumption items in the standard of living, and the number of items included, will have much to do with how much people consume. Advertising can work either on the general attitude toward consumption or on the attitude toward a particular product or service.

The differences between these two approaches should be noted carefully. If advertising can reinforce and increase the importance given to consumption and minimize the importance of thrift and of renunciation of goods, it creates an attitude which is favorable to an increase in the total of goods consumed. When, on the other hand, advertising merely changes the attitude towards a particular good or service, it does not necessarily favor an increase in total consumption. It might be that such advertising would only cause individuals to change their consumption pattern without increasing their consumption [5]. To achieve its purpose advertising must not merely make a product seem desirable, but seem so desirable that it will be purchased out of money that was not destined for immediate consumption. Unless advertising causes the product to be bought out of savings, that is, unless it causes individuals to add to and not merely change their consumption, it will not have the effect of increasing total consumption in the economy. So it is that the following pages must answer two questions.

1. Can advertising reinforce the general propensity to consume?

2. Can advertising influence people to buy particular products out of money not destined for consumption?

---

[5] It is the contention of many economists that much of the advertising does no more than this. *cf.* Mary Jean Bowman and George Leland Bach, *Economic Analysis and Public Policy*, (N.Y.: Prentice-Hall, 1943), p. 318; A. C. Pigou, *The Economics of Welfare*, (4th ed., London: Macmillan, 1932, reprinted in 1952 with new appendices), p. 198-199; Dorothea Braithwaite, « The Economic Effects of Advertising », *Economic Journal*, 38 (1928), p. 18. Nicolas Kaldor, « The Economic Effects of Advertising », *Review of Economic Studies*, 18 (1950-51), p. 5.

A Note on Methods

It must be admitted that there is probably no feasible way of *measuring* directly the influence of advertising on the *general* propensity to consume or on the purchase of products out of money not destined for consumption. This is due to the fact that advertising is only one of numerous factors which influence consumption. Since it is practically impossible to isolate one factor from another, only estimates are possible [6]. There is, however, evidence on the power of propaganda to change attitudes and ideas, and even some evidence on the ability of advertising to influence primary demand for products. While this evidence will not permit one to give a direct and conclusive answer to the questions posed above, it is sufficient to permit one to draw highly probable conclusions with regard to the possibilities and the limits of advertising.

Since much of the material presented in these pages is pertinent to the discussion of the other effects of advertising, and of the responsibility of advertising for these effects, the references are copious. Further, since many of these works may not be readily available, extented citations have been used freely.

Opinions

The opinions given in this section are intended to prepare the reader for what follows by showing that some members of the advertising profession and a fair number of students of business and of social psychology have doubts about the ability of advertising to produce the results mentioned in the previous pages. There is particularly strong scepticism about the ability of advertising to influence underlying attitudes and, while these writers will admit that advertising and propaganda have some

---

[6] Neil H. Borden, *The Economic Effects of Advertising*, (Chicago: Irwin, 1942), p. 121. This work is the only one of its kind and though by no means definitive, does supply much useful evidence which bears on the questions we are treating.

influence, they do not see it as a form of magic which can manipulate people at will.

Three classes of writers are cited: first, members of the advertising profession, second, writers on business, third, social psychologists and sociologists. Though they do not always make it clear whether they are speaking of short-range or long-range effects, there is a convergence of opinion which sets the stage for the following section in which the emphasis is put on short-range effects.

While the *advertising men* seem to be in agreement about their ability to change the standard of living by stimulating desire for individual products[7], there is no general agreement about its power to *augment the general propensity to consume.* The following questions from an unsigned article reveal the doubts that some entertain about advertising.

> Can advertising actually enhance the propensity to consume, or is its impact confined to the details of the partern of consumption? Advertising doubtless has an impact on the consumer-buyer affecting purchasing decisions which are made in anticipation of consumption requirements. Can advertising reach beyond the consumer-buyer and deal with individuals as consumers, thus causing changes in the pattern of life which will accelerate economic activity and technological progress?[8].

Some members of the profession are frankly sceptical about their ability to engineer the consent of the public and to lead it about by the nose[9]. At least one member of the profession has pointed out the fact that anyone familiar with the skill needed to direct an effective campaign, will realize that advertising does not have the magic power sometimes attributed to it[10].

---

[7] It should be noted that many of the authors cited in the previous chapters confine themselves to advertising's effect on the sale of individual products.

[8] « Advertising and the Pursuit of Happiness », *Cost and Profit Outlook*, 9 (1956) no. 6, June, p. 1 (no printed pagination).

[9] Robert L. Heilbroner, « Public Relations - The Invisible Sell », *Harper's*, 214 (1957) June, no. 1285, p. 30.

[10] Douglas J. Murphey, « The Christian Conscience and Economic Growth, II. The Role of Advertising », *Social Order* 7 (1957), p. 159.

Others who have studied advertising from a *scholarly point of view* seem to deny the power of advertising to change basic attitudes or to create needs. The following are typical opinions.

> Advertising creates needs only in the sense that it makes consumers aware that a product offers a satisfactory solution to a need [11].
>
> It is extremly doubtful whether advertising or any other selling tool, can materially alter the desire for comfort, the association of others, health, rapid and safe transportation, self preservation, and emulation . . . It seems quite apparent that basic human wants cannot be created and that even surface wants can be moulded only slightly and gradually by advertising [12].

W. H. Whyte goes even farther and asserts that it is not the consumer who is manipulated, but the advertising man.

> An indictment habitually leveled at the American society is that we are a people in emotional thrall to a set of synthetic symbols cleverly manipulated by a « communications elite ». But is is not the consumer who is in thrall; it is the manipulator — and to a great anonymous dope, the mathematical unit of the Mass Audience, who doesn't exist at all except in statistics [13].

These opinions of economists and writers on business are reinforced by the statements of *sociologists* who have studied the question of advertising and propaganda influence. Though some of the older writers were of a different opinion [14], the prevailing climate today, especially among American scholars seems to be scepticism. The following quotation will illustrate the nature of their opinions.

---

[11] Borden, *op. cit.*, p. 194.

[12] C. H. Sandage, *Advertising Theory and Practice*, (revised edition, Chicago: Irwin, 1939), p. 137., and *cf.* F. Redlich, *Reklame: Begriff, Geschichte, Theorie*, (Stuttgart: Ferdinand Enke, 1935), p. 189. This point will receive further treatment in later sections when advertising's influence on the desire for individual products is studied.

[13] W. H. Whyte, Jr., « The Language of Advertising », *Fortune*, Sept. 1952, p. 186.

[14] *Cf.* S. Chakotin, *The Rape of the Masses*, (London: Routledge and Sons, 1940), This is a translation of the 5th French edition, S. Tcharkotine, *Le Viol des foules par propaganda*, (Paris: N. R. F. 1939), and Gustave Le Bon, *Psychologie des foules*, (Paris: Presses Universitaires de France, printing of 1947). The original printing was at the turn of the century.

Advertising creates (or more accurately stimulates) effective demand where it activates an underlying ego-involvement of a large group, or else, where it manages to change basic attitudes through long-range efforts. The latter is probably quite rare [15].

There is a general insistence on a need for caution in speaking of the power of advertising.

Thus, Powell warns that it would be rash to jump from the assumed efficiency of the technique in certain cases, to the universal efficacy of the technique itself [16]. La Piere points out that the newness of mass communication and advertising may cause us to attribute occult powers to it, which it does not actually possess [17]. Cartwright is even more forthright it stating that « *Significant changes in behavior as a result of campaigns are rather the exception than the rule* » [18].

Opinions on particular campaigns which were designed to change attitudes, though not consumption attitudes, are sometimes even blunter. One commentator on the hundred million dollar Free Enterprise Campaign conducted by the Advertising Council described its results in the following words.

And it is not worth a damm . . . The Free Enterprise Campaign is psychologically unsound, it is abstract, it is defensive, it is negative [19].

Another facture which illustrates the limits of propaganda may be seen in the « educational » work of the American Armed Forces.

---

[15] W. H. Whyte, Jr., « The Language of Advertising », *Fortune*, Sept. 1952, p. 186. By courtesy of *Fortune*.

[16] Norman John Powell, *Anatomy of Public Opinion*, (N. Y.: Prentice-Hall, 1951) chapter 10. *Cf*. also Leonard W. Doob, *Public Opinion and Propaganda*, (London: Cresset Press, 1949), pp. 515 ff. and Joseph T. Klapper, « Mass Media and Persuasion », in Wilbur Schram, (ed.) *The Process and Effects of Mass Communications*, (Urbana, Illinois: University of Illinois Press, 1954), p. 309.

[17] Richard T. La Piere, *A Theory of Social Control*, (N. Y.: Mc-Graw-Hill, 1954), p. 518.

[18] Dorwin Cartwright, « Some Principles of Mass Persuasion » in Katz *et al. Public Opinion and Propaganda*, (N. Y.: Dryden Press, 1954), p. 383. By permission of Holt, Rinehart and Winston, Inc.

[19] Cited in W. H. Whyte, Jr., *Is Anybody Listening?* (N. Y.: Simon and Schuster, 1952), p. 7 and *cf*. pp. 8 and 11. By courtesy of *Fortune*.

During the last war the American Army, acting on the assumption that information on the background of the conflict would induce better attitudes, staged an elaborate program using the « Why We Fight » movies, lectures and discussions. The result?

> Says a top psychologist who worked on the program, « Nothing . . . just about nothing. And to be honest, we still do not know the answer » [20].

Though the foregoing statements express the more or less common opinions of those who have studied the power of propaganda and of advertising, there is one notable and important exception. Thus the Borden study concluded:

> From a longe-range point of view, advertising and aggressive selling have played a large, though not precisely measurable part in the formation of mental attitudes necessary to a high level of consumption, especially such attitudes as expectation of change and the notion of progress. In other words, advertising has helped to develop a mobile as opposed to a static society [21].

In the pages that follow we shall see that the word « large » is hardly justified and that the Borden study itself gives ample evidence of the limits of advertising.

These opinions will suffice to set the stage for the presentation of the evidence which shows the limitations of propaganda and advertising in changing attitudes. However, before going on, it will be well to summarize the ideas presented thus far. First, the advertising profession is not unanimous in affirming its ability to influence the propensity to consume and the attitudes which underlie it [22]. Similarly, other writers on advertising see it as having limited power to create wants, needs, or to influence fundamental desires. Finally, sociologists also indicate the need for a prudent reserve, and tend to believe that significant changes are the exception rather than the rule.

In the following sections we will study the evidence which justifies these opinions and attempt to bring it to

---

[20] Cited in *ibid.*, p. 13.
[21] *op. cit.* XXXV.

bear on the questions posed at the beginning of this chapter. In the first section the effects of the mass media and propaganda in general will be considered. With this as a foundation, we shall then procede to consider the case of advertising itself·

PROPAGANDA AND THE MASS MEDIA

All of the authors, who will be cited in this section, preface their remarks with two warnings. First, their conclusions are tentative. Second, *unless otherwise stated, they refer only to short-range effects*. This seriously limits the value of their work, but it must be admitted that not much is known about the long-range of mass media [23].

Writing in 1948 Lazarsfeld and Merton stated, « It is our tentative judgement that the social role played by the very existence of the mass media has been commonly over-estimated » [24]. In 1957, Klapper in summarizing all the literature which had appeared up to that time seemed to confirm that judgment when he summarized the conclusions of these studies under the following five points [25].

> 1. Mass communication ordinarily does not serve as a necessary and sufficient cause of audience effects, but rather functions among and through a nexus of mediating factors and influences.
> 2. These mediating factors are such that they typically render mass communication a contributory agent, but not the sole cause, in the process of reinforcing the existing con-

---

[22] It has not been possible to determine the majority opinion in this matter. However, interviews indicate that personal opinions are more reserved in affirming the power of advertising than are public statements.

[23] Elihu Katz and Paul F. Lazarsfeld, *Personal Influence: The Part Played by People in the Flow of Mass Communications*, (Glencoe, Illinois: The Free Press, 1955), p. 24 note 16. and *cf. infra* The problem of long-range effects.

[24] Paul F. Lazarsfeld and Robert K. Merton, « Mass Communication, Popular Taste and Organized Social Action », in Lyman Bryson, (ed.), *The Communication of Ideas*, (N.Y.: Institute for Religious and Social Studies, 1948), p. 98.

[25] Joseph T. Klapper, « What We Know about the Effects of Mass Communication: The Brink of Hope », *Public Opinion Quarterly*, 21 (1957), p. 457f ff. Cited by permission of the *Public Opinion Quarterly*. This is also publication A-242 of the Bureau of Applied Social Research at Columbia University.

ditions. (Regardless of the conditions in question — be it the level of public taste, the tendency of audience members towards or away from delinquent behaviour, or their vote intentions — and regardless of whether the effect in question be social or individual, the media are more likely to reinforce than to change).

3. On such occasions as mass communication does function in the service of change, one of two conditions is likely to obtain. Either:

a) The mediating factors will be found to be inoperative, and the effect of the media direct; or

b) The mediating factors will be found to be themselves impelling towards change.

4. There are certain residual situations in which mass communication seems to wreak direct effects, or to directly and of itself serve certain psychological functions.

5. The efficacy of mass communication, either as contributory agents or as agents of direct effect, is affected by various aspects of the media themselves or of the communication situation (including for example, aspects of contextual organization, the availability of channels for overt action, etc).

The main points to be noted in the above summary are: first, mass communication is ordinarily not a necessary or sufficient cause of audience effects. Secondly, mass communication tends to *reinforce rather than change* attitudes and activity. Thirdly, when it does help to effect changes, this is due either to the absence of other factors, or to the fact that other factors are also working for change. Fourthly, there are only a few situations where mass communication seems to have direct effects.

In the pages that follow we shall investigate these *other factors* which are so important in determining the results of mass communication. When these have been explained it will then be possible to see if advertising enjoys the cooperation of these factors in attempting to change or reinforce attitudes which influence the standard of living.

For the sake of clarity, evidence will be presented under the following headings which are expressions of three basic conditions needed for successful propaganda [26].

----

[26] Lazarsfeld and Merton, *op. cit.*, p. 113. Though not all authors express these three conditions in the same way, it will be clear from what follows that they are considered as of decisive importance. *cf.* Also Joseph

1. Monopolization or the absence of conterpropaganda.
2. Canalization rather than change in basic values.
3. Supplementary face-to-face contacts.

MONOPOLIZATION

Monopolization or the absence of counterpropaganda is of such importance that Klapper feels it is a sufficient though not a necessary condition for the success of a campaign[27]. Even if monopoly is not a sufficient cause of success, the fact remains that it has characterized nearly all the very highly successful persuasion campaigns[28]. It would seem obvious that efforts to persuade will be more successful when there are no groups fighting against it, or at least when the propagandist controls all the ordinary institutions by which ideas are spread and attitudes formed.

This monopoly is not easily obtained in democratic societies where there is no central control over radio, television, newspapers, magazines, books, churchs, schools and clubs. Since any counterpropaganda makes people hesitant to accept an opinion by making them aware that it is controversial[29] it would appear that very little opposition would be needed to undo much of the work of a propagandist who did not control all institutions. Since people seem to have a deep distrust of propaganda[29a] the counterpropagandist need only unmask the attempt to influence in order to undo or weaken the intended effects. For these reasons it is rather important that the opposition be excluded as far as possible.

T. Klapper, « Mass Media and Persuasion », in Wilbur Schramm, (ed.) The Process and Effects of Mass Communication pp. 288-320.

[27] Joseph T. Klapper, « Mass Media and Persuasion », in Wilbur Schramm, (ed.) *The Process and Effects of Mass Communication*, p. 299.

[28] *loc. cit.*

[29] *cf.* Carl I. Hoveland and Irving L. Janis *et al.*, *Communication and Persuasion*, (New Haven, Connecticut: Yale U. Press, 1953), pp. 293-297.

[29a] Robert K. Merton, *Social Theory and Social Structure*, (revised ed., Glencoe, Illinois· Free Press, 1957), p. 524.

CANALIZATION

In general, propaganda is successful only when it is in agreement with the basic values of peoples [30], and harnesses rather than tries to change existing forces [31]. It can also be effective when it does not concern any deeply rooted convictions [32], or is concerned only with new issues that are unrelated to existing attitudes [33]. In other words, it works best when it is reinforcing existing tendencies, or when operating in areas where there are no trends either for or against.

Propaganda which seeks to change attitudes and values, and not merely to reinforce them, faces serious obstacles. People tend to resist perceived attacks on their values and attitudes [34], and even to avoid exposure to ideas which do not agree with their own [35]. When, for one reason or another, they do meet with ideas and attitudes which are different, they interpret the data differently [36]. This is a result of the natural propensity to see, remember and reason in accord with one's existing outlook [37]. For these reasons information does not necessarily change attitudes [38], and may even lead to the reinforcing of previous ways of thinking. It is not unknown for a campaign which goes against ideas and values which people hold dear to have a boomerang effect [39].

---

[30] L. Fraser, *Propaganda*, (N.Y.: Oxford, 1957), pp. 191-92.

[31] For the importance of this in Nazi Germany, *cf.* Hadley Cantril, *The Psychology of Social Movements*, (N.Y.: John Wiley, and Sons, 1941), p. 266.

[32] Frazer, *op. cit.*, pp. 191-192.

[33] *loc. cit.* and Klapper, « What we Know about the Effects of Mass Communication », pp. 462-463.

[34] Wilbur Schramm, *Responsibility in Mass Communication*, (N.Y.: Harper and Brothers, 1957), pp. 55-56 and Klapper, « Mass Media and Persuasion », p. 303.

[35] Klapper, « What we Wnow about the Effects of Mass Communication », p. 467 and *cf.* Bernard Berelson, « *Communication and Public Opinion* », in Wilbur Schramm, (ed.) *Communications in Modern Society*, (Urbana; Illinois: U. of Illinois, 1948), p. 170.

[36] Herbert H. Hyman and Paul B. Sheatsley, « Some Reasons Why Information Campaigns Fail », in Katz *et al.*, *Public Opinion and Propaganda*, pp. 523-528.

[37] John Norman Powell, *The Anatomy of Public Opinion*, (N.Y.: Prentice-Hall, 1951), p. 416.

[38] Hyman and Sheatsley, *op. cit.*, pp. 523 ff.

[39] Klapper, « Mass Media and Persuasion », p. 303.

In general mass media propaganda is rather effective in communicating information [40], but this does not mean that the information will be interpreted in line with the wishes of the propagandist. Propaganda is always limited by the spiritual readiness or hostility of the people to whom the message is addressed [41]. It is not an all powerful force which moulds men as it will.

Timasheff and Facey sum up the conclusions of studies on propaganda and advertising in the following words:

> From such study, this conclusion has emerged: large-scale success is possible only when the addressees are at least partially ready to respond in the direction of the recommended objectives. In other words, the most forceful propaganda cannot do much more than reinforce some of the existing attitudes and bring them to prevail over competing attitudes [42].

FACE-TO-FACE CONTACTS AND THE GROUP

The third condition necessary for the successful use of propaganda is the existence of supplementary face-to-face contacts [44]. In some ways this is perhaps the most decisive of the three conditions for, as we shall see, it is these contacts which are largely responsible for the values people hold, and are, moreover, a potent source of counter-

---

[40] *ibid.*, p. 294.

[41] H. J. Prakke, *De Samenspraak in onze samenleving, Inleiting tot de publicistiek*, (Assen, Holland: Van Gorum, 1957), p. 51.

[42] Nicolas S. Timasheff and Paul S. Facey, *Sociology: An Introduction to Social Analysis*, (Milwaukee, Wisconsin; Bruce, 1949), p. 255 ff.

[44] For works which treat extensively of the importance of face-to-face contacts and small groups, *cf.* Katz and Lazarsfeld, *op. cit.* Alfred Mc Clung Lee and Elizabeth Bryant Lee, *The Fine Art of Propaganda: A Study of Fr. Coughlin's Speeches*, N. Y. Harcourt Brace, 1939) and Alfred Mc Clung Lee, *How to Understand Propaganda*, (N.Y. Rinehart, 1951).

For other remarks on the importance of these contacts *cf.* Emory Bogardus, *The Making of Public Opinion*, (N.Y.: Association Press, 1951), pp. 228 ff. Erik Barnow, *Mass Communication: Television, Radio, Film and Press, The Media and their Practice in the United States of America*, (N.Y.: Rinehart, 1956), pp. 86 ff.

In addition to these works and those cited in the following pages *cf.* Paul F. Lazarsfeld and Bernard Berelson *et al. The People's Choice*, (N. Y.: Columbia U. Press, 1948) and Elihu Katz, « The Two-step Flow of Communication: An Up-to-date Report on an Hypothesis », *Public Opinion Quarterly*, 21 (1957), Spring, no. 1, pp. 61-78.

propaganda. Since these contacts take place in the small
groups which form a part of a person's everyday life, we
shall treat the matter under three headings: the group, the
leaders of the group, and the relation of the groups and
the leaders to the mass media.

THE GROUP

Interpersonal relationships within small groups such as
the family or a circle of friends or business associates seem
to be « anchorage » points for the opinions, attitudes and
values of individuals[45]. In so far as people wish to be
identified with these groups, they tend to share the attitudes and ideas held by the group [46], and even to see things
through the eyes of the group [47]. The influence of the
group is so important that authors such as Katona believe
that most needs are actually group-determined [48].

The position of the group in the process of changing
ideas, attitudes and opinions and in determining needs,
makes it a key to successful advertising and propaganda.
If the group disapproves of the content of advertising,
its chances of acceptance are considerably smaller than
in those cases where the group is neutral or friendly.

Now, though these groups are informal, they do have
their leaders. These are the individuals who are consulted
by others and whose opinion is highly valued. In the real
world, these influentials, as they are sometimes called, have
a great deal to do with the selection of the ideas which
are circulated in the group and with the acceptance of
these [48a].

THE LEADERS

The outstanding characteristic of these opinion leaders
is their notably superior level of information. Because of

---

[45] Katz and Lazarsfeld, *op. cit.*, p. 44.
[46] *ibid.*, p. 50.
[47] *ibid.*, p. 70.
[48] George Katona, *Psychological Analysis of Economic Behavior*, (N.Y.:
Mc Graw-Hill, 1951), p. 109.
[48a] Katz and Lazarsfeld, *op. cit.*, p. 130 ff.

his reading and his interest, the influential is a sort of minor expert on certain matters [49]. In the case of political opinion leaders, for example, this interest is manifested in their reading and listening habits. They tend to read more and more varied magazines and newspapers than do others in their group [50]. In addition they tend to have a wider range of acquaintances and to include among them a large number of other opinion leaders [51].

These facts are important since they indicate that the leaders who have much to do with the opinions of the group, are liable to be in a better position to judge propaganda and so more critical. The fact that they compare the opinions given in various newspapers and discuss them with others who are also better informed than the average man, raises the probability that they will not accept what they hear from a single source.

Of course the fact that the leaders are more exposed to the mass media might make it seem that they are also more influenced by them than are other members of the informal groups [52]. However, the leaders themselves say that the personal influence of others was the major factor influencing their decisions [53]. Further, since the group leader is one particularly loyal to group norms, he is strongly influenced by the group itself [54], and so liable to work for the maintenance of those norms. All of this indicates that it is not enough to reach the leaders in order to have an idea accepted either by the leader or by the group. Exposure, in short, does not guarantee acceptance.

Two additional points should be noted. People are influenced by leaders in their own class and immediate group rather than by some figure in a higher group or in an important position [55]. In other words the influence is

---

[49] United States Information Service, « Prestige, Personal Influence and Opinion », in Schramm, *Process and Effects of Mass Communication*, p. 404.

[50] *ibid.*, p. 408.

[51] *ibid.*, p. 405.

[52] Katz, « The Two-Step Flow », p. 75.

[53] *loc. cit.*

[54] Katz and Lazarsfeld, *op. cit.*, pp. 50 ff.

[55] Paul F. Lazarsfeld, « Who Influences Whom? Its the Same for Politics and Advertising », *Printers' Ink*, 211 (1945), no. 10, June 3, p. 36.

horizontal rather than vertical [56]. In short the expert who
is close to people has more influence than does the one
who merely enjoys a position of prestige. Second, the
influence of these informal leaders is specialized. The same
person does not generally influence opinions on brands of
breakfast foods and political issues [57]. This means that a
propagandist or advertiser must not merely get to the influentials, but get to that influential who is considered as an
expert on a particular topic.

The foregoing remarks should indicate that face-to-face
contacts inside small informal groups are important in
determining the success of propaganda. If the leaders do
not pass information on, or if the group refuses to accept
it, the flow of influence is blocked. Further, since the
group leaders are better informed they are harder to
influence so that they may easily reject ideas presented
by the mass media. Finally, since these groups are informal, it would appear that they cannot be easily manipulated
without the aid of agents who infiltrate and establish themselves as members [58].

Mass media may be able to spread information more
rapidly than word-of-mouth, but so long as the group leaders
can block its admission into the thinking of the group,
or so long as the group can reject it, the mass media and
such propaganda as depends on the use of mass media,
cannot guarantee success.

Even this brief treatment of the three conditions
needed for the successful propaganda campaign indicate
why the mass media are not ordinarily a necessary or
sufficient cause of audience effect. The propagandist who
employs the mass media does not enjoy a monopoly but
must face the competition of other groups. He is, moreover,
limited by the attitudes and opinions which are already
in individuals. Finally, he has, generally speaking, no
direct control over the all important small groups which
sit in judgement on ideas and opinions.

---

[56] *loc. cit.*

[57] United States Information Service, *op. cit.*, p. 405 and Katz and
Lazarsfeld, *op. cit.*, p. 97.

[58] The cell movement as used by both Catholic Action and the Com-
munists, attempts to do just this.

THE EFFECTIVENESS OF ADVERTISING

It is now time to turn from propaganda in general to the particular case of advertising. In the concrete, we will want to see how the factors mentioned above effect the ability of advertising to stimulate and reinforce the other factors which are, according to the argument presented in the previous chapter, working to increase consumption. In the concrete these three questions must be answered. First, does advertising in favor of a higher standard of living and of consumption enjoy a monopoly position in its activity? Second, does advertising have to deal with adverse forces in attempting to reinforce and canalize the movement towards a higher standard of consumption? Third, does advertising enjoy the cooperation of small groups and their leaders, or do they limit its power?

THE MONOPOLY OF ADVERTISING

Since most advertising is connected with the sale of consumer goods and services, it would seem as if advertising as a whole might be considered as propaganda for a higher standard of living. Further, since advertising is so insistent and ubiquitous, it might, at first glance, seem to enjoy a sort of monopoly in its effort to promote a higher standard of living. A little reflection, however, shows that all advertising is not directed to raising the standard of living, or better the standard of consumption, and that advertising does not control some of the most important means of spreading ideas and inculcating attitudes.

In the first place, advertising for savings institutions, investment houses and insurance companies aims at increasing savings rather than consumption. Although the sums spent for the purpose of encouraging savings are not great in comparision with those spent on encouraging consumption, the fact remains that all advertising is not working for a higher standard of consumption [60].

---

[60] *Advertising Age*, March 3, 1958 reports that in 1957 The Prudential

Though not much of advertising is devoted to selling the idea of thrift, two institutions which are not controlled by advertisers have considerable importance in encouraging saving and moderation in consumption: the school and the church. At times the advertising associations have attempted to control some of the texts used in American schools [61], but there is no evidence that they have succeeded. While there is no evidence one way or the other with regard to the church, it seems safe to assume that the various religious groups maintain independence and continue to preach and teach moderation in consumption.

While the critics cited in an earlier chapter decried the influence of advertising on the content of the mass media [62], the fact remains that much of this criticism appeared in the very media which advertising is supposed to control. This is not to be taken as a denial of any serious problem in this area, but merely as an indication that advertising does not have a complete monopoly of the mass media.

In the last place it should be noted that advertising does not control the publication of books. The advertising profession, in point of fact, is quite sensitive to the ideas about advertising which are spread not only in books on advertising, but in novels about advertising men [63].

Advertising in favor of a higher standard of consumption does not enjoy a complete monopoly of either the mass media or of the other means of informing and forming the American people. Unlike the dictator who can control the school, the media, the publication of books and in some cases even the churches, the advertiser must face the competition of other parties who are interested in forming and informing the public.

Insurance Company spent $ 2, 919, 073 on national advertising in Magazines and Network Television. *cf.* Kurt Steuber, *Werbung und Wohlstand*, (Zürich: Polygraphischer Verlag, 1958), p. 159 and Mort Weisinger « They're out to Get Your Money », *Reader's Digest* 71 (1957) October pp. 189-191 (Condensed from *Banking*, Sept., 1957).

[61] Otis Pease, *The Responsibilities of American Advertising* (New Haven, Connecticut: Yale U. Press, 1958), pp. 152-153.

[62] On this problem *cf.* Theodore Peterson, *Magazines in the Twentieth Century*, (Urbana, Illinois: U. of Illinois Press, 1956), p. 35.

[63] For examples of this sensibility to criticism cf. « The Myth of Madison Avenue », *Tide*, March 14, 1958, pp. 71-74.

The importance of this monopoly was stressed by at least one social scientist who was asked to answer the question, « How can Americans be persuaded to live at least a third better ». Professor Allen noted that to accomplish this it would be necessary to create and spread new values for both the individual and the collectivity. However, he insisted that success would demand the concerted efforts of the major social institutions-educational, recreational and religious. This, of course, was in addition to the cooperation of the mass media and those large corporations which have goods to sell [64].

Fortunately there is no evidence that advertising can ever hope for such cooperation in its efforts to raise the standard of living and the standard of consumption.

ADVERTISING AND CANALIZATION

Advertising does not enjoy a monopoly position in its effort to sell a higher standard of living, but it may still enjoy the aid of powerful forces which are moving the popoulation to adopt a higher standard of consumption. Indeed, the assumption is that advertising does have these forces to work with and that its task is to reinforce and step them up.

In general, of course, successful advertising does enjoy the advantage of not having to instill new attitudes, and of not being forced to create significantly different behavior patterns, but of being able to harness existing forces [65]. Once people have adopted certain generic patterns of behavior or generic attitudes, these can be channeled in one direction or another since resistence will be slight [66]. La Piere notes, however, that this favorable situation is not always present. He writes:

---

[64] Philip J. Allen cited by Vance Packard, *The Hidden Persuaders*, (London: Longmans, Green and Co., 1957), p. 261. Allen is a professor at the University of Virginia and gave this opinion in answer to questions posed by *Tide* magazine in 1953. No other source information is given by Packard.

[65] *cf*. Lazarsfeld and Merton, *op*. cit., p. 114; Klapper, « Mass Media and Persuasion », p. 299; Nicolas S. Timasheff and Paul W. Facey, *Sociology*, (Milwaukee, Wisconsin: Bruce, 1949), pp. 255-56.

[66] Klapper, « Mass Media and Persuasion », pp. 308-309.

It is perhaps fairly easy to convert the users of soap to the use of a certain brand of soap by dramatic reinterpretation; but there is slight possibility of developing the attitudes, values and manual habits which make for the use of soap by conversional means alone, especially if the would-be-converter stays comfortably at home and attempts to reach his subjects by such impersonal « mass » means of communication as the printed tract or the radio broadcast [67].

If this analysis is just, and it seems to fit in with what is known about propaganda in general, it then becomes important to discover if advertising must do more than canalize existing attitudes which are moving people towards a higher standard of consumption. More precisely expressed, our question asks, « Does advertising have the cooperation of trends and attitudes which not only lead to increased consumption, *but to increased consumption out of money* which was formerly destined for savings »?

The advertising profession and its advisors are not unaware of what this involves. Pease in summing up the attitudes of the profession during the period from 1920 to 1940 writes:

Those engaged in 20th-century advertising in the United States looked on themselves, in effect, as crusaders for the liberation of middle-class people from the tyranny of Puritanism, parimoniousness, and material asceticism [69].

Advertising saw that it must attack the tradition of thrift entrenched in a people who had been taught to save rather than spend [70], but it was the advisors to the advertising profession who saw that this involved very fundamental changes in the very philosophy of a society. Dr. Dichter, one of the more vocal counselors of the advertising world, was particularly insistent that advertising must seek to demonstrate that the hedonistic approach to life was a moral one. In addition, the Doctor felt that advertising must give the consumer permission to enjoy himself and to feel moral even when flirting, or taking two vacations or buying a second or third car [71].

---

[67] By permission from *A Theory of Social Control* by Richard T. La Piere, copyright 1954 McGraw-Hill Book Company, Inc., p. 515.

[69] Pease, *op. cit.*, p. 41.

[70] *ibid.*, p. 23.

[71] Dr. Ernest Dichter writing in his own private circulation magazine,

Dr. Dichter, who does not necessarily speak for the advertising profession, goes even farther in his explanation of what attitudes and values must be changed if America is to consume more freely. He feels that Americans need a new set of spiritual goals which free them from, what he very inaccurately calls, the mediaeval attempt to flee into the hereafter when they cannot cope with life [72]. As if this were not enough he goes on to write, « Similarly, we must reject the image of a heavenly figure who rewards and punishes daily conduct the way a father does [73] ». « In the last analysis man must escape from a cobweb of tradition and moral concepts which, starting with the idea of original sin, have portrayed life as a sequence of misery, worry and toil [74] ».

If Dr. Dichter is right in saying that advertising must change such fundamental attitudes as those towards God and the very meaning of life itself, the resistence to advertising would appear to be almost insurmountable.

Even if advertising does not have to cope with the very basic attitudes presented by Dr. Dichter, it must work against changing attitude towards consumption itself. David Riesman of the University of Chicago states the problem as follows:

> I suggest that there is a tendency for people, once they are accustomed to upper-middle class norms, to lose zest for bounteous spending on consumer goods. It has been the bounty of modern industry... which has done more than almost anything else to make conspicuous consumption obsolete here. It would go much too far to say that consumption bores us, but it no longer has the old self-evident quality [75].

Another sociologist, writing of the consumption patterns of upper class members of society notes that these

---

Motivations, April 1956. Cited by Packard, *op. cit.*, p. 263 Dr. Dichter is said to have objected to the use Packard made of this citation, but Dichter's recent work, *The Strategy of Desire*, (N.Y.: Doubleday, 1960) propounds the same ideas at great length.

[72] Ernest Dicher, « Thinking Ahead: The Psychology of Prosperity », *Harvard Business Review*, 35 (1957), November-December no. 6, p. 22.

[73] *ibid.*, p. 158.

[74] *loc. cit.*

[75] David Riesman cited in *Tide*, March 14, 1958, p. 28. The same idea can be found in Riesman's *The Lonely Crowd*, (New Haven, Connecticut: Yale U. Press, 1950), p. 346.

go in for conspicuous non-consumption. They are so secure in their social position that they need not follow the styles and so can wear the same clothes that were used forty years ago or use an old car instead of the latest model [76]. These people, of course, are also those who are liable to have the greatest percentage of savings.

Such attitudes are not confined to the upper and upper-middle classes, but are also present in the new suburbia which is inhabited by middle class families. Where once the urge to « keep up with the Jones » stimulated consumption, the modern American suburbanite tries to *keep down with* the Jones, that is, to consume no more and no less conspicuously than his neighbor [77]. Paradoxically, the advertising executives who spend their time in trying to persuade consumers to improve their standard of living seem to share this tendency. While the executives do consider that they must maintain a certain standard of living because of their position, they do not attach much importance to most of the commonly accepted prestige symbols [78]. More important, as a group, they tend to have very respectable savings. Only 4% report that they save nothing, and 6% that they save little. A good 23% manage to put away up to 9% of their pay; 32% save 10%; 28% save between 11% and 25% of their pay, while a group of 7% saves between 25% and 50% of their income [79]. It would seem that the advertising executives are unimpressed by their own arguments in favor of high consumption.

Various reasons are given why people are losing their zest for consumption and trying to keep down with the Jones. There is the fact that those who have purchasing power have satiated their hungers, and satisfied their needs [80]. When people have their material and even psychic needs satisfied, they become more fickle and sophisticated. They no longer feel driven by their needs.

---

[76] Margaret C. Pirie, « Excerts from an address to 5th annual seminar of the American Marketing Association, Toronto, January 1958 » *Advertising Age*, April 21, 1958, p. 86.

[77] The Editors of Fortune, *The Changing American Market*, (Garden City, N.Y.: Hanover House, 1953), pp. 79-80.

[78] « Do Admen Keep Up with the Jones? » *Tide*, November 8, 1957, p. 27.

[79] *loc. cit.*

[80] Paul D. Converse *et al. Elements of Marketing*, (6th ed., Englewood Cliffs, New Jersey: Prentice-Hall, 1958), pp. 44.

The conclusion to be drawn from these opinions seems obvious. If upper-middle class people tend to lose their zest for consumption, and if there is social pressure to consume inconspicuously, it would appear that advertising must face forces which militate against its effort to increase the propensity to consume. As we shall see in a later section these trends originate in groups where the influence of advertising, like that of all propaganda, is limited by the nature of the group and of its leader. Though the evidence does not prove that advertising cannot overcome these forces, it casts doubt in its ability to do so [82].

In addition to these psychological and sociological factors which influence the propensity to consume, there is one additional factor, also of a psychological nature, which is of the utmost importance: *consumer optimism* [83]. Consumer spending is greatly influenced by whether people think it is a good time to buy or not [84]. The judgment of consumers in this matter is determined by past and expected changes in their own financial position [85], and by their view of the economic outlook of the whole economy [86]. Now their evaluation of future business conditions appears to depend on significant political events on the international and domestic scene even more than on their own income expectations [87]. In short, consumer optimism is largely determined by objective factors, by people's personal experience, and by the news they get through the papers and radio.

Propaganda, however, is not too effective when the people can compare statements with the facts [88]. So long as the people have their own eyes and the service of a *free press*, advertising is not going to be able to explain

---

[81] *cf. infra*, Advertising and Face-to-Face Contacts.

[82] *cf. infra*, Advertising and Individual Products.

[83] George Katona and Eva Mueller, *Consumer Attitudes and Demand, 1950-1952*, (University of Michigan Research Center, 1953), pp. 2 ff. For proof that business is quite aware of this *cf.*, Packard, *op. cit.*, pp. 224 ff.

[84] Katona and Mueller, *op. cit.*, p. 63.

[85] *ibid.*, pp. 65 and 79.

[86] *ibid.*, p. 69.

[87] *ibid.*, p. 79.

[88] On this point *cf.* Leonard W. Doob, « Goebbel's Principles of Propaganda », in Katz *et al. Public Opinion and Propaganda*, p. 521.

away the facts [89].　This, it is submitted, constitutes an important and perhaps decisive limitation on the power of advertising to control one of the most basic factors which influences spending in an economy [90].

Advertising must face all these limitations on its power: the old value placed on thrift, the pressure to keep-down-with-the-Jones, a possible lack of zest for consumption and shifts in consumer optimism as a result of bad news.　This only proves that it cannot guarantee results, and should not distract one from the fact that, on the whole, the trends and the attitudes in the United States are favorable to increased consumption and a rising standard of living.　Despite the shifts mentioned above and the residue of old values, the general movement is towards an ever increasing standard of living which gives higher value to consumption.

The following points show the general direction and the forces behind it.　First, in the last ten years consumption has increased on an average of three percent a year per capita [91].　Second, even those who keep-down-with-the-Jones are very optimistic and tend to upgrade their purchases and to save very little [92].　Third, Americans, as a whole, seem to have retained their enthusiasm for the « new » and « improved » which is one of the powerful forces behind the sale of new products [93].　In short, advertising seems to have at its disposal a basic trend which favors an increase in consumption and a higher standard of living.

If the actual situation is, generally speaking, favorable

---

[89] There is, unfortunately, evidence that there have been attempts to tamper with free and unbiased news reporting on events which might influence consumer optimism. *cf. Time*, (Atlantic Edition), March 17, 1958, pp. 45-46; and « Suburbia Snubs the Recession », *Fortune*, 57 (1958) May, no. 5, p. 116.

[90] For more on the importance of long-range factors influencing consumption and saving, *cf.*, Milton Friedman, *A Theory of the Consumption Function*, (Princeton, New Jersey, Princeton U. Press, 1957), pp. 221 ff.

On limitations of ordinary propaganda in influencing this long range outlook *cf.* George Katona, *Psychological Analysis of Economic Behavior*, (N. Y.: Mc Graw-Hill, 1951), p. 288.

[91] *Economic Report of the President*, January, 1958 (Washington, D. C. Government Printing Office), p. 2.

[92] *cf.* Whyte, *The Organization Man*, pp. 352 ff.

[93] *cf. The Changing American Market*, p. 14.

to advertising, this does not mean that it can guarantee results either in the long-run, or at any given moment. The probabilities are with it, but advertising is still at the mercy of changes in attitudes.

ADVERTISING AND FACE-TO-FACE CONTACTS

The third basic condition needed for the success of propaganda is supplementary face-to-face contacts. These contacts are after an individual's own personality, probably the most important factor in determining needs, attitudes and likes [94]. As Riesman notes, the effectiveness of advertising in the case of children is due more to the support advertising has from their « peer » groups, than from any intrinsic power of advertising itself [95]. Katona notes that in modern American society most needs are group determined so that even repeated perception, e.g. of advertising, is not sufficient to arouse the forces which drive people to act [96].

At least in certain types of communities the group seems to have an almost dictatorial power in determining consumption patterns and trends. Whyte in describing the « inconspicous consumption » of the new suburbia put it this way.

> *It is the group that determines when a luxury becomes a necessity.* This takes place when there comes together a sort of critical mass. In the early stages when only a few of the housewives in a block have, say, an automatic drier, the word-of-mouth praise of its indispensibility is restricted. But then, as time goes on and the adjacent housewives follow suit, in a mounting ratio others are exposed to more and more talk about its benefits. Soon the nonpossession of the item becomes an almost unsocial act — an unspoken aspersion on the others' judgment or taste. At this point only the most resolute individualist can hold out, for just as the group punishes its members for buying prematurely, so it punishes them for not buying [97].

---

[94] *cf.* Schramm, *Responsibility in Mass Communication*, p. 53. Lazarsfeld, « Who Influences Whom? » p. 32. Klapper, « What we Know about the Effects of Mass Communication », p. 467.

[95] Riesman, *The Lonely Crowd*, p. 339.

[96] Katona, *Psychological Analysis of Economic Behavior*, p. 109.

[97] William H. Whyte, Jr. *The Organization Man*, Garden City, N. Y.:

The amazing thing about this process is that it is only partially determined by national trends, for even within a given neighborhood, there can be a great deal of variation in what luxuries are being turned into necessities [98]. This, of course, fits in with what was said earlier about the nature and influence of the group in general [99]. The mass media may inform the leaders, and even individuals but the group then determines whether or not to act on the information given.

Elmo Roper, one of the more prominent American experts in the field of market research, says that his studies show that the most important factor influencing a woman's buying is what her friends have told her about the product plus her own personal experience [100]. Brooks in commenting on the importance of word-of-mouth advertising says that the facts only confirm the general theory that personal contacts are most effective in changing opinions and behavior [101]. In brief, consumption choices and the attitudes underlying them are due to the group rather than to advertising.

While advertising itself may have little control over these groups and their opinions, advertising, supplemented by personal selling, that is, by personal contact, might be in a position to influence group attitudes and ideas. Whyte has pointed this out [102], and, though the salesman can never be a part of the day to day life of the small groups, he could provide much of the supplementary face-to-face contact necessary for successful propaganda. When properly coordinated with personal selling, advertising would have a relatively good control over the third of the three basic conditions.

Doubleday Anchor Books, 1957), p. 347. Cited by permission of Simon and Schuster the original publishers, copyrighted by the author 1956.

[98] *ibid.*, pp. 347-348.

[99] *cf. supra*, pp. 162 ff.

[100] Elmo Roper, « Women's Buying Habits », *Social Order*, 7 (1957), p. 61.

[101] Robert C. Brooks, Jr., « Word-of-Mouth Advertising in Selling New Products », *Journal of Marketing*, 22 (1957), October no. 2, p. 155.

[102] Whyte, *The Organization Man*, p. 348 note 2 and p. 349 where he describes how the door-to-door salesmen might be used in starting neighborhood trends. The advertising men themselves are quite aware of the importance of this factor and stress the need for overall marketing and effective personal salesmanship. *cf.* Mc Keehan, *op. cit.*, pp. 43-44.

SUMMARY ON ADVERTISING AND THE PROPENSITY TO CONSUME

This first section on advertising and the propensity to consume sought to determine if advertising enjoyed the conditions necessary for effective influence over the attitudes which control that propensity. The opinions of advertising men, sociologists and writers on business showed that its power is viewed as being limited. In the second section we discussed the general conditions necessary for successful propaganda and in the third attempted to see how advertising realized these conditions. The conclusions of these sections may be summarized as follows.

Advertising does not have an ideal situation in its effort to raise the standard of living since it does not enjoy a complete monopoly, nor control of the local groups, nor a trend which is without any opposition. However, on the whole, its position is largely favorable in that the basic forces are in the direction of increased consumption and since it has the possibility of at least some direct influence on the all important groups. *As long as this favorable position continues in the United States, advertising can, in all probability, have some influence in increasing the propensity to consume.*

At the same time *advertising cannot guarantee to influence the propensity to consume* since the basic forces are beyond the control of advertising. Unfavorable news may lower consumer optimism and advertising has not and should not have any control over such news. Consumption might lose its glamor, or people might become bored with the « new » with the result that the overall trend toward increased consumption might slow down.

It must be kept constantly in mind that advertising can harness existing forces, it cannot, generally speaking, create them. Given favorable conditions it can canalize. Given unfavorable conditions it can do little or nothing. Advertising is a catalyst, rather than an essential element, a lubricant rather than a fuel, an instrumental, but not a principal cause. It follows, then, that advertising is a useful economic tool but not exactly a reliable one.

A Note on Long Range Effects

Before going on to consider the second way in which advertising is supposed to increase total consumption, a few words on long-range effects may help to answer some possible objections. In the previous pages, the discussion was confined to short-range effects of propaganda because there is little evidence on possible or actual long-range effects. Some have assumed that advertising has, as a matter of fact, helped in some way to create, over the long-run, mental attitudes favorable to high consumption [103]. Such statements which admit that the effect is not precisely measurable, are based on the assumption that so much advertising aimed at increasing consumption must have had a « large » part in the formation of such attitudes [104]. This is a dangerous assumption since it is always difficult to generalize when treating of propaganda [105].

This is not to deny that the cumulative effects of propaganda *may be* tremendous [106], but merely to say that we have no proof that they are tremendous, or large or significant. Even immediate short-term effects sometimes disappear [106b], so that we cannot conclude that these accumulate in the long-run. We do not know if even brainwashing has significant long-term results for the simple reason that even its short-run effects tend to disappear when the victim is removed from the power of the persuaders and returned to his normal environment [107]. Indeed there are cases where success backfires after a period of time. Thus there are cases of children who succumbed to advertising at the age of six, and developed a hostility to advertising later on because they felt that they had

---

[103] The Advisory Committee of the Borden study, in Borden, *op. cit.,* p. XXXV.

[104] *loc. cit.*

[105] Powell, *op. cit.,* Chapter 10 discusses the reasons why it is difficult to generalize and to extend conclusions beyond the facts on which they are based.

[106] Doob, « *Public Opinion and Propaganda* », p. 520.

[106b] *cf.* Hoveland *et al., Communication and Persuasion,* p. 270.

[107] Joost A. M. Merloo, *Mental Seduction and Menticide, The Psychology of Thought Control and Brainwashing,* (London: Jonathan Cape, 1957), p. 291.

been exploited [108]. On the other hand, there is evidence that some immediate effects may become stronger with time [109].

Common sense may be justified in assuming that propaganda and advertising have *some* effect, it is not justified in assuming that it must have a *particular* effect, or the *intended* effect; nor in assuming that actual effects are permanent or cumulative. In this context the results of one medium-range study on the effects of television ownership are particularly interesting since they illustrate how common sense may be right on one count and wrong on another.

Belson, in an extremely original study, attempted to discover if the mere fact that a family owned a television set had an effect on their initiative and interests [110]. He discovered that in the first year of set ownership there was a gradual fall in initiative, and that interests declined as well though these did not hit their low point till the second year of set ownership. These conclusions seemed to support the common opinion held by many critics of British television. The study went on, however, to discover that at the end of five years both interests and initiative had risen to a level almost equal to that had before ownership of a television set. In short, though the immediate effects confirmed the common sense conclusion, the medium-range effect showed that the change was not permanent, and so not overly significant.

Granted the limitations of our knowledge, it would be rash to assume that we can predict the long-range results of the mass media or of advertising. The social scientists maintain a prudent reserve in this matter and both the advertising profession and the ethician will do well to imitate them in this.

---

[108] cf. *Advertising Age*, October 21, 1957, p. 28 for a report by Lester Rand of the Youth Research Institute.

[109] cf. *Klapper*, « Mass Media and Persuasion », p. 297.

[110] William A. Belson, « The Effects of Television upon the Interests and Initiative of Adult Viewers ». A Paper read at the Annual Meeting of British Association for the Advancement of Science, 1956. (Mimeographed notes of the author). This paper also appeared in the *Australian Quarterly*, December 1957, pp. 59-70. Mr. Belson formerly senior psychologist of the BBC, London, is now a research fellow at the London School of Economics. Those interested in the methods used in this study should consult the bibliography under Belson.

Advertising and Individual Products

The present section seeks to discover if advertising can influence people to buy specific products out of money not destined for immediate consumption. In other words, can advertising for a particular product raise total consumption in the American economy? This is an extremely important and extremely difficult question. As noted earlier in this chapter, it is not enough to show that advertising has increased the sales for a given brand or product-class, since the increase may be offset by a decrease in the consumption of other products. This is to say that, though advertising may influence the pattern of consumption, it does not necessarily increase total consumption in an economy.

Since advertising does not claim to be able to increase the sales for any and all products, the above question can be made more precise and the scope of this inquiry reduced accordingly. In order to be able to increase demand for a product, the advertising profession requires that the product be new or improved [111] and enjoy a favorable trend. Consequently the question should read: can advertising influence people to buy new and improved products with a favorable trend out of money not destined for immediate consumption?

The new products mentioned in connection with this claim include automobiles at the time of their introduction, air conditioners and deodorants [112], the safety, and later, the electric razor [113], radio and television sets [114].

---

[111] The advertising profession does not always distinguish between an improved product, but generally speaks of a new and improved product. Actually, it is difficult to draw any hard and fast line since, when there are enough improvements, the product may be considered as new. Consequently we have not attempted to make a distinction, and have treated the two as one.

[112] Thomas D'Arcy Brophy, « The Role of Advertising in Our Economy », Address to the Advertising Club of New Orleans, June 5, 1956, pp. 2-4 (mimeographed copy).

[113] « *Facts You Should Know about Advertising* », (N. Y.: Better Business Bureau, 1953) p. 8.

[114] *ibid.*, p. 9 and « *What Advertising is ... What it has Done ... What it Can Do Now* ». Reprinted from *Printers' Ink* May 15, 1953, no 8 (no printed pagination).

Among the improved products are instant dessert puddings [115], the new model cars and the changing varieties of baby food combinations [116]. The characteristic of these products is that they either do something which previous products could not, or do it more easily or more rapidly [117].

It is not enough, however, for the product to be merely new and improved [118], it must be in step with the times. It must enjoy a favorable trend, that is, large scale acceptance by consumers. This point is well expressed in the following words:

> If the product is in keeping with the trends . . . advertising can be effective in creating and enlarging markets quickly. But if these conditions do not exist, or if the product has been left behind in the procession by technological or style changes, even heroic doses of advertising cannot make up for the acute lack of product research and styling [119].

If newness and a favorable trend are important in increasing the sales of a product, they must be of even greater importance when they are to cause an increase in total consumption by causing people to buy the product out of money not destined for immediate consumption. The product, in any case, is the key to increased sales, and, *a fortiori*, to increased consumption in the whole economy.

THE EVIDENCE

Though there is probably no way of determining directly whether or not advertising influences people to buy

---

[115] Brophy, *op. cit.*, p. 3.

[116] *The Modern Marketing Concept*, (N. Y.: Mc Cann-Erikson, n. d.) p. 7.

[117] Bernard C. Duffy, « Some Examples of How Advertising Has Increased the Standard of Living », *Advertising to Raise the Standard of Living, Addresses at the fifth annual Chicago Tribune Distribution and Advertising Forum*, May 18, 1954, p. 25 insists on the element of ease and speed.

[116] These products must also, of course, be worthy and capable of living up to their claims. This is true of any product which hopes to profit from advertising. *cf.* Walter Seiler, « How Advertising and Selling Drive Our Fast-Raced Economy », reprinted from *Printers' Ink*, October 21, 1955, (no printed pagination).

[119] Otto Kleppner, « Is there Too Much Advertising? » reprinted from *Harper's*, February 1951, (no printed pagination).

products out of money not destined for immediate consumption, the evidence which bears on its ability to expand *primary* demand [120] for new and improved products will enable us to give some answer to the question with which this section is concerned.

Even before one considers the facts of the case, however, it should be noted that what is known of the effects of propaganda indicate that given a trend, advertising can *reinforce* it. In addition, the facts presented in the previous section create a presupposition that advertising *cannot create* a trend in most circumstances. These presuppositions are confirmed by the facts.

The long quotation which follows summarizes Borden's conclusions on the effects of advertising on primary demand. Since his is the most complete study yet made of the question and since this conclusion seems to have been accepted by all who have written after him [121], it seems safe to build on these conclusions.

> From the many cases analysed and from the industry studies one clear and important generalization can be made, namely, that basic trends of demands for products, which are determined by underlying social and environmental conditions, are more significant in determining the expansion or contraction of primary demand than is the use or the lack of use of advertising . . . Advertising has been effective in expanding demand when the underlying factors favored expansion. In other instances expansion has gone ahead irrespective of whether advertising has been used. Conversely, strong advertising has not overcome contraction of demand when underlying conditions operated to bring contraction.
>
> When advertising has been used, its chief effect on primary demand has been either to speed up the expansion of a demand that naturally would have come without advertising,

---

[120] Primary demand is the demand for a class of goods or services, e. g., automobiles or radios, as opposed to selective demand which is the demand for a brand or make of automobiles or radios, e. g. for Buicks or for RCA.

[121]. C. Chisholm, *The Economic Function of Advertising*, (London: Business Publications, 1943), p. 8. is the only author who, to my knowledge, has any basic criticisms of Borden, and his remarks do not touch on the conclusions which are being used here, except in so far as he thinks Borden should have done more work on advertising by categories and products.

or to check or retard an adverse trend. Consumers' wants for products have been determined by the character of the consumers and by their existing environment. Advertising has not changed people's basic characteristics, nor has it appreciably changed environment. It has merely played upon consumers' buying motives to intensify desire or to build favorable attitudes towards product consumption [122].

The conclusions contained in the above citation are of the utmost importance. First, at best, advertising merely steps up the expansion of a demand that would have come naturally without advertising. Secondly, it is the basic trend which really determines whether demand for a given product will expand. Thirdly, these basic trends are determined by underlying social and environmental conditions. Fourthly, in the absence of favorable trends advertising can do little.

Despite all this, one may still ask if advertising does not have a significant effect on the creation of the trends in question. In general, these trends are probably present even before advertising is applied [123]. Nevertheless, though it would be exaggerated to speak of advertising *creating* a trend, it may be of some significance in encouraging the first sales which may start a trend. In this context Borden writes:

> New products have been accepted, but the demands for them have grown relatively slowly. Once the new products have been accepted by a few consumers, however, consumption has usually expanded through much of the social group . . . While the attitudes which favor consumption of various products are determined by the entire milieu, aggressive selling and advertising have been important forces leading to the acceptance of new products. They have played a particularly important part in bringing first sales, upon which emulative consumption depends [124].

Two points shoud be made with regard to this statement. First, the first sales do not necessarily lead to

---

[122] Borden *op. cit.*, pp. 433-434.

[123] Martin Mayer, « What is Advertising Good For? » *Harper's* February, 1958, p. 29. Mayer's conclusions are based on several hundred interviews with advertising executives.

[124] Borden, *op. cit.*, p. 692.

emulation [125].   Second, the time lag between the first sales
and the beginning of a trend can be so long, that despite
aggressive selling, advertising's contribution can be considered as far less important that Borden's conclusion seems
to indicate.   Thus, in the case of mechanical refrigerators,
the first decade of aggressive selling (1920-1929) induced
only ten percent of the potential users to buy [126].   It is,
further, impossible to say how many of these initial sales
were due to personal selling and how many to advertising [127]. For these reasons, it seems best not to speak of
advertising creating a trend, but of its being some help in
making the initial sales which may or may not snowball
in time [128].

This thesis that advertising cannot create a trend is
further reinforced by what is known of advertising's inability to control fashion.   While this may surprise many
people, the fact remains that many experts think it doubtful
that advertising has ever seriously altered any fashion
trend [129].   Advertising can spread and prolong fads until
they become fashions [130], but, except on rare occasions, it
cannot create them.   Even though style in clothing has
become more and more important in the United States, it
appears that the fashion industry has lost all control over
the changes [131].   Some have, of course, attempted to dominate these shifts, but as Agnew notes, « Advertising grave-
yards are filled with the remains of those who have tried
to dominate style » [132].

Three conclusions may be drawn from this evidence.
First, advertising can reinforce and speed up a trend in

---

[125] *cf. supra* ADVERTISING AND FACE-TO-FACE CONTACTS for the
importance of the group in determining what will be accepted and approved of in the community.
   [126] Borden, *op. cit.*, p. 410.
   [127] *ibid.*, p. 411.
   [128] *cf., ibid.*, p. 301 for the interesting example of dentifrices. On p.
298 the author notes that after 1930 aggressive advertising was unable to
increase per capita consumption of dentifrices, even though a trend
had begun in the previous decade.
   [129] Gorden, *op cit.*, p. 122.
   [130] H. E. Agnew, « Can Standardization Reduce Advertising Costs »,
Annals of the American Academy of Political and Social, 137 (1928) p. 256.
   [131] *The Changing American Market*, p. 178.
   [132] Agnew, *op. cit.*, p. 122.

primary demand. Secondly, in general, it probably has not much power to create this trend. Third, it cannot guarantee to continue this trend, though it may prevent it from reversing itself completely and suddenly.

INFERENCES AND EXAMPLES

The evidence presented above indicates that advertising can help in expanding primary demand, but it does not prove that it can expand aggregate demand and consumption in the entire economy. Though it appears impossible to prove directly that advertising has helped to raise total consumption, the data given provides the basis for an argument in favor of advertising's capacity to do so in certain circumstances. When the trend, which advertising is reinforcing, is itself leading to an increase of total consumption, advertising may have some share in augmenting that aggregate. In other words given the right product and a strong enough trend, advertising does have some contribution to make [133].

The increased sales of American cars in the period after the Second World War seems to represent just such a movement which increased total consumption. This trend was due not merely to the utility of the car, but to its meaning and to the affection which Americans have for the automobile. The Editors of Fortune put it this way:

> Never has an industry produced a machine that has so inflamed the proprietory instinct in so many prospects; never has an industry output so gratified both the senses and the psyches of so many of its customers. [134].

So great was the affection of the American for his car and so powerful the trend generated by this affection that the consumer would turn in his car before it was worn out and buy one of the new and improved models [135].

---

[133] cf. Borden, *op. cit.*, 708 for a similar, though not identical argument.

[134] *The Changing American Market*, p. 152.

[135] *ibid.*, p. 155. For further information on the meaning of the automobile, *cf.* Joseph W. Newman, Motivation Research and *Marketing Ma-*

The fact that auto credit accounts for as much as one half of all consumer credit in the United States [136], indicates that the buyers were willing to expand their consumption in order to have an automobile. Add to this the fact that seventeen percent of all American families had two automobiles in 1957 and that two out of five automobiles sold in that year were bought by two-car families [137], and it becomes clear that the automobile enjoyed a very powerful trend.

Nevertheless, we can still ask if this trend did lead to an expansion of total consumption, and if advertising made any appreciable contribution to the trend itself. The first question cannot be answered here, but two facts indicate that the contribution of advertising was limited. First, despite heavy advertising the trend did slow down when the automobile lost some of its prestige and became only a means of transportation [138]. Secondly, many members of the advertising profession admit that, though they might be able to slow down an unfavorable trend, they could probably not stem it [139]. Though these are only indications, and not proofs, it would seem safe to conclude that in the absence of evidence to the contrary, advertising probably has no appreciable effect on total consumption.

CONCLUSION

The conclusions of this last section, namely that advertising can speed up a favorable trend, but cannot guarantee to create a trend, converges with a the conclusion of the first two sections in the present chapter. Neither propaganda in general, nor advertising for a generally higher standard of living can guarantee results when it

nagement, (Boston: Harvard U. School of Business Administration, 1957) p. 235 and p. 237.

[136] *The Changing American Market,* p. 159.

[137] *Advertising Age,* February 17, 1958 p. 2 reporting on the survey of *U. S. News and World Report.*

[138] « Auto Prestige: Conspicuous Consumption is Waning », *Time,* (Atlantic Edition) March 31, 1958, p. 50.

[139] For the results of a survey and a series of interesting comments on this point, *cf.* « Consumers: to Admen They're a Puzzlement », *Tide,* March, 14, 1958, pp. 49-51.

must work against a trend or the deep rooted attitudes of the public. Given a social atmosphere which favors increased consumption in general, or the increased consumption of a given product, advertising may be of some use. However since advertising has little control over the basic forces which create trends, it cannot give a general and unqualified assurance of its ability to expand consumption.

The fact, that the effectiveness of advertising in expanding consumption depends on forces which are largely beyond its control, means that its usefulness is limited. In the following chapter we shall consider these limitations in relation to the problem of the harmonious growth of the economy.

Even if advertising could give some assurance of its ability to stimulate total personal consumption, this would not necessarily constitute an economic justification of its activity. The stimulation of personal consumption is useful only if it contributes to a better use of resources in an economy. In the following chapter we will study the assumption that the situation in the American economy calls for a stimulation of consumption in view of the economic and social needs of society.

In closing, it should be noted that the present chapter, though largely a preparation for those which follow, contains certain conclusions which are of great importance for any study of the ethics of advertising. The fact that advertising is an instrumental rather than a principal cause, or perhaps better, a reinforcing rather than an activating agent, enables us to locate its position in the traditional scheme of agents who influence the activity of another[140]. Though further refinements are necessary, the socio-psychological analysis given above should be of great help in applying the principles of moral philosophy to the various effects of advertising.

In addition, the conclusions of this chapter also tend to confirm the charge that much advertising merely shifts demand from one firm to another, and so represents a

---

[140] *cf.* for example the scheme of *actus humanus cooperativus* given in F. Hürth and P. M. Abellán, *De Principiis, de Virtutibus et Praeceptis, Pars 1,* (Romae: Pontifica Universitas Gregoriana, 1948), p. 196 ff.

competitive cost which does not serve the consumer and society [141]. This, of course, means that the advertising profession must find other justifications for advertising which attempts to do more than inform consumers about the availability of products [142].

---

[141] *cf.* Oskar Sànger, *Werbung als dominanter Faktor des Absatzprozesses.* (Disseration, Freiburg im Breisgau, 1956), pp. 120-141. Kurt Steuber, *Werbung und Wohlstand.* (Zürich: Polygraphischer Verlag, 1958), pp. 89-126.

[142] Some of these arguments are listed in the introduction. It should be noted, however, that many of these arguments also rest in whole or in part on the assumption that advertising has considerable power to influence consumption.

CHAPTER VII

ECONOMIC ASSUMPTIONS

After the previous chapter there is really no imperative
need for further investigation of the claim that advertising
by stimulating personal consumption can be a prime factor
in encouraging economic progress. However, since some
may doubt the validity of our conclusions, it will be
useful to investigate some of the economic assumptions
which underlie the claim under consideration. Such an
investigation has the additional virtue of laying bare some
of the myths and shibboleths which often play a large role
in discussions of advertising and its place in the economy.

The present chapter, then, seeks to examine two of
the economic assumptions found in the argument proposed
by the advertising profession. Since only a professional
economist can give a definitive answer to the question
posed in the chapter, the following pages only attempt to
show that there is serious doubt about the economic validity
of the case for advertising. The first assumption concerns
the need for an artificial stimulation of consumption in
present-day American economy; the second, the suitability
of advertising as a tool to be used in encouraging harmonious economic growth.

The precise questions to be answered may be phrased
as follow:

1. Does the long-range economic and social situation
in the United States call for an artificial stimulation of
personal consumption?

2. Can advertising be used to promote that economic
stability which is necessary for harmonious economic
growth?

Before going on to define the terms in the above questions, it will be well to avoid confusion by stating certain

positions which have been adopted with regard to two
theories which might be used to support the case in favor
of advertising.

Though the argument presented in the earlier chapters
makes no *explicit* reference to a theory of secular stagnation, it has been suggested that it would be possible to
work out an argument on the basis of a theory which
« attributed unemployment and the lack of resources to
the fact that free enterprise in a mature economy results
in a deficiency of demand »[1]. Such an argument would,
however, be no better than the theory on which it was
built. Now, in the concrete, the validity of such theories
depends on the validity of the hypotheses which support
the theory itself. With respect to these theories and hypotheses, Haberler notes:

> Ces speculations au sujet de l'évolution profonde de l'éco-
> nomie manquent nécessairement d e précision et subissent
> aisément l'influence de l'équation personelle de l'auteur et de
> son milieu. Très souvent, leur force de persuasion dépend
> moins de la puissance du raisonnement que du choix des
> faits invoqués[2].

Samuelson, who presents the theory of secular stagnation in one form, but does not discuss its relative merits,
notes that the ten years since 1945 have proved to be quite
the reverse of any gloomy expectations concerning the
stagnation of a mature economy[3]. His personal view is
that the outlook in the immediate future is inflationary
enough so that secular exhiliration may be no less a danger
than secular stagnation[4].

Even though many economists admit that in the United
States a superfluity of savings and a deficiency of consumption are more likely to hinder growth than the contrary[5],

---

[1] Neil H. Borden, *The Economic Effects of Advertising*, (Chicago:
Irwin, 1942), p. 185.

[2] Gottfried von Haberler, *Prospérité et Dépression: Une étude théorique des cycles économiques*, (nouvelle édition revue et augmentée, Genève: Societé des Nations, 1939), pp. 278-279.

[3] Paul A. Samuelson, *Economics*, (3rd ed. N. Y.: Mc Graw-Hill, 1955),
p. 348.

[4] *ibid.*, p. 349.

[5] W. Arthur Lewis, *The Theory of Economic Growth*, (Homewood,
Illinois; Irwin, 1955), p. 297. Lewis himself notes that it is arguable
whether the actual conditions ever exist. *cf. ibid.*, p. 216.

many are not prepared to regard the theory of secular stagnation as either proved or provable [6]. In view of the fact that these theories are so controversial, no solid argument can be built on them. Consequently we have prescinded from the theories and confined our consideration to opinions which are based on the actual economic situation in the United States.

No matter what may be said of secular stagnation due to a deficiency of demand, it may still be true that at a *given moment* a fall in consumption may contribute to the disruption of the economy [7]. This is to say that an under-consumption theory of the cycle might be invoked in support of the utility of advertising [8]. Rather than attempt to validate or invalidate such theories, we have assumed with the advertising profession that on occasion consumption is an important factor in cyclic fluctuations. Having accepted this assumption which is highly favorable to advertising, we have confined ourselves to a consideration of the suitability of advertising as a tool for the harmonizing of consumption with production in view of an orderly economic growth.

THE DEFINITION OF TERMS

With these positions stated, we may now return to a consideration of our questions and a definition of terms. First, does the long run economic and social situation in the United States call for an artificial stimulation of consumption?

The terms used in this question must be defined carefully in order to avoid misunderstanding. By the long-run situation, we mean that prevailing during the next ten years. The economic aspect of this situation refers to the need for and the possibility of economic growth. The social aspect is concerned with the necessity of attaining

---

[6] Samuelson, *op. cit.*, p. 348.

[7] Samuelson, *op. cit.*, pp. 320 ff for the various reservations and conditions to be placed on such a statement.

[8] *cf.* Haberler, *op. cit.*, pp. 135 ff for different forms of the theory of underconsumption in relation to the cycle.

this growth without compromising the free enterprise system in the United States. By personal consumption is meant the purchase and use of goods and services by individuals. This is opposed to public consumption and expenditures, that is expenditures made by the government for goods or services and the use made of these by the government or by all citizens together.

The most important term in the first question is *artificial stimulation*. The meaning attached to this phrase will best be seen by comparing it to normal stimulation. Normal stimulation of consumption is that which results from changes in the economic and social conditions of the citizens, from the influence of society and education on their standard of living and from information about products, their prices, qualities, availability and the uses which these products can serve because of their intrinsic qualities. In so far as advertising gives such information, it is a part of the normal process of stimulation [9].

By artificial stimulation is meant any attempt to pressure, push, cajol, manipulate, to rearrange values or to endow a product with a psychic value which is not connected with its qualities [10]. Advertising which attempts to stimulate in this way is often called suggestive advertising in that it does not merely inform but attempts to insinuate or suggest [11]. We refer to this as artificial stimulation since ordinarily this type of outside influence is not considered necessary to increase total consumption [12].

These definitions should make it clear that there is no question of the necessity of advertising as a means of giving

---

[9] Such advertising is normally called informative advertising *cf.* Kenneth E. Boulding, *Economic Analysis*, (3rd ed. N. Y. Harper, 1941), pp. 672-673, but with some authors we hold that it is also persuasive both in intent and effect. *cf.* N. Kaldor, « The Economic Effects of Advertising », *Review of Economics*, 18 (1950-51), p. 4.

[10] We prescind from the question of whether these methods are used merely for a competitive reason. For authors who take a different view, *cf.* Edward Hastings Chamberlin, *Theory of Monopolistic Competition*, (6th ed. Cambridge, Mass: Harvard U. Press, 1948) p. 120 and Dorethea Braithwaite, « The Economics of Advertisement », *Economic Journal*, 38 (1928), p. 17.

[11] *cf.* Wilhelm Roepke, *Masse und Mitte*, (Zürich: Rentsch, 1950), p. 209.

[12] *cf.* Kurt Steuber, *Werbung und Wohlstand*, (Zürich: Polygraphischer Verlag, 1958), p. 7. The reason is that the economist sees his problem as the adaptation of scarce means to the fullfillment of given needs.

product information. People who want things must know of their location, price qualities and existence, so that informative advertising is needed in an exchange economy-[13]. Such advertising is a part of the normal process of increasing consumption and no one questions its utility [14]. What is under discussion, however, is the need for artificial stimulation of the type described. Such stimulation is attacked for a number of reasons, both moral and economic, and is in need of justification by such arguments as that which insists on its contribution to economic growth [15]. This is the critical point; the need for artificial stimulation of demand, the need for suggestve advertising.

GROWTH AND PERSONAL CONSUMPTION

Does the long-range economic and social situation of the United States call for an artificial stimulation of personal consumption? In the present section we shall attempt to answer this question in so far as it involves the *economic* situation; in the next section, the social exigencies which are proposed by the advertising profession will be considered apart. In treating of the economic situation during the next ten years, it is assumed that growth is desirable in view of the needs of both the nation and its citizens [16]. It is also assumed that much of this growth can and should be found in the increased production of goods for personal consumption [17]. Our problem concerns not the fact of growth, but the distribution of the fruits of this growth. To be more concrete, we want to know if the percentage of this increase which must come from personal consump-

---

[13] Roepke, *op. cit.*, p. 203 gives an excellent short summary of the need for informative advertising in this type of economy.

[14] While no one questions the utility of information, advertising is often criticized for giving too little actual information at too great a cost. *cf.* Steuber, *op. cit.* p. 22, Roepke, *op. cit.*, p. 207.

[15] Kaldor *op. cit.*, p. 1, notes that the defenders of advertising regard the « external » effects as more important than the direct effects.

[16] *cf. Economic Report of the President*, January 1958, (Washington, D. C., Government Printing Office), p. 3.

[17] *cf.* Rockerfeller Brothers Fund, *The Challenge to America, Its Economic and Social Aspects, Report of Panel IV of the Special Studies Project*, (Garden City, N. Y.: Doubleday, 1958), p. 27.

tion is such as to demand a stimulation of consumption by suggestive advertising.

In attempting to answer this question we shall present first the analysis given by one member of the advertising profession [18], and then compare it with the uses of this new wealth which are proposed by other groups. The conclusion of this section will state: The need for public services and private investment is so great, and the present rate of increase in consumption so high, that there is serious doubt about the need of stimulating consumption by artificial means.

The argument of the advertising profession can be seen in the following quotation:

> The production level of over $ 500 billion possible by 1965 could yield disposable income to individuals after taxes, sufficient for a further 50% increase — to over $ 350 billion of consumer purchases, plus a high level of over $ 20 billion annually in personal savings [19].

Now since the present annual rate of increase in consumption per capita is only three percent [20], consumption will have to be stimulated if it is to increase at an average rate of five percent a year during this period [21]. Even if increases in the population absorb fifteen percent of this increased production, stimulation will be needed [22].

In estimating the need for increased consumption in 1955-1956, Johnson saw the situation as follows. In order to consume everything produced at the 1953 per capita rate, an increase of twenty-seven billion dollars or about twelve percent would be needed [23]. If consumption is to keep up with increasing productivity, an increase of forty billion dollars or about seventeen percent in personal con-

---

[18] This limitation has been forced on the author since most do not give any precise figures which indicate how they think the fruits of growth should be distributed.

[19] Arno H. Johnson, « The Job for Advertising in the Continuing Expansion of Our Economy », *Papers form the 37th Annual Meeting of the A.A.A.A., Group II,* (N. Y.: A.A.A.A., 1955) p. 2.

[20] *Economic Report of the President,* January 1958, p. 2, this is the average increase between 1946 and 1958.

[21] Johnson, *op. cit.,* p. 2.

[22] Stanley Resor, « We Can Sell $ 600 billion of Output », *U. S. News and World Report,* January 4, 1957, p. 72.

[23] Johnson, *op. cit.,* p. 4.

sumption would be required to create the demand for this production[24]. In either case, stimulation would certainly be in order.

These huge increases in personal consumption are seen as possible and necessary because Johnson foresaw expenditures for defense as decreasing from $ 43.6 billion in 1954 to $ 41 billion in 1955-56, while other government expenditures were to rise only slightly from $ 33.9 billion to $ 35 billion[25]. Further, Johnson estimated that the amount devoted to private investment would mount from $ 45.7 billion to $ 50. billion, an increase in the neighborhood of ten percent. In short Johnson assumed that the increased wealth will not be needed for public expenditures and private investment, and so would be available for consumption. In other words the argument assumes that America can afford such a huge increase in personal consumption[26].

Here, then, is a crucial question: can the United States afford such an increase in personal consumption, or are other needs so great that the increase in consumption must be held to present rates or even decreased? While this question cannot be answered with metaphysical certainty, the opinions of experts seem to indicate: 1) that the United States cannot afford such an increase, 2) that the rate of increase might have to be slowed down.

The experts who prepared the Rockefeller Report on the needs and capacities of the American economy during the period between 1957 and 1967 cast up several trial balances of the relations between the rise in national wealth, the increase in consumption, the need for investment, and both low and high estimates of the need for public expenditure. As the following table shows, the estimated rate of per capita increase in consumption never exceeds the present normal rate of three percent[27].

---

[24] Johnson, *op cit.*, p. 13.
[25] *loc. cit.*
[26] Though other authors do not cite figures, they seem to hold this principle. *cf.* Melvin Brorby, *We Ask Ourselves Four Questions*, (N. Y.: A.A.A.A., 1958) pp. 5-6.
[27] Rockefeller Brothers' Fund, *op. cit.*, pp. 71-72, by permission of Doubleday and Company.

BILLIONS OF 1957 DOLLARS

	1957	1967			
		GNP at 3%	GNP at 4%		GNP at 5%
		Government LOW	When Government LOW HIGH		Government HIGH
Gross National Product	434	583	642		707
Government	86	127	127	153	153
Private Investment	67	100	112	112	123
Consumption	281	356	403	377	431
Annual Growth Rate of Per Capita Consumption	—	.8%	2.1%	1.4%	2.8%

The principles which guided this partition of the national revenue are of some importance. First, the authors of the report see the need for restraint and a proper sense of values which causes one to chose the essential rather than the merely desirable [28]. Second, these experts see that the increased expenditures of the government are necessary not only in view of the need for defense and increased provision for welfare, but because many such expenditures are necessary for growth itself [29]. Third, the framers of the report see that growth cannot occur without large sums being devoted to investment. Indeed, these planners project a moderate increase in the ratio of investiment to GNP because they see the need for a rise in private investment in the program of urban renewal [30].

A very similar estimate has been made by the National Planning Association for the period from 1956 to 1965. In the following table column I assumes that defense needs remain stable, but that other public expenditures rise in proportion to the increase of national production; column

---

[28] *ibid.*, pp. 73-74.
[29] *ibid.*, pp. 23-24.
[30] *ibid.*, pp. 70.

II assumes a reduction of some twenty-six billion dollars in the defence budget; column III assumes an increase of some twenty billion dollars in the national security program [31].

	(Billions of dollars in 1956 dollars)			
	1956	1965 I	1965 II	1965 III
Gross National Product	414.7	584.0	584.0	600.00
National Security	42.4	46.5	20.0	66.5
Personal Consumption	267.2	385.0	395.0	377.5
Private Domestic Investment	65.9	88.0	91.0	95.0
Net Foreign Investment	1.4	1.5	4.0	1.0
Other Government Purchases	37.8	63.0	74.0	60.0

Let us look more closely at what lies behind these figures. Of the increase of $ 170 billion in GNP envisioned in columns I and II, the increase in population will account for some $ 70 billion, (assuming the maintenance of recent per capita increases in *basic* needs), while about $ 15 billion will probably be needed for private investment [32]. If the remainder of some $ 85 billion were devoted to consumption, then, it would be the equivalent of an annual per capita increase of close to five percent [33]. However, in view of the fact that the United States needs to spend between $ 20 billion and $ 36 billion (in 1956 dollars) for such items as education, health, research, resource conservation, highways and skyways [34], Colm concludes as follows.

> It is most likely that the great rise in potential production would be devoted to a combination of these various purposes. It would be used to increase the level of living by a continuing raise in real wages and by wiping out the remnants of poverty. An average annual increase of perhaps 2 percent in the per capita level of living appears compatible with the expected increase in production and the necessity of making appropriate allowances for improvement of health services, education and training, research, conservation and development of natural resources, transportation, productive plant and equipment, foreign investment and so on. When and if it

---

[31] Gerhard Colm and Theodore Geiger with the assistance of Manuel Helzner, *The Economy of the American People: Problems, Progress and Prospects*, (Washington, D. C., National Planning Association, 1958), pp. 162-163 by permission of the NPA.

[32] *ibid.*, p. 83.

[33] *ibid.*, p. 84.

[34] *ibid.*, pp. 83-84.

becomes necessary further to increase national security expenditures, the improvement in the standard of living and in some non defense areas of government services would have to proceed more slowly [35].

The conclusion is clear. If the United States is to provide for the welfare of all its citizens and to assure the continued existence of the nation, it will have to limit the growth of personal consumption to a rate equal to, or below that which has prevailed during the previous decade [36]. In short even the richest nation in the history of the world still finds that the sum of its needs and aspirations, challenges its ability to produce [37].

Though there may be some dispute about the details of the distribution of revenue proposed by the various groups cited in the previous pages, it should be clear that even with a high rate of growth in the economy, the increasing need for public expenditures and for private investment will limit the increase in personal consumption to a level which will require no stimulating since it will probably be below that of the trend in increased demand for consumer goods. It seems safe to conclude that there is *serious doubt about the need for stimulating the desire for consumers goods, and therefore serious doubt about the social utility of advertising in attempting to change the standard of living.*

One can go even farther, however, and charge advertising with trying to affect a misallocation of resources by

---

[35] *ibid.*, p. 84 by permission of the National Planning Association.

[36] This limitation may be all the more necessary if expansion is to be paid for out of real savings. While the advertising people may point to a high rate of savings as a danger sign, (*cf.* Resor, *op. cit.*, p. 74), others believe that savings must be increased if the financing of the economy is to be on a sound basis. (*cf.* Marcus Wallenberg, « The High Cost of Money », *Fortune* December 1957, pp. 134-135). Some writers go so far as to say that the demand for investment capital will be so great in the next twenty years, that one of the greatest economic problems will be the limitation of the amount of capital investment to a level which can be met primarily from real savings. (*cf.* « For the Next Twenty Years » *Newsweek*, European edition) June 16, 1958, pp. 46-49.

[37] *cf.* Colm, *op. cit.*, p. 84; Rockerfeller Brothers Fund, *op. cit.*, p. 73 and *Economic Report of the President*, January 1958, pp. 2-3. For another projection of expenditures which corresponds with the two given *cf.* Thomas R. Carskadon and George Soule, *USA in New Dimensions: The Measure and Promise of America's Resources, A Twentieth Century Fund Survey*, (N. Y.: Macmillan, 1957) pp. 14-15.

exalting personal consumption at the expense of those services and investment which the public needs. This charge is made very forcibly by Galbraith in his controversial book *The Affluent Society,* His case may be seen in the following citations.

> Advertising operates excusively, and emulation mainly on behalf of privately produced goods and services. Since management and emulative effects operate on behalf of private production, public services will have an inherent tendency to lag behind. Automobile demand which is expensively synthesized will inevitably have a much larger claim on income than parks or public health or even roads where no such influence operates [38].
>
> The same forces which bring us our plentitude of private goods and leave us poverty-striken in public services also act to distort the distribution of investment as between ordinary material capital and what we may denote as the personal capital of the country [39].

In the last analysis advertising is reinforcing the tendency of people to seek their own immediate interest without regard to those services which the public weal demands. Its job is easier because many must pay more than they get personally and directly from the public sphere [40]. In short, advertising, as propaganda for private consumption, can work for the distortion of the economy by causing people to neglect their duty to allot money for public services.

Rebuttal and Counter Rebuttal

The argument as presented by the advertising profession has an answer for this charge and for the conclusions already stated. The advertising profession will admit that all these needs exist and should be satisfied, indeed their argument in favor growth cites the same needs [41]. Their objection is not against the satisfaction but against the method, and the results of the method.

---

[38] John Kenneth Galbraith, *The Affluent Society*, (Boston: Houghton Mifflin, 1958), pp. 260-261.

[39] *ibid.*, p. 270. Personal capital means investment in human beings, in education, health and welfare.

[40] *ibid.*, p. 267.

[41] *cf.*, chapter II and chapter III.

The rebuttal might be worded as follows: If these public needs are satisfied by decreasing the total share given
to consumers and increasing the total share given to public services, you will kill incentives and destroy the dynamism that drives the economic system.   At the same
time, by increasing the share given to government you
run the risk of interference, of a planned economy and
finally of collectivism.   Therefore, we must increase private consumption in order to produce so much wealth
that incentives remain and the share taken by the government remains constant or decreases.   Any other course
will destroy the system which has given us our wealth
and guarantees our freedom.

Each of these points demands consideration.   First,
increasing the government's functions prematurely, and
so increasing taxes will kill initiative.   This point has
been considered by the authors of the reports previously
cited.   Here are two statements of the problem.

> Some analysists of the American tax system believe that
> the taxes imposed on business profits and individual incomes
> in the higher brackets are so severe that they have undesir-
> able effects on economical management and on incentives
> for investment and work.   In contrast, it has been pointed
> out that during the last decade the relatively high taxes have
> not prevented a very high and sustained rate of investment
> and no general lack of incentive to work, save, and invest
> has been noticed.   Even so, tax rates imposed on business
> profits and high incomes are probably approaching limits
> beyond which their unfavorable effect on management and
> management and incentives would outweight any possible
> desirable effect on income distribution [42].
>
> As presently constituted, our tax system presents a series
> of important impediments to growth. The very high graduated
> rates in the personal income tax structure reduce the incentive
> and the ability to accumulate capital and put it to productive
> use.   The failure to develop averaging devices presents an
> impediment to certain groups. The very high corporate tax
> rates and present depreciation provisions slow the growth of
> corporate enterprise [43].

Now these two opinions come from the very groups
whose estimates were used to prove that we do not need

---

[42] Colm, *op. cit.*, p. 99.
[43] Rockerfeller Brothers Fund, *op. cit.*, p. 22.

to stimulate consumer demand. How, then, do they reconcile their opinions on incentives with their proposal for large government expenditures? Both groups admit that an overall reduction would be ideal [44], but feel that a change in the tax structure which would equalize burdens without decreasing overall tax revenue would do the job of raising incentives [45]. In short, the danger to incentive comes not so much from the size of the taxes but from their distribution.

The advertising profession is quite right in contending that one must not destroy economic incentive, but the facts seem to indicate that though government expenditures have doubled since 1929 [46], there has been no noticeable diminution of incentives. Further, it is the opinion of responsible men who are devoted to the free enterprise system, that the danger is not so much from high taxes, but from a poorly organized distribution of the tax burden. In the actual order, then, the first argument of the advertising profession may have little weight in its simplified form [47].

The second point urged in favor of increasing wealth in the private sphere so as to prevent the continuing encroachements of government comes down to limiting the share of governement in the total national income so that its influence is also limited. The implication is that if government increases its share, it will tend to interfere, to plan and finally to introduce collectivism. Therefore, in order to protect our way of life and meet our needs, we must increase total private production and consumption so that the share of government does not increase.

Here again one may agree with the principle: the government's share should not increase; and disagree with the facts: i.e. governments share will increase if we allot resources under the plans outlined above. Let us examine

---

[44] Colm, *op. cit.*, p. 100, and Rockerfeller Brothers Fund, *op. cit.*, p. 27.

[45] Rockerfeller Brothers Fund, *op. cit.*, p. 23, Colm, *op. cit.*, p. 99.

[46] Carskadon, *op. cit.*, p. 14.

[47] For a few interesting remarks on the incentive to work as related to income, *cf.*, William H. Whyte, Jr., *The Organization Man*, (Garden City, N. Y.: Doubleday Anchor Books, 1957), pp. 157-159. His conclusion: Big executives may complain about high taxes, but they work just as hard as ever.

the share of government in the different balances cast up by the Rockefeller report whose authors agree that the share of the government should not be increased [48].

	1957		1967	
		GNP at 3% Growth Rate	GNP at 4% Growth Rate	GNP at 5% Growt Rate
Share of Government Annual Growth	19+%	21%	19+% *or* 23%	20+%
Rate of Per Capita Consumption	—	0.8%	2.1% *or* 1.4%	2.8%

Two points should be noted in the above [49]. First, except in the second alternative at a growth rate of four percent (an alternative which presupposes need for a large increase in public expenditures) the share of the government remains at approximately one-fifth of the national revenue [50]. This is to say that it is held relatively constant. Second, the increase in consumption in no case goes over the three percent annual increase which has characterized the last decade [51]. In short, the government's share is maintained more or less constant, while consumption is allowed to increase at a rate which does not require artificial stimulation.

SUMMARY

The facts which have been presented and the analysis of these cannot settle the question once and for all. However, they do indicate that responsible groups do consider it possible to have a full employment economy [52] which

---

[48] Rockerfeller Brothers Fund, *op. cit.*, p. 27.

[49] Percentages of government's share based on figures given in *ibid.*, pp. 71-72.

[50] This has been the percentage during the past decade or so, *cf.* Carskadon, *op. cit.*, p. 14.

[51] *Economic Report of the President*, January 1958, p. 2.

[52] It should be noted that all these plans have relatively full employment in mind, i. e., a state in which not more than three percent of the labor force are without work. *cf.*, Carskadon, *op. cit.*, p. 3; Colm, *op. cit.*, p. 162.

protects incentives, and freedom, fulfills the public needs of society and still allows for an increase in personal consumption, and *that without the need for artificial stimulation of consumer demand*, without the *need of any outside force to change the basic attitudes towards consumption*.

Since demand is determined by underlying social and economic factors, the fact that these are still operating in the direction of increased consumption indicates that demand will probably continue to grow. The advertising profession itself has mentioned these factors: the trend towards family life and to the suburbs, a rise in educational levels, the astounding increase in the population, a more equal distribution of wealth and the introduction of new products which have found a favorable reception [53]. These are the real and the principal causes of demand [54]. As shown in the previous chapter, advertising does not create these forces, but at its best only reinforces them. In addition this reinforcement probably results from the information given by advertising rather than from its suggestive character [56]. As already noted basic trends in primary demand are largely independent of advertising, whether it be informative or suggestive, and this reinforces the opinion which denies the need for suggestive advertising in maintaining demand no matter what its possible uses in speeding it up [57].

To put it yet another way, we may say that given the tendency to increase consumption, a tendency which implies that people desire a great many things, there is no need to push, pressure or cajol, but merely to inform in such a way as to facilitate purchases [58]. At the same time, it should be noted, that if the defense needs of the nation make it imperative to increase government expenditures,

---

[53] *cf.*, Johnson, *op. cit.*, pp. 4-11.

[54] *cf.*, Chapter VI.

[55] *cf.*, especially, Borden, *op. cit.*, pp. 410 and 692.

[56] Steuber, *op. cit.*, p. 20 and p. 22 and p. 123.

[57] *cf.* Chapter VI.

[58] Of course such manipulation might be extremely profitable for an individual company, but this would not prove its value to the economy as a whole. *cf.* Oskar Sänger, *Werbung als dominanter Faktor des Absatzprozesses*, (Diss. Freiburg im Breisgau, Mimeographed, 1956), p. 128 and p. 141.

and so to decrease the rate of increase in consumption, it may be necessary to limit even informative advertising [59].

In conclusion, then, it can be said that there is great doubt about the necessity of stimulating consumption artificially in the long-range projections given. Further, it remains very probable that personal consumption may have to be cut below the levels foreseen as a result of recent per capita average increases.

ADVERTISING AND HARMONIOUS GROWTH

In the present section we shall seek to answer the second question posed at the beginning of this chapter. Can advertising stimulate consumption in such a way as to help in the attainment of the economic and social goals of society? To put it another way, is advertising as an instrument and as a part of the business life of a nation capable of contributing to the harmonious and orderly progress of an economy? In order to understand the meaning of these question, it will be necessary to preface the answer with a few remarks on the problem of stable growth.

It should be quite obvious that growth implies change and adjustment, and that an economy does not grow at an even rate either as a totality or in its parts [60]. Now, national economic policy seeks to attain an even rate of growth, limiting fluctuations to a relatively narrow area around a rising trend [61]. On the one hand, government and private measures seek to resist extended lapses from normal rates of growth in order to prevent depressions and unemployment [62]. On the other hand, and this is particularly true in the present day American economy, policy seeks to moderate splurges which go beyond rates which can be maintained for a long time and which might lead to inflationary pressures [63].

---

[59] As was the case during the last war both in the United States and England, *cf.* F. P. Bishop, *Advertising and Employment*, (London, Advertising Association, 1944), p. 9.

[60] Rockefellers Brothers Fund, *op. cit.*, p. 8.

[61] *Economic Report of the President*, January 1958, p. 3.

[62] *ibid.*, p. 3.

[63] *ibid.*, p. 4.

Because the causes of recessions and of inflation are complex, the efforts made to study them have given rise to a variety of explanatory theories [65]. Those theories which blame the down turn on an insufficiency of consumer demand [66], the underconsumption theories, provide a natural basis for an argument in favor of advertising being used to stabilize the economy. Even if no long-range, artificial stimulation of demand is required to assure growth, advertising might still be very useful at a given moment, when according to the theory of underconsumption, a fall in demand has started a down turn. The advertising profession has framed such an argument in an effort to justify both informative and suggestive advertising [67]. The possibility of such a contribution to economic stability must be considered.

A recession is, however, only one of the movements which interfere with a continuous and regular growth of the economy. Inflation is a second evil which can have an adverse effect on both the economy as a whole and on large groups within it [68]. Now though various factors may cause inflation, it is generally admitted that it is due to a demand for goods, services and investment capital which is greater than the available supply [69]. When an economy is faced with this situation, it must moderate demand until the supply of goods can be increased. On the whole not much has been said with regard to the possibility of using advertising to control an inflation, though some few of the defenders of the profession have pointed out that it could be used to increase savings or the sale of government bonds [70], and might help to lower prices by lowering costs [71]. Some of the critics of advertising have,

---

[65] *cf.*, Samuelson, *op. cit.*, pp. 320 ff. or any other introductory text for lists of these theories.

[66] *cf.*, Harberler, *op. cit.*, pp. 133 ff. for a discussion of the various theories, which stress underconsumption as a cause of the cycle.

[67] *cf.*, the various authors cited in the following pages for the names of those who have proposed this argument.

[68] *Economic Report of the President*, January 1958, p. 4.

[69] Samuelson, *op. cit.*, p. 350; *Economic Report of the President, loc. cit.*; Boulding, *op. cit.*, p. 305.

[70] F. P. Bishop, *op. cit.*, p. 9.

[71] Advertising Association, *Notes for Speakers: Talking Points*, series 12, May 1956, p. 1.

however, pointed out that if it raises demand at the wrong time, it may increase inflationary pressure [72], and lead to over expansion in some industries [73]. This implies that just as it might be useful to increase advertising in times of decline, it might be necessary to reduce it when the upswing is causing inflation [74]. If the advertising profession is sincerely interested in making a contribution to economic stability and healthy growth, it must face up to the possibility that the public weal may demand a mitigation of advertising as well as an increase.

Since harmonious and healthy economic growth demands that both recessions and harmful inflation be avoided, it is necessary to ask if advertising can be used in such a way as to mitigate both of these tendencies. *Assuming for the sake of argument* that consumer demand is an important factor in both inflation and in recessions, and that variations in this demand could be used to avoid or soften the effects of the movements which are leading to one extreme of the other, we will ask if advertising can be increased or diminished in such a way as to help in the maintenance of the desired long-range movement. We are not merely interested in discovering if the presence or absence of advertising can influence demand, but whether it can influence it in such a way as to produce the needed short-range effect, and that in view of the long-range goals of the economy. The possibility of an effective use of advertising can be determined only after one has answered the question: How should advertising be used in order to have the proper effects?

CONDITIONS

In order to have the proper effect advertising would have to be applied in the *right amounts*, and at the *right*

---

[72] Galbraith, *op. cit.*, p. 232.

[73] F. P. Bishop, *The Economics of Advertising*, (London: Robert Hale, 1946), p. 139. Bishop is on the whole favorable to advertising and should perhaps not be classed with the critics.

[74] Bishop, *Advertising and Employment*, p. 9, and Roland S. Vaile, « Comment on Cyclic Policy and the Advertising Appropriation », *Journal of Marketing*, 16 (1951), Jan. no. 1. p. 81.

time [75]. Further the advertising efforts of the various companies would have to be *coordinated* among themselves and with the fiscal policies of the government [76]. Without a coordinated and controlled application of advertising based on an accurate knowledge of the actual situation in the economy [77], advertising might only aggravate the situation and increase rather than reduce fluctuations [78].

A closer look at each of the above points will indicate why they are important. First, advertising must be applied in the right amounts. Because the margin between scarcity and over supply is very small when compared to aggregate demand [79], too much advertising could overstimulate demand and give rise to inflationary pressures [80]. Theoretically it is also possible that too little advertising might cause demand to drop below the level necessary to maintain full capacity. If the object of the advertising profession is to bring demand and supply into balance, the amount of advertising must be proportionate to the effect desired, that is, to the amount of demand needed to attain the proper equilibrium.

It is not, however, merely a question of the right amount, but of the right amount at the right time. As in

---

[75] Lever, *op. cit.*, p. 60.

[76] *cf.* Galbraith, *op. cit.*, p. 232, and J. F. ten Doesschate, « Enkele schuchtere opmerkingen over de maatshappelijke beteknis van het reclame », *De Functie van de reclame in het economisch bestel, 16e Nederlandse Reclamecongres*, (Scheveningen: Genootschap voor Reclame, 1953), pp. 29-30. J. G. Stridiron, « De financiering der reclame en crisis-tijden », *Reclame en de crisis, erste Nederlandsche Reclame-Congres*, (Amsterdam: Genootschap voor Reclame, 1932), p. 19 and p. 30. For other remarks bearing on this point, *cf.* Louis C. Wagner, « Advertising and the Business Cycle », *Journal of Marketing*, 6 (1941), October, p. 135. C. H. Sandage, *Advertising Theory and Practice*, (revised ed. Chicago: Irwin, 1939), pp. 40-42.

[77] Advertising, of course, suffers the same basic limitation as other tools used to assure stability, namely, the lack of accurate information which enables one to foresee movements. On this point cf., Rockefeller Brothers Fund, *op. cit.*, p. 15; *Economic Report of the President*, January, 1958, p. 73.

[78] *cf.* Vaile. *op. cit.*, pp. 81-82; F. W. Taylor, *The Economics of Advertising*, (London: Allen and Unwin, 1934), p. 64. Borden, *op. cit.*, pp. 732 ff. Charles S. Wyand, *The Economics of Consumption*, (N. Y.: Macmillan, 1937), pp. 435-436.

[79] Gilbert Burch, « Why do People Buy », in The Editors of Fortune, *Why do People Buy*, (N. Y.: Mc Graw-Hill, 1953), p. 13.

[80] Bishop seems to have such an effect in mind when he speaks of the need for restraint in *Advertising and Employment*, p. 10.

the case of fiscal policies designed to control adverse
movements, the question of timing is essential[81]. The
advertising profession, or at least some of its members,
recognize the fact that to be effective in time of decline,
advertising would have to be applied while purchasing
power was still high[82]. Vaile sees the need for proper
timing on the up-swing as well, and thinks that advertising
would be most effective if cut before rising consumer demand caused business to over-expand[83]. Timing, then, has
its importance if advertising is to be used effectively.

In addition to the right amount at the right time, it
is necessary that advertising be coordinated with other
forces in the economy, and that the advertising of the
various companies be coordinated in view of the public
weal. The need for cooperation with government policies
would appear to be almost self-evident. If advertising is
working to increase demand at a time when the government is seeking to restrain it, the end result may that the
expensive efforts merely negate each other[84]. Similarly, if
the advertising effort slackens at a time when the government is trying to increase demand, it is at least theoretically
possible that the government policy would be much less
effective than if selling effort has been maintained[85].

The advertisers must cooperate not only with the
government but with each other. First the effect of advertising is cumulative and those who have discussed the
possibility of using advertising as an instrument of stabi-
lization, see that a large number would have to raise or
lower their advertising for the effect to be significant[86].
However, when there is question of cutting advertising, the
businessman may hesitate since if his competitors do not

---

[81] Samuelson, *op. cit.*, p. 342.
[82] Advertising Association, *Notes for Speakers*, no. 9, March 1955,
p. 3.
[83] Vaile, *op. cit.*, p. 81 f.
[84] Galbraith, *op. cit.*, p. 232.
[85] This is, of course, part of the argument advanced in favor of the
increased use of advertising in time of decline. If advertising cooperates,
it is serving the public weal. See, for example, William C. Mc Keehan,
« If We as a People ... The Challenge to American Enterprise », *Papers
from the 37th Annual Meeting of the A.A.A.A., Group II*, (N. Y. A.A.A.A.,
1955), p. 30.
[86] D. Seligman, « How Much for Advertising », *Fortune*, 54 (1956),
December, p. 123.

follow suit, he may lose business [87]. Cooperation would be especially necessary if this fear were to be removed.

The need for cooperation may be particularly great when the excess of deficiency of demand is localized in particular industries. Thus, it is quite possible to have inflationary demand for non-durable goods, while the demand for durable goods has dropped and caused some unemployment [88]. Since all goods and services are to some extent in competition with one another [89], increased advertising in fields where demand is already high might draw away demand from fields where it is low. For advertising to be effective it would have to be increased in one field, and possibly lowered in another [90]. Unless cooperation were forthcoming in such situations, there could be no guarantee that demand would be shifted in accord with the needs of the public weal [91].

REALIZATION OF CONDITIONS

Having explained the three basic conditions (the right amount, at the right time, and in a coordinate fashion) we must now ask if advertising can be used in accord with these conditions. Since the possibility of cooperation determines to a large extent the possibility of applying the right amounts at the right time, this question will be treated first. Then, assuming for the sake of argument that such cooperation is possible, we shall examine the technical possibilities of an accurate use of advertising.

---

[87] Howard Bowen, *Social Responsibility of the Businessman*, (N. Y.: Harper and Brothers, 1953), p. 219.

[88] Just such a situation seems to have been present in the American economy during 1957-58. *Cf.*, *Economic Report of the President*, January 1958, p. 25 on the inflationary demand in retail markets and p. 17 following on demand and employment relative to durable goods.

[89] *cf.*, Mary Jean Bowman and George Leland Bach, *Economic Analysis and Public Policy*, (N. Y.: Prentice Hall, 1943), p. 318.

[90] Alfred Sauvy, *Les faits et les opinions*, (Paris: Cours de Droit), 1954-55, Vol. II, p. 251. This author notes that for the effect of advertising to be favorable in the short run, it would have to orient consumption in such a way that it increases the use of resources (both men and capital) in those sectors where there is unemployment.

[91] Steuber, *op. cit.*, p. 158 notes that mere shifts of demand are not necessarily beneficial.

Our first question with regard to the necessary coordination of advertising with government policies and other factors is the following. Can advertising be used to mitigate fluctuations by being increased on the down swing and cut down on the upswing? In the abstract such a use is possible, but in the concrete such a use would involve a change in the psychology and sales tactics of the businessmen who control advertising. The past uses of advertising and the reasons behind these uses will indicate the nature of the obstacle.

In the past advertising was generally used cyclically, that is to say, expenditures on it rose in good times and declined in poor times [92]. Though, as we shall see, this policy is no longer followed, by all companies, the past use of advertising relative to the cycle leads most to conclude that advertising has made no considerable contribution to economic stability [93]. This is not merely an accident, but due to the factors which influence the advertising appropriation.

In the first place the outlook of the entrepreneur influences his use of advertising. When times are good, he looks on advertising as a valuable means of increasing sales, while in bad times, his pessimism makes him feel that no amount of advertising would help against the powerful forces causing the decline [94]. In short, the expectations of businessmen have much to do with their willingness to advertise [95], and since general business conditions and the future outlook influence these expectations, they will generally influence the advertising appropriation itself. If the entrepreneur foresees no additional profit as a result of an increased appropriation for advertising, he will hardly increase his expenditures on this item [96]. On the other

---

[92] *cf.*, Advisory Commitee to the Borden Study, in Borden, *op. cit.*, p. XXXVI; Steuber, *op. cit.*, p. 150; Lever, *op. cit.*, p. 77.

[93] *cf.*, Dexter Keezer *et al.*, *Making Capitalism Work*, (N. Y.: Mc Graw-Hill, 1950), p. 169. Many authors even think that advertising may have contributed to economic instability for a variety of reasons. *cf.*, Vaile, *op. cit.*, p. 81; Taylor, *op. cit.*, p. 64; Borden, *op. cit.*, p. 732; Sandage, *op. cit.*, p. 42. Wyand, *op. cit.*, pp. 435-437.

[94] Steuber, *op. cit.*, p. 152.

[95] cf. Bowman and Bach, *op. cit.*, pp. 660-661 for the importance of these expectations, and *cf.*, Haberler, *op. cit.*, p. 169 for a résumé of psychological theories of the cycle.

[96] Bowen, *op. cit.*, p. 219; Borden, *op. cit.*, p. 735 notes that it is

hand, if the outlook is good and he foresees increased profits resulting from advertising, he will hardly be ready to cut down his budget, or maintain it constant [97].

Pessimism based on a poor profit outlook is not, however, the only obstacle to a countercyclic application of advertising. In times of decline the money for increased advertising may not be available [98], and since large sums are needed for most effective advertising, [99] this is a serious difficulty. As Sauvy has pointed out, it is precisely those companies which need to increase sales who may be without the funds necessary for additional advertising [100].

This last difficulty is not insurmountable, since, as some economists have pointed out, companies might set aside funded reserves for use in time of declining demand [101]. Nevertheless, such measures must face certain obstacles. With the present excess profits tax, a company paying taxes at the rate of eighty-two percent, would have to earn $ 5.56 for every dollar it put away into such a fund [102]. Since the temptation is to spend today's « cheap » dollars today [103], it would be necessary to change the whole long-run outlook before the majority would be willing to follow such a course. Indeed, such a plan might prove so expensive that the cost might offset the advantages of greater regularity of sales [104].

Despite the difficulties which arise from the profit outlook and the lack of advertising funds, it must be admitted that at least in the case of the last few recessions in the

---

not enough to induce people to consume more in order to bring the economy out of a decline. The surest remedy is a revival of the spirit of enterprise and risk taking. Keezer, *op. cit.*, p. 169 also notes that such use of advertising would demand great leadership and courage on the part of business.

[97] Bowen, *loc. cit.*, mentions that fear of being displaced by competitors would hold the businessman back. Bowmen and Bach, *op. cit.*, p. 319 note that there is great danger in curtailing advertising in those situations where it represents an important competitive weapon.

[98] Burch, in « *Why do People Buy?* » p. 262.

[99] Borden, *op. cit.*, p. 424 lists the conditions favoring the successful use of advertising and notes that the availability of substantial sums is important.

[100] Sauvy, *op. cit.*, p. 251.

[101] Burch, *loc. cit.*

[102] *ibid.*, p. 266.

[103] *loc. cit.*

[104] F. L. Vaughan, *Marketing and Advertising, An Economic Appraisal*, (Princeton, N. J. 1928), p. 101.

United States, total advertising has gone up despite a drop
in production and employment [105]. This has been due to
two factors. First advertising is now looked on as an
investment by many businessmen [106], and secondly, there
has been a decrease in the general tendency to curtail
long-range plans because of short-range changes in sales [107].
If and when such attitudes become general, they may make
coordination possible, at least in times of threatening decline. While there seems to be no evidence pointing to a
new tendency to moderate advertising when demand is
excessive, Burch has pointed out the possibilities of « funded reserves » helping to prevent business from « forcing »
markets at the top of the cycle [108].

The evidence presented above indicates that it is difficult, but not impossible to have some coordination of
advertising with the general movement of the business
cycle in times of decline. What, however, is to be said of
the possibility of using advertising properly when the decline or the inflationary pressure is local? This last question
refers to situations such as that which was present in the
American recession of 1957-58 when there was severe unemployment in such industries as those devoted to the manu-
facture of automobiles, while retail sales continued to
rise [109]. In such situations it is not sufficient merely to
raise total demand. The task is rather to increase demand
in the areas that are suffering from a deficiency, and
possibly decrease it in other sectors where demand is
excessive and is forcing up prices [110].

It should be almost self-evident that those who are
enjoying a heavy demand and high profits will not cut
down on advertising so long as they think it profitable.
Those industries which are suffering are, of course, likely
to find themselves in a position where they are without
enough funds to advertise effectively, or they may be con-

---

[105] Resor, *op. cit.*, p. 76; D. Seligman, *op. cit.*, p. 123.
[106] Resor, *loc. cit.*, Seligman, *loc. cit.*
[107] Colm, *op. cit.*, p. 88.
[108] Burch, *op. cit.*, p. 262.
[109] *cf.*, *Time*, (Atlantic ed.), March 24, 1958, pp. 58-59.
[110] Sandage, *op. cit.*, p. 42 notes that many firms use advertising to
increase momentary profit by lowering unit costs and maintaining profits
which if plowed back into expansion may reduce the purchasing power
of the consumer.

vinced that the return on advertising would not be sufficient to justify its being increased. In addition, the product itself may not be suitable for advertising [111], or the
reason for the deficiency of demand may be of such a nature that advertising could not work effectively against it.

The advertising profession is not unaware of these
difficulties, and it is interesting to note that in the recession
of 1957-58 many did not see increased advertising as the
solution to the problems faced by their own companies.
A poll of *Tide's* Advertising Leadership Panel yielded the
following illustrative cross-section of opinion. Only five
percent thought that the drop in buying was due to the
fact that consumers had not been persuaded to raise their
standard of living sufficiently [112]. More interesting, however, is the reply to the question, what would do most to
boost your company's sales [113].

44% - the biggest group believed that a vastly improved
product would do most to boost their company's sales;
38% thought that a considerably more efficient distribution
system would do most to step up their sales; 22% maintained that a substantial cut in their product's price would
do most to step up their sales. The smallest group of
advertising executives, 21% insisted that a greatly increased advertising budget would be the most useful stimulus.
These opinions would seem to indicate that the advertising
profession itself is quite aware of the limited importance
which advertising has in a time of recession.

A particular example will help to explain the opinions
given above. Despite the fact that the automobile is one
of the most heavily advertised products in the United
States [114], car sales dropped severely during the recession
of 1957-58. When one studies the phenomenon, it becomes
evident that advertising was ineffective because more
powerful forces were determining the structure of demand.

---

[111] Borden, *op. cit.*, XXVII and p. 424 ff. *cf.*, Resor, *op. cit.*, p. 77
where he admits that the usefulness of advertising depends on the industry and the potential market.

[112] « Consumers: — to Admen they're a Puzzlement », *Tide*, March 14,
1958, p. 50.

[113] *ibid.*, p. 52.

[114] *Fortune*, September, 1956, p. 110. The cigarette companies and
soap manufacturers generally share these top honors.

First, the rising population and the rising prices of food
and services caused a larger part of income to be devoted
to necessities so that the discretionary income had actually
decreased [115]. In short the consumer was spending much of
his money on things that he did need, and so had less over
for automobiles [116]. Secondly, the consumer having discovered new status symbols, such as boats, summer homes
and swimming pools, and at the same time desiring certain
new products [117], shifted his discretionary income to the
purchase of such items. It would seem fair to say that advertising was not enough because the consumer knew what
he needed and bought what he desired out of what money
was available to him [118].

In conclusion, it appears that advertising cannot in all
circumstances be of great help when the economic trouble
is localized. First, those firms who foresee higher profits
as a result of the maintenance or increase of advertising
can hardly be expected to cut back expenditures. Secondly,
those firms who are suffering losses may lack the necessary
funds for increased advertising. Thirdly, even granted
that they have the necessary money, they may foresee no
profits as a result of increased advertising. Fourthly, this
latter judgment may be based on such sound reasons as
the following: the unsuitability of the product for advertising, the existence of strong counter trends, which would
render advertising unduly expensive relative to its results [119].

---

[115] Edwin B. George of Dun and Bradstreet, cited in *Printers' Ink,*
263 (1958), May 16, no. 7, p. 34. In the same place the author also noted
that he did not think this recession was due to consumers alone.
    [116] *loc. cit.*
    [117] *Time,* (Atlantic), December 29, 1958, p. 42.
    [118] This point is well made by the editors of *Tide* and by a panel
of experts in an editorial survey « Advertising's Enigma, The Changing
Consumer », *Tide,* March 14, 1958 pp. 21-30.
    [119] In the thirties and before, it seemed as if the businessmen who
cut down advertising in time of recession and raised it in boom times,
followed the wiser policy from a short-run point of view. *cf.* Wagner,
op. cit., p. 135. It is, however, extremely hard to generalize. For some
companies advertising will increase both sales and profits, for others
it will increase sales but not profits. Again, advertising may assure future profits when a decline is over, even though it was not of much
help in the recession itself. For illustration of these various effects

In the previous paragraphs our attempt to explain the difficulties faced in attempting to coordinate advertising in such a way as to mitigate fluctuations or localized imbalances, necessarily involved some consideration of the businessman's judgment on the effectiveness of advertising. In the present section which considers the suitability of advertising as an instrument, we shall see that their judgment is not without foundation. Thus a lack of cooperation makes the application of the right amount at the right time rather difficult, but the difficulties inherent in the use of advertising itself also help to explain why this cooperation is not forthcoming.

As in the previous pages, we shall first consider the use of advertising in times of general decline or inflation, and then in periods when the trouble is highy localized. First, however, it is necessary to explain what is meant by the right amount at the right time.

The right amount of advertising is that which will have the desired effect at a reasonable cost and without leading to undesirable aftermaths. In the concrete case of a decline, this would be a quantity capable of bringing demand into line with supply without leading to excessive demand. The right time to apply advertising is the moment when, because countertrends are not yet strong, it will have maximum effect at a minimum cost.

In order to judge the right amount it would be necessary to know the size of the deficiency (or in the case of inflation, of the excess) of demand relative to supply and capacity [120]. Second, it would be necessary to know what effect the advertising would have [121]. In order to know the effectiveness of advertising, however, it would

---

cf., Roland S. Vaile, « Use of Advertising during a Depression », *Harvard Business Review*, 5 (1927), and, « The Effects of Advertising on a Depression », *Priters'Ink*, 94, (1931), January 1, no. 1.

[120] In short, excellent marketing research would be needed, as well as extremely accurate economic indicators which would be capable of telling businessmen which way consumers were going to move. *cf.*, J.-H. Vleamminck, « Quelques incidences économiques de l'effort publicitaire », *Annales de Sciences Economiques Appliquées*, 12 (1954), December, no. 5, p. 485. For an explanation of the attempts being made to obtain such information, *cf.*, George Katona and Eva Mueller, *Consumer Attitudes and Demand, 1950-1952*, (University of Michigan Research Center, 1953).

[121] *cf.*, H. J. A. Hermans, « *De Bedrijfseconomische Beteknis van de Reclame*, (Leiden, Holland: H. E. Steinfert-Kroese, 1949), p. 322-323.

be necessary to know the strength and the direction of the trend which was shifting demand upwards or downwards. In order to judge the right moment for the application of advertising, it would be necessary to foresee the speed of the trend, and to judge the time it would take advertising to be effective [122]. If advertising needs, let us say, three months to have its effect, it would have to be applied three months before the critical turning point in order to have its effect at the proper moment.

Without knowledge of the magnitude and direction and speed of various trends, and without knowledge of the effects of a given amount of advertising and of the time needed for these effects to be realized, any policy based on a use of advertising would face great dangers. Speaking of the general problem of economic policy the Rockefeller report notes:

> One of the great dangers of attempting to minimize economic fluctuation is that we will take action either prematurely or too late, and that the type and extent of action will not be closely related to the economic threat [123].

In the absence of evidence to the contrary, it is submitted that there is no way of knowing what the effect of increased or decreased advertising would be on the economy as a whole. Further, it is submitted that there is no way at present of properly estimating the time necessary for advertising to have its effect.

The proof of the above statements is necessarily indirect, but the following facts seem to indicate that they are basically sound. As already noted, it is practically impossible to judge the contribution of advertising to a given sales campaign *even after the fact* [124]. It would seem logical to suppose that it would be even more difficult to foresee its effects. Further, if this is true even of the advertising of individual companies, it would seem

---

[122] Gaëtan Pirou, « La publicité et la théorie économique », *Mélanges dédiés à M. le Professeur Henri Truchy*, (Paris: Sirey, 1938), p. 455 notes that the time needed is very variable, and may be as long as three years when it is a question of maximum effect.

[123] *op. cit.*, p. 15.

[124] Borden, *op. cit.*, pp. 121 ff; Steuber, *op. cit.*, p. 158.

to be even truer of the advertising of all companies taken together [125].

When one considers the question of timing, the statement of the Advisory Committee in the Borden study seems to express the difficulty very exactly.

> Advertising is not a business stimulator that can be turned on and off at will with the assurance that the results will be commensurate with the expenditures [126].

The basic difficulty is found in the fact that advertising like all propaganda is not magic. The effects depend on the trends which in turn depend on the reaction of people to what they see and hear [127]. In attempting to time and control advertising effects, these other forces must be taken into consideration, and these forces are liable to be unpredictable. Katona has given tentative expression to some of the factors which influence consumer optimism, and these factors seem rather hard to foresee, much less to control.

Katona notes that past and expected changes in people's financial situation appear to have a stronger influence on consumer buying than the level of satisfaction with one's current income [128]. Further, the attitudes towards the economic outlook are determined by significant political events on the international and local scene, and these have a great influence on buying [129]. Such events and the reactions to them are difficult or impossible to foresee with the result that the trend based on them (a trend which determines the effectiveness of advertising) is always subject to changes and shifts.

Since it appears practically impossible to foresee the effects of advertising, or the amount of time needed to

---

[125] Even granted cooperation, it would be almost impossible to make allowances for the differences in *quality* in such a way as to be able to sum all advertising and arrive at an estimate of total predicted effectiveness.

[126] *op. cit.*, p. XXVI, Borden.

[127] Even Goebbels found his propaganda ineffective when the facts contradicted it. *cf.*, Leonard W. Doob, « Goebbel's Principles of Propaganda ». in Katz *et al.*, *Public Opinion and Propaganda*, (N. Y.: Dryden Press, 1954).

[128] Katona, *op. cit.*, p. 79.

[129] *ibid.*, p. 69-70.

11

attain the required results, advertising appears to be a
poor tool to use in attempting any systematic control of
fluctuations in the economy as a whole. This would be
true even if all were willing to cooperate and coordinate
their efforts. However, since such cooperation in itself
is difficult to get, the final conclusion is that in the concrete advertising would be an impractical instrument to
use at least so long as it remains unpredictable [130].

Granted that advertising is too unpredictable to be
used safely and effectively against general economic movements, one may still ask if it might not be useful when
the trouble is confined to certain sectors of the economy.
What has been said above applies here. The right amount
of advertising to increase sales may be too expensive relative to the profits desired and this because the product
is not right, the causes of decline too powerful and the
length of time needed to get results so indefinite that the
risk may be too great. If a decline were due to mere
lagging interest, then advertising might have some effect
without costing too much [131], but when the causes are more
profound, you cannot advertise yourself out of a recession [132]. These points are well illustrated by comments of
the advertising profession on the recession of 1957-58 when
the difficulty was localized, generally in the hard goods
industries. The conclusion to be drawn from all of these
is that advertising is not a universally useful tool even in
these limited cases and so no certain help even in the
limited decline. The following citations will illustrate why
the advertising profession sees this clearly.

First, the consumers are more critical and have many
of their needs satisfied.

> Today, as the greatest sales boom in U.S. history slackens,
> the first phase of the marketing revolution is over. The
> consumer advertising executives face today, is very different
> from his postwar brother. He has matured. He's more price-

---

[130] This explains why some see advertising as just as likely to accentuate the cycle as to smooth it out. *cf.* Taylor, *op. cit.*, p. 64; Wyand,
op. cit., p. 435; Wroe Alderson, *Marketing Behavior and Executive Action*,
(Homewood, Illinois: Irwin, 1957); Borden, *op. cit.*, pp. 732-734.

[131] *cf.* Keezer, *op. cit.*, p. 167; Robert Brandon, *The Truth about
Advertising*, (London: Chapman and Hall, 1949), p. 194.

[132] This was the comment of the editors of *Tide*, June 13, 1958, p. 13.

conscious, discriminating, better educated. His pressing needs have been satisfied (autos, ranch-style homes, appliances) [133].

Secondly, the decline in sales of durable goods is explained by changes in family composition which leave less money for these.

> This trend to more older children in larger families may mean that the consumer who spent heavily on durable goods in the past must now devote more of the family budget to food, clothing and education... Harder times are ahead for durable goods advertisers who, such as major appliance makers, depend on the now declining second stage of the life cycle for 51% of their total sales [134].

Thirdly, many of the products for which demand fell were not new enough to have the necessary appeal.

> Many appliances are near 'saturation' and new models show relatively unimportant improvements [135].
> Here Panel members are somewhat more in agreement. Most believe that consumers on the whole will buy new products only if they have really new advantages. But they add that a sizable number of consumers now insist on quality and taste as well as newness [136].

Now these statements merely recognize the truth of what has been said in the previous chapter about the effectiveness of advertising [137]. If advertising has a new product which will have an appeal even without advertising, it may help to step up demand, though it cannot guarantee to do this rapidly [138]. Further, advertising cannot overcome a trend which is rooted in society, though it might modify it slightly. When advertising faces a localized fall in demand due to such factors as those listed above, even the advertising profession does not seem to think they can do a great deal of good.

The conclusion is that advertising is of very limited utility even in localized declines. In any event, it cannot

---

[133] *Tide*, March 14, 1958, p. 21.
[134] *ibid.*, p. 25. Note that this trend is seen as lasting for some time.
[135] *Tide*, March 4, 1958, citation of Louis F. Cahn, p. 51.
[136] *ibid.*, editorial summary p. 51.
[137] *cf.* the previous chapter, « Advertising and the Individual product ».
[138] Borden, *op. cit.*, p. 692.

legitimately present itself as a tool which by its very nature is capable of relieving the trouble.

Now in all of this section we have assumed that consumer buying was an important factor in the fluctuation. It is not, however, the only factor, nor according to many economists, the most important factor[139]. This leads one to believe that a complete study of the economic assumptions would show the case for advertising as a tool to be used in obtaining economic growth of a harmonious kind, would be even weaker[140], than our own presentation has shown it to be even when judged on its own assumption.

Consumer Credit

Before summarizing the entire chapter, a few words should be said about the relationship between stable economic growth and two particular methods advocated by the advertising profession: consumer credit and model or psychological obsolescence. Since each of these methods should be investigated separately and at great length, our remarks only seek to indicate that there is some doubt about the suitability of using them to promote a sound and stable growth.

There would seem to be little doubt that the intensive use of consumer credit increases the amplitude of both

---

[139] Samuelson, *op. cit.*, pp. 320 ff, Bowman and Bach, *op. cit.*, pp. 657 ff. Steuber, *op. cit.*, pp. 33 ff.

[140] Steuber, *op. cit.*, pp. 121-125 discusses some of these assumptions and concludes against the utility of both suggestive and competitive advertising as being of any significance in growth.

J. F. ten Doesschate, *op. cit.*, pp. 29 ff. also raises some questions as to the validity of the assumption that the real trouble is in the consumers' failure to buy.

It is interesting to note that during the depression of 1957-1958 when many advertising men were publicly claiming that advertising was a depression medicine, (*cf.* Robert B. Mc Intyre « Advertising Called Depression Medicine », *Editor and Publisher*, April 12, 1958, p. 16 where he gives a series of opinions), that the economists, including those consulted by the advertising profession were not always in agreement with this analysis. *cf.*, a series of such opinions in « The Challenge of Our Economy: How Advertising Can Speed Recovery, Today », *Printers' Ink*, 263 (1958), May 16, no. 7, p. 34. *cf.* also Sumner H. Slichter of Harvard cited in *Advertising Age*, March 3, 1958, p. 55.

the upward and downward movements of the cycle [141].
Galbraith, for one, believes that the real danger in the
way wants are created in modern society lies in the related
process of debt creation [142]. As consumer demand comes
to depend more and more on the willingness to incur debt,
economic behaviour becomes more uncertain [143]. This is
particularly true since consumer debt tends to expand
during periods of confidence when purchasing power is
least needed, and to be retired during times of decline
when purchasing power should be kept up [144]. For these
reasons advertising which encourages debt-financed consumption might increase consumption at times when it
should be slowed down, and because of its general dependence on the trends, be unable to maintain consumption
in time of decline.

In addition to amplifying the movements of the cycle,
credit buying can also set up inflationary pressures [145].
One writer puts it thus:

> Il n'y a pas de doute qu'en augmentant le pouvoir d'achat
> actuel au-delà de son volume réel par le tirage de traites sur
> l'avenir, le système de la vente à tempérament, si celle-ci
> prend de grandes proportions, peut avoir des effects infla-
> tionnistes [146].

Though we do not know the extent of this danger [147],
the uncontrolled stimulation of credit buying might well
increase it to a considerable degree. The advertising
profession does not seem to have given much thought to

---

[141] Wilhelm Röpke, *Vorgegessen Brot: Kritische Nachlese zur Diskussion über das Borkkaufwesen*, (Köln: Carl Heymanns, 1955), p. 10. This
author notes that there is no American economist who would deny this
unstabilizing effect and he goes so far as to state that there is no
economist who still has a reputation left who would publicly defend
installment buying.

[142] Galbraith, *op. cit.*, p. 199.

[143] *ibid.*, p. 205.

[144] *loc. cit.*

[145] For a brief analysis of the effects of consumer credit in various
situations, *cf.* J. A. H. Delzing, « Economische, sociale en financiële overwegingen », *Revue der Reclame*, 16 (1956), p. 252.

[146] P.-R. Rosset, *La Vente à tempérament: ses aspects économiques et
juridiques*, (Fascicule XII des Publications de la Societé Neuchâteloise de
Science Economique, n. d.), p. 10.

[147] Galbraith, *op. cit.*, p. 207.

this possibility, nor to the fact that resentment over inflation can lead to a curtailment of spending [148].

In the last place it must be recalled that if an increase
in consumer credit detracts from the real savings needed
to finance expansion, it can retard necessary growth or
at least misdirect the expansion [149]. This possibility, as
we saw earlier in the present chapter is not merely imaginary, and recent years have seen the government forced
to pay high rates because of a shortage of credit [150].

Lest anyone think these dangers are purely imaginary,
it will be useful to see the results of the credit phase of
the advertising proposal of 1954. Writing in that year
Johnson called for an increase of 68% in consumer credit
for 1956, most of this to be used in financing the purchase
of automobiles [151]. Actually, even though the amount of
credit actually extended in 1956 fell some ten billion dollars below the sum envisaged by Johnson, it still had an
unstabilizing effect on the economy [152]. Thus the Economic
Report of the President notes that automobiles sales fell
off dramatically during the recession of 1957-58, and as-
signs as one of the reasons the fact that a sharp easing of
credit terms in 1955 had lead to a saturation of the
market [153]. If credit had been expanded an additional ten
billion, the effect would probably have been even more
pronounced.

The theoretical dangers of increased consumer credit
and the actual results of its expansion, all point to a need
for careful consideration of this aspect of the advertising
proposal. So long as stable growth is desired, there would
appear to be some doubt about the soundness of this
phase of the plan.

---

[148] Eva Mueller, « Consumer Reactions to Inflation », *Quarterly Journal
of Economics*, 73 (1959), p. 261.

[149] Rosset, *op. cit.*, p. 10.

[150] *cf. The Economic Report of the President*, January, 1958, p. 6.

[151] Johnson, *op. cit.*, p. 20 and p. 7.

[152] *ibid.*, p. 20 and *The Economic Report of the President*, January,
1959, p. 192 (Washington, D. C.: Government Printing Office).

[153] *Economic Report of the President*, January, 1959, p. 3.

Psychological Obsolescence

Model and psychological obsolescence together with credit buying have been used to explain the dynamism of the American economy[154]. These methods, are, however, not without their difficulties.

An article may be said to be physically obsolescent when it is worn out or when it is significantly inferior in efficiency to a newer article designed to perfom the same general function. While there is a great deal of relativity in these definitions their general meaning should be clear. A tire is worn out when it is no longer considered safe to drive on it. The horse and carriage became obsolescent when the automobile was not only a faster but a cheaper means of transportation.

Model obsolescence occurs when a product, while remaining basically the same, is produced with features which increase its efficiency and functional utility, though not to such an extent that the former model is significantly inferior. Here again, the definition is relativistic since there is no hard and fast rule for determining what is and what is not significantly superior. Ordinarily, however, the functional improvements in an automobile do not make the model from the previous year physically obsolescent.

Psychological obsolescence proper is had when in the absence of functional improvements, a new model is considered superior because it is new, or because style changes gratify some desire which is not related to the natural function of the object. The older style is obsolete because it no longer satisfies the psychic needs of the consumer. In the case of clothing fashions, for example, last year's latest style no longer denotes superiority even though it may be more than adequate as clothing and as decoration[155]. Last year's car may no longer demonstrate one's status in society and so be useless as a prestige symbol[156].

---

[154] Mazur, *op. cit.*, p. 129.

[155] *cf.* Gorden, *op. cit.*, pp. 122 ff. for a discussion of fashion and its significance.

[156] *cf.* Joseph W. Newman, *Motivation Research and Marketing Management*, (Boston: Harvard University School of Business Administration, (Boston: Harvard University School of Business Administration, 1957), p. 237 for various motives for automobile ownership.

In actual practice model and psychological are often found together. For the sake of clarity, however, we shall treat them separately.

For the individual, model obsolescence is often legitimate. In the case of an automobile, for example, it can actually be more economical to buy a new car since the cost of major repairs tends to increase proportionately more than the price of the latest model [157]. Further, for an individual an improvement may be significant because of his circumstances. An air conditioning unit might be of great utility to a traveling salesman in a tropic or subtropic zone. Finally, it should be noted that the accumulation of changes in a product does in many cases amount to a real and significant improvement in functioning [158].

When one turns from the consideration of the benefits which model obsolescence may bring to the individual and consider its effect on the economy as a whole, the picture becomes blurred. On the one hand model obsolescence enables some industries to maintain a high sales volume [159], while on the other it can lead to an expensive scrapage of machine tools [160], if not of the products themselves [161]. In some cases model obsolescence can even lead to the more serious consequences described by Kapp.

> In the automobile industry, the policy of « degrading » consumers' goods by the periodic introduction of new models has given rise to intermittent periods of peak production (and unemployment) and partial utilization of existing equipment with a high percentage of enforced idleness of relatively highly skilled workers and specialized capital equipment [162].

Model obsolescence not only causes seasonal variations in employment and waste as a result of only partial

---

[157] The Editors of Fortune, *The Changing American Market*, (Garden City, N. Y.: Hanover House, 1953), p. 162.

[158] *ibid.*, p. 159.

[159] K. William Kapp, *The Social Costs of Private Enterprise*, (Cambridge, Mass.: Harvard U. Press, 1950), p. 178.

[160] Ronald S. Vaile *et al.*, *Marketing in the American Economy*, (N.Y.: Ronald Press, 1952), p. 101.

[161] The products themselves can still be sold in the second-hand market and passed along until they are worn out physically. Consequently, the psychological obsolescence is often only apparent.

[162] Kapp, *op. cit.*, p. 178.

utilization of existing resources, but can make demand itself highly unstable and increase the uncertainty and risk connected with future demand [163]. Such unstable demand becomes extremely dangerous in time of economic decline for as income goes down those goods whose appeal rests on superficial values become rapidly less desirable [164]. When the obsolescence has been attached to durable products whose replacement can be postponed, the instability becomes even greater [165].

The waste and the instability connected with model obsolescence are even greater in the case of psychological obsolescence for the « style » appeal is even more unstable since consumers may easily find another means of satisfying their desire for prestige. The American economy had rather tragic evidence of this in the recession of 1957-58. After the automobile manufacturers had spent one and one half billion dollars to retool in the hopes of a huge sale [166], they discovered that prestige buying had declined because people had other ways of buying this quality [167].

While the economic significance of model and psychological obsolescence demands further investigation, there are certainly very serious doubts about their value to the economy as a whole. Even when such practices succeed in increasing or maintaining sales volume for a given firm or industry, there is no guarantee that they will increase sales in the economy as a whole, much less that they will direct resources to those uses which are most desirable.

When it is recalled that installment credit, model and psychological obsolescence are found together in the case of many consumer durables which by their very nature have an unstable demand, it becomes evident that advertising used to encourage consumption based on such foundations, may if successful have an unsettling effect on the

---

[163] Charles S. Wyand, *The Economics of Consumption*, (N. Y.: Macmillan, 1937), p. 435.

[164] *ibid.*, p. 436.

[165] At least one commentator believes that this situation constitutes an obvious danger for the American economy. *cf.*, Christopher Buxton, *A British Assessment of the American Economy*, (London: United States Information Service, n. d. but ca. 1958), no pagination.

[166] *Time* (Atlantic Edition), November 4, 1957, p. 61.

[167] *Time* (Atlantic Edition) March 31, 1958, p. 50.

economy.   Since advertising itself is more effective in the
up swing than on the down turn, it is liable to amplify
the effects of both these methods on the cycle. In short,
the three factors together: advertising, installment credit
and non-physical obsolescence might tend to reinforce each
other in exaggerating the swings of the economy.

Conclusions

We are now in a position to give an answer to the
questions posed at the beginning of this chapter. First,
does the long run economic social and political situation in
the United States call for an artificial stimulation of personal consumption? Secondly, can advertising be used in
favor of that economic stability necessary for harmonious
economic growth?
The answer to the first question is given in the following four statements.   ,
First, at the present moment there appears to be no
need of stimulating personal consumption artificially. The
need for public services and private investment is so great
that even if the growth of the economy is stepped up,
the « normal » per capita increase in personal consumption
will take care of the remainder.
Secondly, it is the opinion of at least some experts
that such growth and distribution of resources will be
sufficient to provide full-employment and to protect incentives as well as freedom.
Thirdly, informative advertising still has an important
function in facilitating the normal growth of personal
consumption.
Fourthly, while a theory of secular stagnation resulting
from a declining propensity to consume might give some
support to the case of advertising, the advertising profession has not explicitly appealed to such a theory. Further, such a theory is not generally accepted either as
proved or provable.
From these statements it follows that *suggestive* advertising is not justified on the grounds that it is needed

to stimulate economic growth in the present day American economy.

The answers to our second question assume for the sake of argument that declines in economic activity and inflationary pressures are due to shifts in consumer demand. They further assume that advertising can have *some* influence on demand. With these assumptions in mind, we conclude that advertising does not appear to be a suitable instrument for the systematic and efficient mitigation of either recessions or inflationary pressures.

First, advertising as a tool is unpredictable and to a large extent uncontrollable. For this reason its use would necessarily be controlled by mere guess work and run the danger that too much too soon would cause an unfavorable reaction, while too little too late would merely be a waste of resources.

Secondly, since this instrument is used by many businessmen, its effectiveness would in the concrete be dependent on the attitudes and judgments of these men. These attitudes are such that there is little reason to hope that they would mitigate their advertising in an effort to reduce inflationary pressure, or to shift demand to those sectors where it was deficient. Further, it would be most difficult even in times of decline to coordinate the activity of all in view of the desired result.

Thirdly, in time of decline, businessmen might be reasonably unwilling to increase advertising for the following reasons. If they lack the funds necessary for increased advertising, they will not be in a position to adjust counter-cyclically. Even if they have funds, it may be that they can see no additional profit resulting from increased expenditures on advertising. Further, their product may not be suitable for advertising promotion. Finally, the trends and forces causing a deficiency of demand in the whole economy or in particular sectors may be so strong that advertising could not hope to have any appreciable effect on them.

In addition, the fact that the advertising profession proposes to encourage the use of consumer credit and of psychological obsolescence, creates at least the suspicion that the proposal, *if successful* might actually lead to an increase of economic instability.

Applications to the Ethical Problem

The conclusions of the present and the previous chapter contain the reply to the important question posed at the end of the chapter on the ethics of consumption. *Is the proposal of the advertising profession consistent with the obligation to use wealth for the satisfaction of the needs of all who live in a society?* To put it another way, would and could the advertising proposal lead to a proper allocation of resources in an economy such as that of the United States?

In the first place, the fact that the long-range economic situation of the United States demands no artificial stimulation of consumption shows that the proposal of the advertising profession is in some ways a solution to a nonexistent problem. The situation is such that suggestive advertising, even if it were not unethical, would have no contribution to make to economic growth. Secondly, since it is the judgment of some experts that personal consumption may have to be curtailed, the proposal might, *if successful*, actually lead to diverting wealth from more urgent needs. This leads to the double conclusion that artificial stimulation is not necessary and might be dangerous.

Though admittedly a stimulation of consumption might be useful in certain limited situations, the evidence available suggests that advertising would not be a suitable tool for encouraging harmonious growth. Indeed, advertising is so limited and its effects so difficult to foresee and control that it might actually contribute to economic instability. In view of these facts, it would probably be wasteful to increase advertising expeditures with an eye to dampening the fluctuations of the economy.

All of this does not deny that advertising, especially informative advertising, has its uses. It does, however, show that the advertising profession must look elsewhere for a social justification of its activity. At the same time the critics of advertising would do well to revise their charges which, like the claims of the advertising men, are often built on an exaggerated idea of the power of propaganda.

CHAPTER VIII

CONCLUSIONS

Having conpleted our long analysis of the various
aspects of the proposal of the advertising profession, it
is now possible to form at least a tentative judgment of
its value and liceity. It should be kept in mind that our
conclusions which have been arrived at in terms of this
proposal have in many cases only a limited value. Thus, the
conclusions concerning the utility and necessity of advertising apply primarily to the present day United States, and
should be applied to other societies only after the factual
situation has been carefully investigated. Further, though
our conclusions as to the ethical or unethical nature of certain techniques have a universal value, the principles involved must be applied with care.

THE ETHICS OF PERSUASION

The first and, perhaps, the most important conclusion
of the present work concerns the liceity of the various *general* methods of persuasion used in advertising. Truthful
informative advertising is, of course, licit in and of itself.
Persuasive advertising, however, poses a real problem
since *some* of the persuasive *techniques* used are *intended*
to by-pass the intellect and reduce rationality, and *may,
if successful*, lead to improvident actions. Techniques which
are used with such an intention, or are of their nature
calculated to produce such an effect are to be condemned
on the grounds that they imply a contempt for human
nature and include a willingness to harm one's fellow man.
These unethical techniques, which we have called « suggestive » advertising in order to set them off from other

and legitimate forms of persuasion, demand further study. Though the intent is always wrong, the harmful effects seem to be rather limited. However, it will be possible to say which techniques are illicit even aside from an intention to lower rationality, only after careful psychological studies.

In the following sections we will consider the desirability of the economic effects which are supposed to flow from informative and non-suggestive persuasive advertising. Here, however, it should be noted that suggestive advertising, because its intent is of itself unethical, cannot be justified by alleged contributions to economic growth. The end does not justify the means when the means is unethical of itself.

In addition to the above conclusion, mention must also be made of the possible dangers arising from the position of advertising in the communication structure of the United States. In attempting to influence consumption and to further economic progress, the advertising profession must refrain from any direct interference with the *practical* freedom of the mass media and from the exercise of indirect influence over the content of the media. Unless such restraint is observed, the attempt to stimulate growth might lead to a diminution of that freedom which is of such importance in democratic societies.

The Ethics of Individual Consumption

Even though truthful informative advertising and non-suggestive persuasive advertising are in and of themselves legitimate, their morality also depends on the products they attempt to sell, and on the effects of this selling, on both the individual and the economy as a whole.

When informative advertising and non-suggestive persuasive advertising are used to encourage the consumption of products which have a real, though perhaps, limited utility, they are legitimate and possibly useful to the individual. However, because advertising for such products is often connected with an increase in consumer credit, a definitive judgment must wait on an examination of the full significance of installment buying. Further, as we shall see in the next section, the social effects of such consumption must also be considered.

Informative and non-suggestive persuasion which aims at promoting the sale of intangible qualities and of products of little worth may be licit so long as it does not encourage immoderate or dangerous uses of these. Moreover, the advertiser who observes such moderation and avoids suggestive advertising as defined in the previous section, is not generally responsible for foolish buying or improvidence since these are only accidental and not caused by the advertising itself.

Though our work has not given any extensive consideration to the problem of the motivation presented in advertising, it must be recognized that much of it is ambiguous and based on pseudo or half values. However, in the absence of evidence that the advertisers *actually intend* to promote a distorted scale or values, or *necessarily* do promote such a distortion, they cannot be condemned. Some, of course, do intend to exploit human weakness, but the more common attitude seems to be an ignorance of the need for a certain restraint or moderation. In this area, then, there is need for additional investigation of both the intentions of the advertisers and the effects of the motivation presented.

INCREASED PERSONAL CONSUMPTION AND THE PUBLIC GOOD

Advertising which observes the norms given in the preceding sections is acceptable from the standpoint of individual ethics. However, since the individual must fulfill certain social obligations with regard to his use of material goods and services, the complete acceptability of advertising depends on its conformity to these social needs. In other words, advertising designed to increase consumption must respect not only the needs of individuals, but of society as a whole.

The factual sections of Chapter VII indicated that in

all probability there is from the long-range point of view no
need for any artificial stimulation of consumption. Further,
there are signs that the present annual per capita increases
in the rate of personal consumption may have to be curtailed
in view of the social needs of American society.

It follows, then, that in the concrete situation there is
no real need for a forced or artificial stimulation of personal
consumption. Indeed, if the public needs of American society
increase, efforts to stimulate such consumption might harm
the nation. Though these facts indicate that the needs of
the economy do not justify persuasive advertising and especially in its suggestive, non-rational form, they do not eliminate the need for informative advertising about such
products as are useful in a very real sense. Such informative
advertising, at least if kept within reasonable limits, must
be considered a necessary means for the ordinary functioning of a healthy economy. Indeed, if we are to be perfectly
accurate, even non-suggestive persuasive advertising in favor
of products with real objective utility can be justified except
in those instances where any increase in personal consumption, howsoever small, would harm the public good. In the
concrete, then, we can only disapprove stimulation by means
of suggestive advertising, or by persuasive advertising in
favor of products of little or only secondary utility.

All this goes to show that the proposal of the advertising
profession rests on very shaky premises and that it does not
supply the solution to any real problem. In addition, it
tends to show that if advertising did have the power to
increase total consumption, it might actually interfere with
the proper allocation of resources in the economy. In other
words, *if advertising were actually effective* in increasing
total consumption, it would probably cause social and economic maladjustments.

The Potential Utility of Advertising

The phrase, « if actually effective », was underlined in
the previous paragraph, because Chapter VI showed that
advertising in general, whether informative, suggestive, or

persuasive in an acceptable manner, is not a force which can guarantee to stimulate consumption in any and all circumstances. This conclusion is of the utmost importance since it indicates that advertising is not a reliable tool for stimulating or harmonizing the movements of the economy. The consequences of this conclusion which strike at the very heart of the proposal of the advertising profession are far reaching.

In the first place, since there is no certainty of advertising's ability to stimulate aggregate consumption, the economists are probably correct when they charge that non-informative advertising is to a large extent a cause of waste. This is to say that advertising if effective in the case of individual companies, probably only shifts demand without increasing it in the economy as a whole. Though the present thesis does not pass judgment on this charge, our conclusions do indicate that the proposal of the advertising profession does not answer it [1].

In the second place, the conclusion that advertising is not a suitable tool for ensuring harmonious growth shows that, whatever may be said of the other alleged benefits of advertising, it cannot be justified on the grounds of its stabilizing influence in the economy. Further, the connection between advertising, consumer credit and psychological obsolescence raises the suspicion that advertising, *if successful*, might actually increase instability.

RESPONSIBILITY

Our treatment of the power of advertising, although admittedly only an introduction to the question, also casts some light on the responsibility of advertisers. The fact that advertising is not a principal cause of changes in consumption even in those cases where it is successful, places the burden or responsibility for changes in consumption, whether they be good or bad, on other agents in society.

---

[1] There may, of course, be other replies to this charge. *cf.*, For example Chapter II for the other claims of the advertising profession, and *infra* POINTS FOR FURTHER STUDY.

12

Though further study is needed before this responsibility can be assigned with any accuracy, the consumer, himself, must bear much of the burden.

Subject again to correction in the light of more detailed studies, it seems almost certain that the advertiser who refrains from suggestive techniques, and in particular those who use only informative advertising, are not to be considered responsible for improvidence and foolish buying. In all probability ethically acceptable techniques are only accidental causes of improvidence. So long as this improvidence is not intended, the techniques may be used in view of the legitimate and useful goals of the advertiser.

POINTS FOR FURTHER STUDY

Since the present thesis is only an introduction, a tentative exploration of a limited number of questions, it has of necessity omitted mention of many problems and of many claims for and charges against advertising. A glance at the contents of Chapter II will provide some idea of the work which remains to be done. Until these additional questions have been treated our own conclusions must remain incomplete and in many cases hesitant. The following points are suggested for future study.

Are the alleged wastes which result from advertising off-set by the fact that advertising supposedly makes mass production possible and enables manufacturers to lower prices? Are the higher costs associated with many advertised products justified on the grounds that advertising is a guarantee of quality and that it stimulates product improvement?[2] It will also be useful to determine if many of the supposedly harmful effects of advertising are accidental or necessary consequences of advertising. In addition, further study is needed to determine to what extent the ad-

---

[2] The present work was already completed when a study of these very topics appeared. *cf.* Ralph Harris and Arthur Seldon, *Advertising in a Free Society*, (London: Institute of Economic Affairs, 1959). Though this is an interesting study, it suffers from two great defects. First, there is a hedonistic bias which makes the subjective satisfaction of the consumer an ultimate norm. (*cf.* p. 70, *op. cit.*) Second, implicitly at least,

vertiser can eliminate supposedly harmful effects without at the same time depriving the consumer of the normal benefits of advertising [3].

Finally, there is need of much research on the morality of *individual* advertising techniques. For example, it is still necessary to determine whether or not repetitive slogans actually tend to by-pass the mind of the consumer. It would be equally interesting to discover whether the female form is used to arouse erotic associations or merely serves to attract attention to pertinent information. The list of possible problems is large and interesting.

A FINAL WORD

Now at the very end of the study, it should be clear why this work has been presented as an introduction, as an attempt to explore and to map out the problems of modern advertising. While the existence of so many reserves, distinctions and unanswered questions may be annoying and unsatisfactory, the newness of the subject and the complexity of the matter have dictated such a presentation. Despite these defects the present work is presented in the hope that it will ease the task of future students and stimulate the investigation of problems whose solution is desired by the advertising profession as well as by society as a whole.

A CHECK LIST

In judging the liceity of any given advertisement, advertising campaign or general movement in advertising as a whole, the ethician must consider a large number of factors. The following questions cover many of these points and may serve as a preliminary check list.

---

the good effects of some advertising which did succeed are attributed to advertising as a whole. However, the book does make a real contribution to the study of the problem.

[3] Even Steuber (*Werbung und Wohlstand*, Zürich: Polygraphischer Verlag, 1958) who is rather severe in his criticism takes cognizance of these problems. *cf., op. cit.* pp. 108-118 and pp. 163-200.

General questions:

1. What does the advertiser intend to do?
2. What are the actual effects of his advertising on the individual and on society as a whole?
3. Are these effects accidental, or do they result almost necessarily from the techniques used?

With regard to technique:

1. Does the advertisement inform, or does it seek to persuade?
2. If persuasive, does the advertisement attempt to by-pass the intellect?

With regard to content:

1. Is the information truthful?
2. Are the motives presented valid reasons for acting?
With regard to psychological effects:
1. Does the advertising seriously disturb the psychic equilibrium of the individual without sufficient reason?
2. Does the advertising distort the hierarchy of values?

With regard to personal consumption:

1. Does it lead to a misuse of individual resources relative to the real needs of an individual?
2. Does it lead to an immoderate use of any particular product?

With regard to social consumption:

1. Does it lead to a misuse of national resources in the actual economic situation of the nation?

Final judgement:

When the intent and technique are not evil in and of themselves, and where the harmful effects are not necessary, are there other effects which out weigh the harmful results?

ABBREVIATIONS

A. A. A. A. . American Association of Advertising Agencies.

Annals . . *Annals of the American Academy of Political and Social Science.*

HBR . . . . . *Harvard Business Review.*

PI . . . . . . *Printers' Ink.*

JM . . . . . *Journal of Marketing.*

JAA . . . . . *Journal of the Advertising Association.*

mimeo . . . *mimeographed.*

n. d . . . . no date of publication.

n. p. . . . . no place of publication.

n. pag. . . . no printed pagination.

POQ . . . . *Public Opinion Quarterly*

P. U. F. . . . Presses Universitaires de France

U. . . . . . . University.

ASSOCIATIONS AND SPECIALIZED LIBRARIES

BELGIUM: (Bruxelles)

    Comité Belge de la Distribution
    Comité Nationale Belge de l'Organisation Scientifique
    Fédération Belge de la Publicité
    Office Belge pour l'Accroissement de la Productivité
    Union Belge des Annonceurs

ENGLAND: (London)

    The Advertising Association
    British Institute of Management
    British Library of Political and Economic Science
    Institute of Practioners in Advertising
    London Chamber of Commerce
    Library of the British Broadcasting Corporation

FRANCE: (Paris)

    L'Association Internationale des Etudes et
    Recherches sur L'Information
    Chambre de Commerce de Paris
    Centre d'Etudes Sociologiques
    Fédération Française de la Publicité
    Union Fédérale de la Consommation

GERMANY: (Frankfurt a. M.)

    Bibliothek des Instituts für Wirtschaftswissenschaft
    Industrie- und Handelskammer
    G. W. A. Gesellschaft Werbeagenturen
    Verband Deutscher Werbungsmittler und Werbeagenturen
    Zentralausschuss der Werbewirtschaft

HOLLAND: (Amsterdam)
    Bond van Adverteerders
    Centraal Bureau voor Courante Publiciteit
    Genootschap voor Reclame
    Institute voor de Persschap
    Stichtung voor Reclame-Onderwijs
    Vereniging voor Erkende Advertentie-Bureaux

ITALY:

> Centro Nazionale di Documentazione e Studi sui Problemi
> dell'Informazione. (Rome)
> Federazione Italiana Pubblicità. (Milano)

SWITZERLAND: (Zürich)

> Association Suisse de la Publicité
> Archiv für Handel und Industrie
> International Press Institute
> Schweizerisches Sozialarchiv

THE UNITED STATES: (New York)

> American Association of Advertising Agencies
> Advertising Federation of America
> Advertising Research Foundation
> Magazine Advertising Bureau.

SPECIALIZED BIBLIOGRAPHIES

American Association of Advertising Agencies. *Bibliography of Material Discussing the Contribution of Advertising to Our Economy and Way of Life.* N.Y., 1948, 4 pp. mimeographed.

Advertising Federation of America. *Books for the Advertising Man,* N. Y., 1957, 37 pp.

Advertising Research Foundation, *Introductory Bibliography of Motivation Research.* N. Y.: 1953.

— *Directory of Organizations which Conduct Motivation Research.* N. Y.: 1954.

— *Directory of Social Scientists interested in Motivation Research.* N. Y.: 1954.

— *A Bibliography of Theory and Research Techniques in the Field of Human Motivation.* N. Y. 1956.

Bird, Charles W. « Suggestion and Suggestibility: A Bibliography », *Psychological Bulletin.* 36 (1939), pp. 264-283.

Bowman, Jan C. « Bibliography on Filmology as related to the Social Sciences », *Cahiers du Centre de Documentation de l'Unesco,* February, 1954, No. 9.

Broderich, G. G. and H. Moskowitz. *Radio and Television Bibliography.* Washington, D. C.: U. S. Federal Security Agency, Office of Education, Bulletin No. 17, 1948.

Columbia Broadcasting System, *Radio and Television Bibliography.* 4th ed. 1941 with supplements 1942 and 1943.

Correspondance de la Presse et Publicité. Numéro Spécial, 1957.

« L'Information: index bibliographique », *Etudes de Presse,* 8 (1955), no. 13.

Erny, Karl. « Bibliographie der Werbe-Literatur », *Schweizer Reklame,* 1958, Jan. pp. 17-19; February, pp. 46-49; May, pp. 154-155.

Fearing, F. and Genevieve Rogge. « A Selected and Annotated Bibliography in Communications Research », *The Quarterly of Films, Radio and Television,* 6 (1951), pp. 283-315.

Gazett, Published by the Institute of the Science of the Press, Amsterdam. Each issue has an excellent bibliography of current material.

Catalogus Biblioteek Genootschap voor Reclame. Amsterdam, n. d., 20 pp.

Kaindl, J. J. *Bibliographie der deutschen Reklame-Plakat- und Zeitung Literatur.* Wien, 1918.

Keesing, Felix M. *Cultural Change: An Analysis and Bibliography of Anthropological Sources to 1952.* Stanford, California: Stanford University Press, IX, 242 pp.

Verzeichnis der Bücher im Institut für Publizistik. Münster: 1951, 91 pp. 1954, 246 pp. (typed).

Istituto di Pubblicismo, *Bibliographia italiana sull'informazione* (1955-56) estratto da *Saggi e studi di pubblicistica*, Serie, VII-VIII, Roma, 45 pp.

Institute of Practioners in Advertising. *Catalogue of Books*. London: 1957, 32 pp.

Jones, Donald H. *100 Books on Advertising*. 6th ed. Columbia, Missouri: U. of Missouri, 1932, 25 pp.

Lasswell, Harold D. and Ralph D. Casey and Bruce Lannes Smith, *Propaganda and Promotional Activities: An Annotated Bibliography*. Minneapolis, Minnesota: U. of Minnesota, 1935; XVII, 450 pp.

Laude, C., L. Thomas and M. Vincienne, « Bibliographie Choisie: formation et développement des attitudes et opinions », *Recherches Sociologiques*, 4 (1957), no 1, pp. 89-94.

A London Bibliography of the Social Sciences, London School of Economics and Political Science, 1952.

Catalogus van de Nederlandse Persbiblioteek. Amsterdam, 1957; 195 pp. and 10 pp. mimeo, supplement, 1958.

Neese, Gottfried. « Literatur zur Werbeforschung », *Publizistik*, 1 (1956), pp. 187-190.

Redi, Riccardo e Franco Venturini. *Bibliographia generale del Cinema*. Roma: Edizione dell'Ateneo, 1953, 251 pp.

Reuel, Denny and Mary Lea Meyersohn, « A Preliminary Bibliography on Leisure », *American Journal of Sociology*, 62 (1956-1957), pp. 602-615.

Revzan, David A. *A Comprehensive Classified Marketing Bibliography*. Los Angeles: U. of California, 1951; 2 vols.

Rose, Oscar, (ed.) *Radio Broadcasting and Television: An Annotated Bibliography*. N. Y. Wilson and C., 1947.

Smith, Bruce Lannes and Chitra M. Smith, *International Communication and Political Opinion, A Guide to the Literature*. Princeton, New Jersey: Princeton U. Press, 1956, XI, 325 pp.

Smith, Bruce L., Harold D. Lasswell and Ralph D. Casey, *Propaganda, Communication and Public Opinion*. Princeton, N. J.: Princeton U. Press, 1946.

UNESCO, « Public Opinion Research », *International Social Science Bulletin*, 5 (1953), no 3, pp. 467-570.

— *Reports and Papers on Mass Communications*. Paris: 1957, 60 pp.

Wales, Hugh G. and Robert Ferber, *A Basic Bibliography on Marketing Research*. American Marketing Association Bibliographical Series, no 1, 1956.

PROFESSIONAL CODES OF ETHICS

Association Suisse de Publicité. *Statuts*. Zürich, 1931, 10 pp.

British Code of Standards relating to the Advertising of Medicines and Treatments, 4th ed. 1958, 6 pp.

Burnett, Verne. *Self-Regulation of Advertising: A Guidebook of Ma-*

jor Facilities. N. Y. American Association of Advertising Agencies, 1950; 84 pp. (mimeographed).

Bureau de Vérification de la Publicité. *Statuts.* Paris, n. d.

Fédération francaise de la publicité, *Code des usages de la publicité.* Paris, 1950, 40 pp.

Federazione Italiana della Pubblicità. *Usi e consuetudini vigenti in materia di pubblicità,* Milano, n. d., 16 pp. (mimeographed).

Independent Television Authority. *Principles for Television Advertising,* 2nd. ed. London, 1958, 16 pp.

International Chamber of Commerce. *Code of Standards of Advertising Practice. revised edition,* Paris, 1955.

Raad van Orde en Tucht voor het Advertentiewezen, (Council of Order and Discipline in Ducht Press Advertising). *Rules for Dutch Press Advertising,* Amsterdam, 1957, 60 pp.

Verband deutscher Werbungsmittler und Werbeagenturen, *Berufsgrundsätze für Werbungsmittler und Werbeagenturen,* Frankfurt a. M., 1958, 13 pp.

BOOKS

Albaucher, G. *La publicité commerciale et son rôle économique.* Paris: P. U. F. 1923; 140 pp.

Albig, William. *Modern Public Opinion.* N. Y.: Mc Graw-Hill, 1956; XII, 518 pp.

Alderson, Wroe. *Marketing Behaviour and Executive Action.* Homewood, Illinois: Irwin, 1957; VIII, 487 pp.

American Academy of Political and Social Science. *Standardization and the Consumer: Annals,* 137 (1928).

— *Marketing in Our American Economy: Annals,* 209 (1940).

— *The Ultimate Consumer, A Study in Economic Illiteracy: Annals,* 173 (1934).

— *Communication and Social Action: Annals.* 250 (1947).

Arnou, André. *Elements d'économie politique.* Paris: Spes, n. d. 733 pp.

Azpiazu, Gioacchino. *L'uomo d'affari.* Roma: Civiltà Cattolica, 1953; 484 pp.

Barnouw, Erik. *Mass Communication: Television, Radio, Film, Press: The Media and their Practice in the United States of America.* N. Y.: Rinehart, 1956, 280 pp. (biblio.)

Barton, Roger. *Advertising Handbook.* N. Y.: Prentice Hall, 1950, 1015 pp.

Baster, A. S. J. *Advertising Reconsidered.* London: P. S. King and Son; 1935; VI, 128 pp.

Baudhuin, F. *Déontologie des affaires.* 4th ed. Louvain, Belgique: Societé d'études morales, sociales et juridiques, 1950; 227 pp.

Becker, Karl and Karl-August Siegel. *Rundfunk und Fernsehen im Blick der Kirche.* Frankfurt a. M. Josef Knecht, 1957; 371 pp.

Bendix, Reinhard and Seymor Martin Lipset. (eds.). *Class, Status and Power: A Reader in Social Stratification.* Glencoe, Illinois: Free Press, 1953; 725 pp.

Berelson, Bernard and Morris Janowitz, (eds.). *Reader in Public Opinion and Communication.* enlarged ed. Glencoe, Illinois: Free Press, 1950; XI, 611 pp. (biblio.).

Bernays, Edward L., (ed.) *The Engineering of Consent.* Norman, Oklahoma: U. of Oklahoma, 1955; VIII, 246 pp.

Bishop, F. P. *The Economics of Advertising.* London: Robert Hale, 1946; 200 pp.

— *The Ethics of Advertising.* London: Robert Hale, 1949; 255 pp.

— *Advertising and the Law.* revised edition by P. N. S. Farrell, 2nd ed., London: Ernest Benn, 1952; IX, 221 pp.

Bogardus, Emory S. *The Making of Public Opinion. N. Y.:* Association Press, 1951; X, 265 pp. (biblio.).

Bogart, Leo. *The Age of Television: A Study of Viewing Habits and the Impact of Television on American Life.* N. Y.: Frederich Ungar, 1956; XII, 347 pp. (biblio.).

Borden, Neil H. *The Economic Effects of Advertising.* Chicago: Irwin, 1942; XL, 988 pp.

— *Advertising in Our Economy.* Chicago: Irwin, 1947; XI, 301 pp.

Boulding, Kenneth E. *Economic Analysis,* 3rd ed. N. Y.: Harper and Brothers, 1955, XX, 905 pp.

— *The Organizational Revolution: A Study in the Ethics of Economic Organization,* (with a commentary by Reinhold Niebuhr), N. Y.: Harper and Brothers, 1953; XXXIV, 286 pp.

Bowen, Howard R. *Social Responsibilities of the Businessman,* (with a commentary by Ernest Johnson), N. Y.: Harper and Brothers, 1953; XII, 276 pp.

— and John C. Bennet *et al. Christian Values and Economic Life.* N. Y.: Harper and Brothers, 1954.

Bowman, Mary Jean and George Bach, *Economic Analysis and Public Policy.* N. Y.: Prentice-Hall, 1943; XIX, 935 pp.

Boyd, M. *Crisis in Communication: A Christian Examination of the Mass Media.* N. Y.: Doubleday, 1957; 128 pp.

Brandon, Robert. *The Truth About Advertising.* London: Chapman and Hall, 1949; XV, 262 pp.

Brembeck, W. L. and W. S. Howell. *Persuasion: A Means of Social Control.* N. Y.: Prentice-Hall, 1952; XI, 488 pp. (biblio.).

Britt, S. H. *Social Psychology of Modern Life.* revised ed. N. Y.: Rinehart, 1949.

Brown, Leo C. *et al. Social Orientations.* Chicago: Loyola U. Press, 1954; VII, 680 pp.

Brunner, Emil, *Justice and the Social Order.* (translated by Mary Hottinger). N. Y.: Harper and Brothers, 1945; 304 pp.

Bryson, Lyman. (ed.). *The Communication of Ideas.* N. Y.: Institute for Religious and Social Studies, 1948; 296 pp.

— *et al.* (eds.) *Approaches to Group Understanding: Sixth Symposium of the Conference on Science, Philosophy and Religion.* N. Y.: Harper and Brothers, 1947.

Burtt, Harold Ernest. *Psychology of Advertising.* Boston: Houghton Mifflin, 1938; 473 pp.

Cairncross, Alec. *Introduction to Economics.* 2nd. ed. revised impression. London: Butterworth, 1955; VIII, 588 pp.

Cantril, Hadley. *The Psychology of Social Movements*. N. Y.: J. Wiley and Sons, 1941; XV, 274 pp.

Canoyer, H. G. and R. S. Vaile. *Economics of Income and Consumption*. N. Y.: Ronald Press, 1951.

Carskadon, Thomas R. and George Soule. *U. S. A. in New Dimensions: The Measure and the Promise of America's Resources: A Twentieth Century Fund Survey*. N. Y.: Macmillan, 1957; 124 pp.

Caton, Dennis. *Advertising Explained*. London: George Allen and Unwin, 1949; 111 pp.

Chafee Zechariah, Jr. *Government and Mass Communication: A Report from the Commission on Freedom of the Press*. Chicago: U. of Chicago Press, 1947; 2 vols.

Chakotin, S. *The Rape of the Masses: The Psychology of Totalitarian Political Propaganda*. (translated from the 5th French edition). London: Routledge and Sons, 1940; 300 pp.

Chamberlin, Edward Hastings. *The Theory of Monopolistic Competition*. 6th ed. Cambridge, Mass.: Harvard U. Press, 1948; XIV, 314 pp. (biblio.).

Chase, Stuart. *The Tragedy of Waste*, N. Y.: Macmillan, 1928.

Cherington, P. T. *Advertising as a Business Force*, London: 1919 XV. 569 pp. also N. Y. Doubleday-Page, 1913.

Childs, Marquis W. and Douglas Cater. *Ethics in a Business Society*. N. Y.: Harper and Brothers, 1954; X, 191 pp.

Clark, Blake. *The Advertising Smokescreen*. N. Y.: Harper and Brothers, 1944; IX, 228 pp.

Clark, John Maurice. *Preface to Social Economics*. N. Y.: Farrar and Rinehart, 1936; XXI, 435 pp.

— *Social Control of Business*. 2nd ed., N. Y.: Mc Graw-Hill, 1939; XVI, 537 pp.

— *Economic Institutions and Human Welfare*. N. Y.: Knopf, 1957; XII, 283, x pp.

Cochrane, Willard W. and Carolyn Shaw Bell, *The Economics of Consumption*. N. Y.: Mc Graw-Hill, 1956; VIII, 481 pp.

Coggle, Bertrand J. and John P. K. Byrnes. *Christian Social Ethics*. London: Epworth Press, 1956; VI, 178 pp.

Cole, Robert H. (ed.), *Consumer Behavior and Motivation: 1955 Marketing Symposium*. Urbana, Illinois: U. of Illinois, 1956; 121 pp. (biblio).

Collins, G. Rowland, *The Advertising Appropriation and the Business Cycle*. N. Y.: N. Y. U. School of Business, 1948.

Colm, Gerhard and Theodore Geiger. *The Economy of the American People: Progress, Problems, Prospects*. Washington, D. C.: National Planning Association, 1958; VIII, 165 pp.

Columbia University Bureau of Applied Social Research. *Psychological Impact of Newspaper and Radio Advertisements*. N. Y.: American Newspaper Publishers Association. 1949.

Commission on the Freedom of the Press. *A Free and Responsible Press: A General Report on Mass Communication: Radio, Motion Pictures, Magazines and Books*. Chicago: U. of Chicago Press, 1947.

Converse, Paul D. *et al. Elements of Marketing.* 6th ed. Englewood Cliffs, New Jersey: Prentice-Hall, 1958; XXI, 883, XV pp. (biblio.).

Crum, W. L. *Advertising Fluctuations, Seasonal and Cyclic.* Chicago. W. W. Shaw, 1927; XXVII, 308 pp.

de Farcy, Henri. *L'agriculture à la conquête de son marché.* Paris: Spes, 1958. 492 pp.

de Finance, Josephus, *Ethica Generalis.* Romae: Pontificia Universitas Gregoriana, 1959.

de Plas, Bernard and Henri Verdier. *La Publicité.* Paris: P. U. F. 1957; 127 pp.

Dickenson, Zenas Clark, *Economic Motives.* Cambridge, Mass.: Harvard U. Press, 1922; VII, 304 pp.

Doob, Leonard W. *Public Opinion and Propaganda.* London: Cresset Press, 1949; VII, 600 pp.

— *Social Psychology.* N. Y. Henry Holt, 1952; XIX, 583 pp.

Domenach, J.-M. *La propagande politique,* Paris: P. U. F., 1955, 127 pp.

Driencourt, Jacques. *La propagande: nouvelle force politique,* Paris: Armand Colin, 1950, VII, 282 pp.

Economic Report of the President, January 1957, 1958, 1959. Washington, D. C., Government Printing Office.

Eich, Jürgen. *Wenn Milch und Honig fliessen: eine wirtschaftskritische Studie.* Düsseldorf: Droste Verlag, 1958; 318 pp.

Elvinger, Francis. *La marque, son lancement, sa vente, sa publicité.* Paris: n. d.

Elliott, William Y. (ed.), *Television's Impact on American Culture.* East Lansing, Michigan: Michigan State U., 1956; XVI, 382 pp.

Ferlet, R. *La force de la propagande.* Paris: Girardot, n. d., 80 pp.

Ferber, Robert and Hugh G. Wales, *Motivation Research.* Homewood, Illinois: Irwin, 1957.

— *Motivation and Market Behavior.* American Marketing Association, 1958; 437 pp.

Ford, John C. and Gerald Kelly, *Contemporary Moral Theology. Vol. 1. Questions in Fundamental Moral Theology.* Westminster, Maryland: Newman, 1958; VII, 368 pp.

Fortune, Editors of. *Why do People Buy?* N. Y. Graw-Hill, 1953; 270 pp.

— *The Changing American Market,* N. Y. Hanover House, 1955; 304 pp.

— *This Amazing Advertising Business.* N. Y. Simon and Schuster, 1957.

Fraser, L. *Propaganda.* N. Y. Oxford, 1957, X, 218 pp.

Friedman, Milton, *A Theory of the Consumer Function.* Princeton, New Jersey: Princeton U. Press., 1957; XVI, 243 pp.

Fromm, Erich, *The Fear of Freedom.* London: Kegan Paul, Trench and Trubner, 1942; XI, 257 pp.

— *Man for Himself.* London: Routledge and Kegan Paul, 1949; XIV, 254 pp.

— *The Sane Society.* London: Routledge and Kegan Paul, 1956; XIII, 370 pp.

Fusi, M. e S. Cervellera. *Codice della Pubblicità.* Milano: Franco Angeli. 608 pp.

Galbraith, John K. *American Capitalism*: *The Concept of Counter-vailing Power*. revised ed. Boston: Houghton Mifflin, 1956, XI, 208 pp.

— *The Affluent Society*. Boston: Houghton Mifflin, 1958; XII, 368 pp.

Galliot, Marcel, *La publicité à travers les âges*. Paris: Edition Hommes et Techniques, 1955, 159 pp.

— *Essai sur la langue de la réclame contemporaine* Toulouse: Collection Universitas, XXXI, 579 pp. (biblio.).

Garcia-Jimenez, Jesus. *Luz en las antenas*: *deontologia del hombre y del programa*. Madrid: Euramerica, 1957; 238 pp.

Geller, Max A. *Advertising at the Crossroads*. N. Y. Ronald Press, 1952.

Giezendanner, P. *Streifzug durch das Reklamerecht*. Zürich: Schweizer kaufmännischer Verein, 1953, 87 pp.

Gonzalez-Moral, Irenaeus. *Philosophia Moralis*. 4th ed. Santander, Hispania: Sal Terrae, 1955, 714 pp.

Gorden, Leland J. *Economics for Consumers*. 2nd ed. N.Y.: American Book Co., 1944; IX, 666 pp.

Haas, C. R. *La Publicité*. 2nd ed. Paris: Dunod, 1958, 490 pp.

Haberler, Gottfried von, *Prospérité et dépression*, nouvelle ed. Genève: Société des Nations, 1939; XX, 519 pp.

Haecker, Theodor. *Was ist der Mensch*? Frankfurt am Main.: Ulstein, 1959; 172 pp.

Henry, Harry. *Motivation Research*. London: Crosby Lockwood and Son, 1958; 240 pp.

Hepner, Harry Walker, *Modern Advertising Practices and Principles*. 3rd ed. N. Y.: Mc Graw-Hill, 1956; X, 740 pp.

Herbin, Pierre. *Comment concevoir et rédiger votre publicité*. Paris. Editions de la revue 'la Publicité', 1938; X, 240 pp.

Hermans, H. J. A. *De bedrijfseconomische beteknis van de reclame*. Leiden, Holland: H. E. Steinfert Kroese, 1949, VII, 404 pp.

Hess, H. W. *Advertising*: *Its Economics, Philosophy and Technique*. Philadelphia: J. B. Lippincott, 1931; XIII, 516 pp.

Hickman, C. A. and M. H. Kuhn. *Individuals, Groups and Economic Behavior*. N. Y.: Dryden Press, 1956; 266 pp.

Hole, E. S. and John Hart. *Advertising and Progress*. London: Review of Reviews, 1914; 271 pp.

Hoggart Richard. *The Uses of Literacy*: *Aspects of Working-class Life, with Special Reference to Publications and Entertainments*. London: Chatto and Windus, 1957; 319 pp.

Horney, Karen. *The Neurotic Personality of Our Time*. N. Y.: W. Norton, 1937; XII, 299 pp.

Hoveland, Carl I. *et al. Communication and Persuasion*: *Psychological Studies of Opinion Change*. New Haven, Connecticut: Yale U. Press, 1953; XII, 315 pp.

— *et al. Experiments on Mass Communication*. Princeton, N. J.: Princeton U. Press. 1949.

— *Personality and Persuasibility*. New Haven, Connecticut: Yale U. Press, 1959; 284 pp.

Hower, Ralph M. *The History of an Advertising Agency*: *N. W. Ayer and Sons at Work 1869-1949.* revised ed. Cambridge, Mass.: Harvard U. Press. 1949; XIII, 647 pp.

Hoyt, Elizabeth, *et al. American Income and Its Use.* N. Y.: Harper and Brothers, 1954; XXI, 362 pp.

Hundhausen, Carl. *Wesen und Formen der Werbung*: *Grundriss der Werbung* no. 3. Essen: W. Girardet, 1954, 304 pp.

Hürth, F. and P.M. Abellán. *De principiis, de virtutibus et praeceptis.* Romae: Pontificia Universitas Gregoriana, 1948; 362 pp. (ad usum privatum auditorum).

Inkeles, Alex. *Public Opinion in Soviet Russia*: *A Study in Mass Persuasion.* Cambridge, Mass.: Harvard U. Press, 1950; XVIII, 378 pp.

International Advertising Association, *Report of the International Advertising Conference (Great Britain), 1951.* London: Advertising Association, 1951, 151 pp.

— *Report of the Second International Advertising Conference in Europe, (The Hague),* Amsterdam: Netherlands: Advertising Association, 1947; 123 pp.

International Chamber of Commerce, *Advertising*: *Conditions and Regulations in Various Countries.* Basel: Verlag für Recht und Gesellschaft, 1953, n. pag.

Kaldor, Nicolas and Rodney Silverman, *A Statistical Analysis of Advertising* 1948. Cambridge, England: University Press, XIV, 200 pp.

Kapp. K. William, *The Social Costs of Private Enterprise.* Cambridge, Mass.: Harvard U. Press, 1950; XII, 287 pp.

Katona, George. *Psychological Analysis of Economic Behavior.* N. Y.: Mc Graw-Hill, 1951, IX, 347 pp.

— and Eva Mueller. *Consumer Attitudes and Demand, 1950-1952.* University of Michigan Survey Research Center, 1953; V, 119 pp.

Katz, Daniel, *et al. Public Opinion and Propaganda.* N.Y. Dryden Press, 1954; XX, 779 pp.

Katz, Elihu and Paul F. Lazarsfeld. *Personal Influence*: *The Part Played by People in the Flow of Mass Communication.* Glencoe, Illinois: Free Press, 1955; XX, 400 pp.

Keezer, Dexter Merriam. *et al. Making Capitalism Work.* N. Y.: Mc Graw-Hill, 1950; IX, 316 pp.

Kenner, H. K. *The Fight for Truth in Advertising.* N. Y.: Round Table Press, 1936.

Knight, Frank H. *The Ethics of Competition and Other Essays.* London: George Allen and Unwin, 1935; 363 pp.

Kropff, H. F. J. *Neue Psychologie in der neuen Werbung*: *methodische Grundlagen für die praktische Anwendung.* Stuttgart: C. E. Poeschel, 1951; 367 pp.

Kyrk, Hazel. *A Theory of Consumption.* N. Y.: Houghton Mifflin, 1923; XIV, 298 pp.

Laloire, Marcel. *Précis théorique et technique de publicité.* Bruxelles: Editions comptables, commerciales et financières, n. d. 220 pp.

Lauterbach, H. *Man, Motives and Money*: *Psychological Frontiers of Economics,* Ithica, N.Y.: Cornell U. Press, 1954; XIV, 366 pp.

Lazarsfeld, Paul F. and Bernard Berelson and Helen Gaudet, *The People's Choice*. N. Y.: Columbia U. Press, 1948.

— and Patricia L. Kendall. *Radio Listening in America*: The People Look at Radio Again. N. Y.: Prentice-Hall, 1948; V, 178 pp.

Lapiere, Richard T. *A Theory of Social Control*. N. Y.: Mc Graw Hill, 1954; XI, 568 pp.

Le Bon, Gustave. *Psychologie des foules*. Paris: P. U. F. 1947; 141 pp.

Lebret, L-J. *et al. Economie et civilisation*. Paris: Editions ouvrières, 1956 and 1958; 2 Vols. Vol. 1. *Niveau de vie: besoins et civilisation*. Vol. 2. *Science économique et developpement*.

Lee, Alfred Mc Clung. *The Daily Newspaper in America*. N. Y.: Macmillan, 1937.

— *How to Understand Propaganda*. N. Y.: Rinehart, 1951.

— and Elizabeth Briant Lee. *The Fine Art of Propaganda*: A Study of Fr. Coughlin's Speeches. N. Y.: Harcourt, Brace, 1939; XI, 140 pp.

Lever, E. A. *Advertising and Economic Theory*. London: Oxford, 1947; XI, 132 pp.

Lewis, W. Arthur. *The Theory of Economic Growth*. Homewood, Illinois: Irwin, 1955; 453 pp.

Linegarger, Paul M. A. *Psychological Warfare*. Washington, D. C.: Infantry Journal Press, 1948; XIII, 259 pp.

Lottin, Odon. *Morale Fondamentale*. Paris: Desclée, 1954; 546 pp.

Lumley, F. E. *The Propaganda Menace*. N. Y.: Century 1933; IX, 445 pp.

Lynch, William. *The Image Industries*. N. Y.: Sheed and Ward, 1959; 159 pp.

Lynd, Robert S. and Helen Merrell Lynd. *Middletown*: A Study in American Culture. N. Y.: Harcourt, Brace, X, 534 pp.

— *Middletown in Transition*: A Study in Cultural Conflicts. N. Y.: Harcourt, Brace, 1937; XVIII, 604 pp.

Mataja, V. *Die Reklame*. 4 th ed. Munich: Duncker und Humbolt, 1926; VIII, 391 pp.

Mauduit, Roger. *La réclame: étude de sociologie économique*. Paris: Alcan, 1933; 172 pp.

Maurer, Emil. *Die volks- und betriebswirtschaftliche Bedeutung der Wirtschaftswerbung*. Berlin: Carl Heymann, 1939; VI, 229 pp.

Mayer, Martin. *Madison Avenue, U. S. A.* N. Y.: Harper and Brothers, 1958; 332 pp.

Mazur, Paul. *The Standards We Raise*. N. Y.: Harper and Brothers, 1953; XIII, 173 pp.

Meerloo, Joost A. M. *Mental Seduction and Menticide*: The Psychology of Thought Control and Brainwashing. London: Jonathan Cape, 1957; 324 pp.

Megret, M. *La Guerre Psychologique*. Paris: P. U. F. 1956; 128 pp.

Merton, Robert K. *Mass Persuasion*: The Social Psychology of a War Bond Drive. N. Y.: Harper and Brothers, 1946; XIII, 210 pp.

— *Social Theory and Social Structure*. revised ed. Glencoe, Illinois: Free Press, 1957; 645 pp.

Messner, Johannes, *Kulturethik*. Innsbruck: Tyrolia, 1954; 681 pp.

— *Die soziale Frage*. 6th ed. Innsbruck: Tyrolia, 1956; 742 pp.

— *Ethik: Kompendium der Gesamtethik.* Innsbruck: Tyrolia, 1955; XV, 531 pp.

— *Das Naturrecht.* 3rd ed. Innsbruck: Tyrolia, 1958; 1205 pp.

Mitnitsky, Alexandre. *La psychologie de la publicité: aspects historiques et effets juridiques.* Lausanne, Suisse: Roth and Roth, 1948; 194 pp.

Mouroux, Jean. *Sens Chrétien de l'homme.* Paris: Aubier, 1945 247 pp.

Muller, Albert, *La morale et la vie des Affaires.* Tournai: Casterman, 1951; 235 pp.

Mc Ewan, John. *Advertising as a Service to Society.* London: Macdonald and Ewan, 1956; (7), 124 pp.

Nell-Breuning, Oswald von. *Wirtschaft und Gesellschaft.* I *Grundfragen.* Freiburg i. Br.: Herder, 1956; VIII, 461 pp.

Newman, Joseph W. *Motivation Research and Marketing Management.* Boston: Harvard U. School of Business Administration, 1957; XIV, 525 pp.

Packard, Vance. *The Hidden Persuaders.* London: Longmans, Green and Co., 1957; VII, 275 pp.

Park, R. E. *Society: Collective Behaviour, News and Opinion, Sociology and Modern Society.* Glencoe, Illinois: Free Press, 1955; 358 pp.

Pease, Otis. *The Responsibilities of American Advertising: Private Control and Public Influence, 1920-1940.* New Haven, Connecticut: Yale U. Press, 1958; XV, 232 pp.

Peterson, Theodore. *Magazines in the Twentieth Century.* Urbana, Illinois: U. of Illinois Press; 1956; X, 457 pp.

Pitkin, Walter B. *The Consumer: His Nature and His Changing Habits.* N. Y.: Mc Graw-Hill, 1932; XIII, 421 pp.

Prakke, H. J. *De Samenspraak in onze samenleving: Inleiding tot de publicistiek.* Assen, Holland: Van Gorcum, 1957; 208 pp.

Potter, David M. *People of Plenty: Economic Abundance and the American Character.* Chicago: U. of Chicago Press, 1954; XXVII, 219 pp.

Powell, Norman John. *Anatomy of Public Opinion.* N. Y.: Prentice-Hall, 1951; XI, 619 pp.

Redlich, F. *Reklame, Begriff, Geschichte, Theorie.* Stuttgart: Ferdinand Enke, 1935; 272 pp.

Regatillo, E. F. and M. Zalba. *Theologiae Moralis Summa, vol. I Theologia Moralis Fundamentalis.* Madrid: Biblioteca de Autores Cristianos, 1942; 965 pp.

Reid, Margaret G. *Consumers and the Market.* 3rd revised ed. New Haven, Connecticut: Yale U. Press, 1942; 634 pp.

Riesman, David. *et al. The Lonely Crowd: A Study of the Changing American Character.* New Haven, Connecticut: Yale U. Press, 1950; XVII, 386 pp.

Roepke, W. *Civitas Humana: Grundfragen der Gesellschaft und Wirtschaftsreform.* 3rd ed. Zürich: Rentsch, 1944; 421 pp.

— *Die Gesellschaftskrisis der Gegenwart.* Zürich: Rentsch, 1942, 410 pp.

— *Masse und Mitte.* Zürich: Rentsch, 1950; 261 pp.

— *Jenseits von Angebot und Nachfrage.* Zürich: Rentsch, 1958; 368 pp.

Rosenberg, Bernard and David Manning White. *Mass Culture: The Popular Arts in America.* Glencoe, Illinois: Free Press, 1957; X, 561 pp.

Roucek, Joseph S. *et al. Social Control.* 2nd ed. Princeton, New Jersey: D. Van Nostrand, 1956.

Russell, Thomas. *Commercial Advertising: Six Lectures at the London School of Economics and Political Science.* London: 1919; X, 306 pp.

Samueslon, Paul A. *Economics: An Introductory Analysis.* 3rd ed. N.Y.: Mc Graw-Hill, 1955; XXII, 753 pp.

Sandage, C. H. *Advertising Theory and Practice.* revised ed. Chicago: Irwin, 1939; XIII, 747 pp.

Sargent, William. *The Battle for the Mind.* London: Heinemann, 1957.

Sauvy, Alfred. *Le pouvoir et l'opinion: essai de psychologie politique et sociale.* Paris: Payot, 1949; 188 pp.

— *L'opinion publique.* Paris: P.U.F., 1956; 127 pp.

— *Les faits et les opinions,* Paris: Cours de Droit, 1954-1955; 722 pp.

Schöllgen, Werner. *Die soziologischen Grundlagen der katholischen Sittenlehre.* Düsseldorf: Patmos, 1953; 410 pp.

Schramm, Wilbur. (ed.), *Communications in Modern Society.* Urbana, Illinois: U. of Illinois, 1948; VI, 252 pp. (biblio.).

— (ed.). *The Process and Effects of Mass Communication.* Urbana, Illinois: U. of Illinois Press, 1954; 586 pp.

— *Responsibility in Mass Communication.* N.Y.: Harper and Brothers, 1957; XXIII, 391 pp.

36e Semaine Sociale de France, (Lille) *Réalisme économique et progrès social.* Lyon: Chronique Sociale de France, 1949; 421 pp.

39e Semaine Sociale de France, (Dijon). *Richesse et Misère.* Lyon: Chronique Sociale de France, 1952; 359 pp.

42e Semaine Sociale de France, (Nancy). *Les techniques de diffusion dans la civilisation contemporaine.* Lyon: Chronique Sociale de France, 1955; 414 pp.

43e Semaine Sociale de France, (Marseille). *Les exigences humaines de l'expansion économique.* Lyon: Chronique Sociale de France, 1956; 397 pp.

Sesmant, Hubert. *L'information moderne.* Paris: Maison Mame, 1941; 289 pp.

Seyffert, Rudolf. *Wirtschaftliche Werbelehre.* 4th ed. Wiesbaden: Th. Gabler. 1952; 240 pp.

Sheed, F. J. *Society and Sanity.* London: Steed and Ward, 1953; 225 pp.

Schilling, Otto. *Katholische Wirtschaftsethik.* München: Max Hueber, 1933; 338 pp.

Siepmann, Charles A. *Radio, Television and Society.* N.Y.: Oxford U. Press, 1950; VII, 410 pp.

Silverman, Rodney. *Advertising Expenditures in 1948.* London: Advertising Association, 1951; XI, 99 pp.

— *Advertising Expenditures in 1952*. London: Advertising Association, 1954; 64 pp.

Simon, Morton J. *The Law for Advertising and Marketing* N. Y.: W. W. Norton and Co., 1956; XXXII, 645 pp.

Smith, George Horsley. *Motivation Research in Advertising and Marketing*. N. Y.: Mc Graw-Hill, 1954; XIV, 242 pp.

Steinberg, Charles S. *The Mass Communicators*. N. Y.: Harper and Brothers, 1958; 470 pp.

Steuber, Kurt. *Werbung und Wohlstand*: *eine volkswirtschaftliche Untersuchung der Werbung*. Zürich: Polygraphischer Verlag, 1958; 211 pp.

Stewart, P. W. and J. F. Dewhurst. *Does Distribution Cost too Much?* N. Y.: Twentieth Century Fund, 1939; 403 pp.

Taeusch, Carl. F. *Policy and Ethics in Business*. 1st ed. N. Y.: Mc Graw-Hill. 1931; XI, 624 pp.

Tawney, R. H. *The Acquisitive Society*. London: G. Bell and Sons, 1943; 242 pp.

Taylor, F. W. *The Economics of Advertising*. London: Allen and Unwin, 1934; 248 pp.

Thomas Aquinas. *Summa Theologica*. Romae: Marietti, 1948.

Thompson, Denys. *Voice of Civilization*. London: Muller, 1943.

Timasheff, Nicolas S. and Paul W. Facey. *Sociology*. Milwaukee, Wisconsin: Bruce, 1949; XIV, 399 pp.

Tosdel, Harry R. *Selling in Our Economy*: *An Economic and Social Analysis of Selling and Advertising*. Chicago: Irwin, 1957; XI; 333 pp.

Troelstrup, Arch W. *Consumer Problems*. N. Y.: Mc Graw-Hill, 1952; XV, 458 pp.

Trotabas, Louis. (ed.). *L'opinion publique*. Paris: P. U. F. 1957; 446 pp.

Turner, E. S. *The Shocking History of Advertising*. London: Michael Joseph, 1952; 302 pp.

Union International d'Etudes Sociales (Malines). *Code social. nouvelle synthèse*. Paris: Spes. 1948; 123 pp.

— *Code de moral politique*. Paris: Spes. 1957; 218 pp.

Utz, Arthur-Fridolin. *Sozialethik*: *1. Teil*: *Die Prinzipien der Gesellschaftslehre*. Heidelberg: F. H. Kerle, 1958; XXII, 520 pp.

Vaile, Ronald S. *The Economics of Advertising*. N. Y.: Ronald Press, 1927.

— *et al. Marketing in the American Economy*. N. Y. Ronald Press, 1952; XVIII, 737 pp.

Baarle, W. H. van. *et al. Het advertentiewezen*. Leiden: Stenfort-Kroese, 1954; VIII, 93 pp.

— *Reclamekunde en reclameleer*. Leiden: H. E. Stenfort-Kroese, 1956; XVII, 696 pp.

Vaughan, F. L. *Marketing and Advertising*: *An Economic Appraisal*. Princeton, New Jersey: Princeton U. Press, 1928; XI, 255 pp.

Vawter Foundation Lectures in Business Ethics. *The Ethical Problems of Modern Advertising*. N. Y.: Ronald Press, 1930; 134 pp.

Waite, Warren C. and Ralph Cassady Jr. *The Consumer and the Economic Order*, 2nd ed. N. Y.: Mc Graw-Hill, 1949; X, 427 pp.

Waples, Douglas, (ed.), *Print, Radio and Film in a Democracy*. Chicago: U. of Chicago Press, 1942; XIV, 197 pp.

Ward, A. Dudley. (ed.), *Goals of Economic Life*. N. Y.: Harper and Brothers, 1953; X, 470 pp.

— *The American Economy: Attitudes and Opinions*, N. Y.: Harper and Brothers. 1955; XX, 199 pp.

Weiler, E. *La publicité: sa psychologie, son origine, sa fonction économique*, Paris: Sirey, 1932; 158 pp.

Welty, Eberhard, *Herders Sozialkatechismus*. Freiburg i. Br.: Herder, 1951-1958; 3 vols.

Whyte, William. H. Jr. *The Organization Man*. Garden City, N. Y.: Doubleday Anchor Books, 1957; VI, 471 pp.

— and the Editors of Fortune. *Is Anybody Listening?* N. Y.: Simon and Schuster, 1952; 239 pp.

Wild, John. *Introduction to Realistic Philosophy*. N. Y.: Harper and Brothers, 1948; XI, 516 pp.

Williamson, Harold F. and John A. Buttrick, (eds.), *Economic Development: Principles and Patterns*: N. Y.: Prentice-Hall, 1954; XII, 576 pp.

Wright, David Mc Cord. *Capitalism*, 1st ed. N. Y.: Mc Graw-Hill, 1951; XVII; 246 pp.

Wyand, Charles S. *The Economics of Consumption*. N. Y.: Macmillan, 1937; XIII, 565 pp.

Wüst, René-Henri. *La Guerre psychologique*. Lausanne, Suisse: Payot, 1954; 162 pp.

PAMPHLETS

Baynes, Michael. *Advertising on Trial: The Case for the Consumer*. London: Bow Group, 1956; 47 pp.

Better Business Bureau. *Facts You Should Know About Advertising*. N. Y.: 1953; 14 pp.

Bishop, F. P. *Advertising and Employment*. London: Advertising Association, 1944; 12 pp.

Borton, Elon G. *Some Questions and Answers about Advertising*. N. Y.: Advertising Federation of America. n. d., n. pag.

Brorby, Melvin. *We Ask Ourselves Four Questions*. N. Y.: A. A. A. A. 1958; 16 pp.

Buxton, Christopher. *A British Assessment of the American Economy*. London: U. S. Information Service, n. d. n. pag.

Chisholm, C. *Economic Function of Advertising*. London: Business Publications, 1943; 20 pp.

Fellows, Harold E. *Advertising Stopped at 10 o'clock This Morning*. Washington, D. C.: National Association of Radio and Television Broadcasters, n. d., 11 pp.

Gamble, Frederic R. *The Role of Advertising in Economic Development. Address at the XVth Congress of the International Chamber of Commerce, Tokyo, May 18, 1955*. N. Y.: A. A. A. A., 1955, n. pag.

Haley, Sir William. *Moral Values in Broadcasting*. London: B. B. C., 1948; 12 pp.

13

Motivation Research, London: Institute of Practitioners in Advertising, 1957; 18 pp.

Subliminal Communication. London: Institute of Practitioners in Advertising, 1958; 34 pp.

Kleppner, Otto. *Where Does Advertising Fit In?* N. Y.: A. A. A. A. 1952; 25 pp.

Murray, Albert Victor. *The Ethics and Techniques of Persuasion.* Cardiff, Wales: Temperance Collegiate Association, 1953; 16 pp.

Mc Cann-Erickson Inc. *Who has the Ultimate Weapon?* N. Y., 1958; 35 pp.

O'Connor, John Joseph. *Philosophical Aspects of Communication: A Study in Social Philosophy.* Washington, D. C. Catholic U. of America Philosophical Studies, no. 145, 1953; VI, 29 pp.

Rockefeller Brothers Fund. *The Callenge to America: Its Economic and Social Aspects.* Garden City, N. Y.: Doubelday, 1958, VIII, 78 pp.

Roepke, Wilhelm. *Borgkauf im Lichte sozialethischer Kritik*, Köln: C. Heymanns, 1954; 21 pp.

— *Vorgegessen Brot: kritische Nachlese zur Diskussion über das Borgkaufwesen.* Köln: C. Heymanns, 1955; 32 pp.

Rosset, P. R. *La vente à tempérament: ses aspects économiques et juridiques.* Fascicule XII des publications de la Société Neuchâteloise de Science Economique, n. d. 24 pp.

Sauvy, Alfred. *Publicité et développement économique.* Bordeaux: Imprimerie Bière, 1957; 24 pp.

Articles and Essays in Collections

Abrams, Mark, « The Function of Advertising in the Economy » *Advertising: A Financial Times Survey*, April 1957, p. 5.

« Advertising has Vital Role to Play », *Advertising Age*, July 5, 1954; p. 1.

(Youth Research Center), *Advertising Age*, October, 21, 1957, p. 28.

« Buyers of New Cars Concentrated in Upper Income Groups », *Advertising Age*, February 17, 1958. pp. 7, 49-50.

(Professor Slichter on the Recession), *Advertising Age*, March 3, 1958; pp. 55.

« 100 Top Magazine and Television Advertisers in 1957 », *Advertising Age*, March 3, 1957, p. 62.

« Advertising has an Important Role in a Recession Economy », *Advertising Agency*, March 8, 1958, pp. 14-21.

« Advertising Role Bigger than Ever », *ibid.* June 6, 1958, pp. 12-13.

A. A. Forum. « Propaganda and the Product », *Journal of the Advertising Association.* 5 (1951), March No. 12, pp. 12-15.

— « The National Income and Advertising Expenditure », *ibid.* 6 (1953), November no 9, pp. 2-9.

— « Critics at Large », *ibid.*, 7 (1955), January no 1, pp. 21-23.

Abramson, A. V. « Advertising and Economic Theory: A Criticism », *American Economic Review.* 21 (1931), pp. 685-691.

Agnew, H. E. « Can Standardization Reduce Advertising Costs? » *Annals.* 137 (1928), pp. 253-258.

Albig, William. « Publicity, Advertising and Propaganda in the United States of America », *Gazette.* 4 (1958), no. 1, pp. 23-32.

Alderson and Sessions Inc. « Advertising and the Pursuit of Happiness », *Cost and Profit Outlook.* June 1957 n. pag.

Alderson, Wroe. « Psychology for Marketing and Economics ». *Journal of Marketing.* 17 (1952) no. 2, pp. 119-135.

« Code for Advertisers », *America,* December 12, 1953, p. 287.

« Immoral Advertising in Rome », *America,* April 6, 1957. p. 2.

« Admen Morally Worried ». *America,* March 14, 1959.

Argence, Pierre. « La publicité et la propaganda peuvent-elles stimuler la consommation?-» *Vendre.* 26 (1957), *août,* no. 105, pp. 401-407.

Balch, W. R. « Advertising and Ethics ». *JAA.* 6 (1954), pp. 24-28.

Baragli, E. « Premesse e promesse della pubblicistica ». *La Civiltà Cattolica.* agosto 18, 1958, pp. 400-408.

Barton, Bruce. « Advertising: Its Contribution to the American Way of Life ». *Reader's Digest,* April 1955, pp. 103-107.

Bell, Daniel. « La Publicité: son impact sur la société ». *Rond point de la publicité dans le monde.* 2 (1958), mars, no. 9. pp. 29-39.

Belson, William « A. Technique for Studying the Effects of a Television Broadcast ». *Applied Statistics.* 5 (1956), no. 3; pp. 195-202.

— « Learning and Attitude Changes Resulting from Viewing a Television Series: ' Bon Voyage ' ». *British Journal of Educational Psychology.* 26 (1956), part 1, pp. 31-38.

— « The Effects of Television ». *The Australian Quarterly,* December, 1957, pp. 59-70.

— « Selective Perception in Viewing a Television Broadcast ». *Audio Visual Communications Review.* 6 (1958), winter, no. 1, pp. 23-32.

— « Measuring the Effects of Television: A Description of Method ». *POQ.* 22 (1958), spring no. 1, pp. 11-18.

Bennett, John C. « The Theological Conception of Goals for Economic Life », in A. Dudley Ward, (ed.), *Goals for Economic Life.* pp. 397-432.

— « The Christian Conscience and Economic Growth: 1. The Next Moral Dilemma » *Social Order,* 7 (1957), pp. 155-156.

Berelson, Bernard, « Communications and Public Opinion », in Schramm. *Communications and Modern Society.* pp. 167-185.

Boulding, Kenneth E. « Religious Fundations of Economic Progress », *HBR,* 30 (1952), May-June, no. 3, pp. 33-40.

Bourke, Vernon J. « La morale thomiste et la question de la possession matérielle », in Marvin Faber, (ed.), *L'Activitè philosophique en France et aux Etats-Unis.* (Paris: P. U. F. 1950, 2 vols.) vol 1, pp. 302-320.

— « The Christian Conscience and Economic Growth, V. Need we be Embarassed? » *Social Order,* 7 (1957), pp. 164-166.

Braithwaite, Dorothea. « The Economic Effects of Advertisment ». *Economic Journal.* 38 (1928), pp. 16-32.

Brooks, Robert C. Jr. « Word-of-mouth' Advertising in Selling New Products », *JM,* 22 (1957), October, no. 2, pp. 154-161.

Brown, Harold Chapman. « Advertising and Propaganda ». *International Journal of Ethics,* (presently Ethics) 40 (1929), October, no. 1, pp. 31-55.

Bryson, George D. « What Advertising Can Give the Consumer », *The International Advertising Conference. (Great Britain)*, London: Advertising Association, 1951, p. 24.

Burch, Gilbert, « Who'll Buck a Trend? » in The Editors of Fortune, *Why do People Buy?* pp. 249-270.

— « Why do People Buy? » in *ibid.* pp. 7-25.

Canoyer, Helen G. « National Brand Advertising and Monopolistic Competition », *The Journal of Marketing*, 7 (1942), October, pp. 152-157.

Cartwright, Dorwin, « Some Principles of Mass Persuasion: Selected Findings of Research on the Sale of United States War Bonds », in Katz *et al. Public Opinion and Propaganda*, pp 382-393.

Chamberlin, Edward, H. « Advertising Costs and Equilibrium: A Correction », *Review of Economic Studies*, 12 (1944-1945), pp. 116-120.

Charbonneau, B. « La publicité », *Esprit*, 3 (1935), April, n. 31, pp. 6-14.

Chase, Stuart, « The Ethics of Advertising as Viewed by the Consumer », in *Vawter Lectures, 1930*, pp. 98-111.

Chastaing, Maxime, « Réclame, publicité, verité relative ». *Vente et Publicité*, November 1956, pp. 26-30.

Clark, Colin, « Economics », in John M. Todd, (ed.), *The Springs of Morality, a Catholic Symposium*, London: Burns and Oates, 1956, pp. 107-118.

— « The Horrible Proposals of J. K. Galbraith », *National Review*, October 11, 1958, pp. 237-239, 255.

Clark, F. E. « An Appraisal of Certain Criticisms of Advertising », *American Economic Review*, 15 supplement (1925), pp. 5-13.

Coffey, T. P. « Advertising Techniques and the Moral Law », *Catholic World*, December, 1957, pp. 174-179.

Cone, Fairfax M. « Advertising is Not a Plot: A Reply to Vance Packard », *The Atlantic*, January, 1958, pp. 71-73.

Copeland, Morris A. « The Economics of Advertising: Discussion », *American Economic Review*, 15 supplement, (1925), pp. 38-41.

Curtis, Vanderveer, « The Place of Ethics in the Field of Advertising », in *Vawter Lectures 1930*, pp. 3-27.

Darms, Louis, « Le consommateur a-t-il démissionné? » *Organisation Scientifique*, février, 1959, reprint, n. pag.

Dean, Joel, « Cyclic Policy on the Advertising Appropriation ». *JM.* 15 (1951), January, pp. 265-73.

de Farcy, Henri, « Publicité et agriculture », *Cahier des Ingénieurs Agronomes*, 125 (1958), avril, pp. 25-29.

De Leener, Georges, « Comment stimuler la consommation? Rôle des producteurs et des distributeurs », *Bulletin du Comité National Belge de l'Organisation Scientifique*, 11 (1937), mai, no. 5, pp. 122-130; juin, no. 6, pp. 148-156.

Delzing, J. A. H. « Economische, sociale en financiële overwegingen », *Revue der Reclame*, 16 (1956), pp. 252-258.

Dessau, Einar, « The Responsibility and Ethics of World-wide Advertising », *Second International Advertising Conference in Eu-*

rope, The Hague: Netherlands Advertising Association, 1957, pp. 31-40.

Di Rovasenda, Enrico, « Problemi attuali circa la destinazione dei beni e l'uso del superfluo », *XXIX Settimana Sociale dei Cattolici d'Italia: Vita Economica ed Ordine Morale,* Bergamo: I. C. A. S. 1956; pp. 197-227.

Dichter, Ernest, « The Psychology of Prosperity », *HBR.* 35 (1957), November-December, pp. 19 ff, 158 ff.

Doesschate, J. F. ten, « Enkle schuchtere opmerkingen over de maatschappelijke beteknis von reclame », in *16e Nederlandse Reclamecongres,* Amsterdam: Genootschap voor Reclame, 1953; pp. 29-38.

Doob, Leonard W. « Goebel's Principies of Propaganda », in Katz *et al. Public Opinion and Propaganda,* pp. 509-521.

Ducommun, Charles F. « L'incidence sociale de la publicité », *Revue économique et sociale,* (Suisse), 9 (1951), pp. 248-265.

Duff, Edward, « Introducing a Symposium: The Christian Conscience and Economic Growth », *Social Order,* 7 (1957), pp. 145-148.

Ellefsen, Olaf, « Has the Advertiser a Moral Responsibility to Support the Press? » *JAA.* 8 (1958), April no. 2, pp. 3-9.

Folliet, Joseph, « L'action psychologique devant la morale », *Chronique Sociale de France,* 67 (1959), avril, pp. 169-184.

« Why do People Buy? » *Fortune,* April, 1952, pp. 105-107; 194 ff

(Advertising Expenditures) *Fortune,* September 1956, p. 110.

« Suburbia Snubs the Recession », *Fortune,* May, 1958, pp. 114-116.

Frank, Glenn, « The Dignity and Duties of the Advertising Profession », *Printers' Ink,* April 14, 1927, pp. 81-89 and 150-157.

Fraser, J. Campbell, « Advertising and Economic Theory », *JAA,* 7 (1955), August, no. 3, pp. 11-17.

Fund for the Republic, *The Press and the People.* (13 reprints of Television Programs produced by W. G. B. H., Mass. n. d.)

Galbraith, J. K. « The Unseemly Economics of Opulence », *Harper's* January, 1952, pp. 58-63.

— « Is Overproduction the Fault of Advertising », *Tide,* October 25, 1957, pp. 19-21.

Garrett, Thomas M., « Moral en advertenies », *De Linie* (Brussel) vrijdag, oktober 24, 1958, no. 525, p. 5.

— « Les éléments éthiques de la publicité moderne », *Crieur Public,* December, 1958, no. 64, p. 17.

— « Die Ethik der Propaganda », *Orientierung,* 23 (1959), March 31, no. 6, pp. 65-68.

— « Motivforschung und Tiefenpropaganda als ethisches Problem », *Achte Internationale Studientagung Stiftung Genossenschafts-Institut « Im Grüene »* Rüschlikon-Zürich, 1959, 8 pp. (French and English Versions in mineographed form).

Gonin, Marius, « L'aspect moral du problème de la publicité », in *23e Semaine Sociale de France, La morale chrétienne et les affaires.* Lyon: Gabalda, 1931; pp. 479-500.

Grosclaude, J. « Le contrôle de la publicité » *Economie et réalités mondiales,* January, 1954; pp; pp. 28-30.

Hayakawa, S. I. « Poetry and Advertising », in Lyman Bryson *et al*,
    (eds.), *Approaches to Group Understanding*, pp. 369-374.
Heilbroner, Robert L. « Public Relations: The Invisible Sell », *Harper's*, June, 1957, pp. 23-27.
Hicks, J. R. « Distribution Costs and Economic Progress: Revised
    Version », *Review of Economic Studies*, 4 (1936), pp. 1-12.
Hotchkiss, G. B. « An Economic Defense of Advertising », *American
    Economic Review*, 15 supplement (1925), pp. 14-22.
Hoveland, Carl I., « Effects of the Mass Media of Communication »,
    in Gardner Lindzey, (ed.), *Handbook of Social Psychology*, Cambridge, Mass.: Addison-Wesley, 1954, vol. I, pp. 1062-1102.
Hutchins, Robert M. « Is Democracy Possible? » *Bulletin of the
    Fund for the Republic*, February, 1959, pp. 1-7.
Huxley, Aldous, « Tyranny over the Mind », *Newsday* (Long Island
    New York), May 31, 1958, special supplement, 24 pp.
Hyman, Herbert H. and Paul B. Sheatsley, « Some Reasons Why
    Information Campaigns Fail », in Katz *et al. Public Opinion and
    Propaganda* pp. 522-531.
Jaspers, Karl, « Wahrheit, Freiheit und Friede », *Frankfurter Allgemeine Zeitung*, Donnerstag, September 30, 1958, p. 6.
« The Function of Advertising in the Conditions of Today », *JAA*,
    5 (1947), pp. 25-31. May, no. 1.
« Advertising's Evidence Analysed », *JAA*. 5 (1948), April, no. 5 pp.
    10-15.
« Advertising in an Expanding Market », *JAA*. 5 (1949), March, no.
    7, pp. 6-10.
« What Economists Think about Advertising », *JAA*. 6 (1953), January, no. 6, pp. 15-19.   (
« Advertising and the Marginal Theory », *JAA*. 6 (1953), July, no. 8,
    pp. 21-24.
Kaldor, Nicholas, « The Economic Effects of Advertising », *Review
    of Economic Studies*. 18 (1950-51)), pp. 1-27.
Katz, Elihu, « The Two-step Flow of Communication: An Up-to-date
    Report on an Hypothesis », *POQ*. 21 (1957), Spring, no. 1,
    pp. 61-78.
Kennedy, William F. « The Christian Conscience and Economic
    Growth », *Social Order*, 7 (1957), pp. 149-154.
Klapper, Joseph T. « The Comparative Effects of the Various Mass
    Media », in Schramm, *Process and Effects of Mass Communication*, pp. 91-105.
— « Mass Media and Persuasion », in Schramm, *Process and Effects
    of Mass Communication*, pp. 288-320.
— « What we Know about the Effects of Mass Communications:
    The Brink of Hope », *POQ*. 21 (1957), Winter, no. 4, pp. 453-474.
Land, P. S. « Role of Advertising in a Recession », *America*, March
    20, 1954, pp. 649-51.
— « People of Plenty », *Social Order*, 5 (1955), pp. 213-219.
Laurent, R. P., « Progrès technique, progrès économique, progrès
    humain », in *43e Semaine Sociale de France*, pp. 99-114.
Lazersfeld, P. F. « Who Influences Whom- Its the Same for Politics
    and Advertising ». *Printers' Ink*, June 8, 1945, pp. 32-36.

— « Some Remarks on the Role of Mass Media in so-called Tolerance Propaganda », *Journal of Social Issues*, 3 (1947), Summer, no. 3, pp. 17-25.

— « Why is so Little Known about the Effects of Television on Children and What can be Done? » *POQ.* 19 (1955), pp. 243-251.

— and Robert K. Merton, « Mass Communication, Popular Taste and Organized Social Action », in Lyman Bryson, (ed.) *The Communication of Ideas,* pp. 95-118.

Lee, Alfred Mc Clung, « Social Determinants of Public Opinions », in Katz *et al. Public Opinion and Propaganda,* pp. 94-104.

Leiter, Robert D. « Advertising, Resource Allocation and Employment,» *JM.* 15 (1951), pp. 158-166.

Lever, E. A. « The Application of First Principles », *JAA.* 5 (1950), December, no. 11, pp. 6-11.

Lyon, Leverett S. « Advertising » in *Encyclopaedia of the Social Sciences.* Edited by Edwin R. A. Seligman. N. Y.: Macmillan, 1930, vol. I, pp. 469-475.

Maclachlan, John M. « Propaganda », in Rouceck (ed.) *Social Control.* pp. 408-427.

Mack, Ruth P. « Economics of Consumption », in Bernard F. Haley, (ed.), *A Survey of Contemporary Economics.* Homewood, Illinois: Irwin, 1952; vol. 2, pp. 39-78.

Maisel, Albert A. « Wizardry in the Washing Machines; A Report to Consumers », *Reader's Digest,* October, 1958; pp. 236-239.

Mataje, Victor, « Reklame », *Handwörterbuch der Staatswissenschaften.* 4th edition edited by Ludwig Elster *et al.* Jena: Gustav Fischer, 1925; vol. 7, pp. 1229-1244.

Mayer, Martin, « What is Advertising Good For? » *Harper's* February, 1958; pp. 25-31.

Mazur, Paul, « The Advertising Force: Its Challenge and Potentials in Today's Economy », *PI.* September 18, 1953; pp. 47-49. (notes from reprint, n. pag.)

Mead, Margaret, « The Pattern of Leisure in Contemporary American Culture », in *Annals.* 313 (1957), May, pp. 11-15.

— « Some Cultural Approaches to Communication Problems », in Lyman Bryson, (ed.), *The Communication of Ideas.* pp. 9-26.

Meerens, M., « Over benadering en mediakeuze bij de verkoop op afbetaling », *Revue der Reclame,* 16 (1956), pp. 279-280.

Moriarity, W. D., « An Appraisal of the Present Status of Advertising », *American Economic Review,* 15° supplement (1925), pp. 23-35.

Mullen, W. H., « Advertising Volume Grows and Costs Decrease », *Journalism Quarterly,* 25 (1948), September, pp. 220-22.

Mueller, Eva, « Consumer Reactions to Inflation », *Quarterly Journal of Economics,* 73 (1959), pp. 246-262.

Murphey, Douglas J. « The Christian Conscience and Economic Growth, II The Role of Advertising », *Social Order,* 7 (1957), pp. 157-159.

Mc Intyre, Robert B., « Advertising Called Recession Medicine », *Editor and Publisher,* April 12, 1948, p. 16.

Mc Intyre, Robert B., « Key to Recession is ' Buy ' says Ike »,
    Editor and Publisher, April 19, 1958, pp. 28-29.
— « Role of PR Advertising in Battle of Recession », *Editor and*
    Publisher, April 26, 1958, pp. 25-26.
Mc Kenna, Joseph P., « Consumption Patterns » in Willaimson and
    Buttrick, *Economic Development,* pp. 242-276.
— « The Christian Conscience and Economic Growth, III, Facts
    and Myths », *Social Order,* 7 (1957), pp. 160-161.
Reinhold Neihbuhr, « Introduction » to Schramm, *Responsibility in*
    Mass Communication, pp. 1-XXIII.
« For the Next Twenty Years », *Newsweek,* (European Ed.) June 16,
    1958; pp. 46-49.
Nye, G. Vernon, « Four Broadcasts on Advertising: — A Review »,
    JAA. 7 (1957), April, no. 10, pp. 22-27.
Packard, Vance, « The Growing Power of Admen », *The Atlantic,*
    September, 1957; pp. 55-59.
— « The Mass Manipulation of Human Behaviour », *America,* De-
    cember 14, 1957, pp. 342-344.
Palmer, Dewey H. and Frederich J. Schlink, « Education and the
    Consumer », *Annals,* 173 (1934), May, pp. 188-197.
Pearlin, Leonard I. and Morris Rosenberg. « Propaganda Techniques
    in Institutional Advertising », in Katz *et al. Public Opinion and*
    Propaganda, pp. 478-490.
Pezet, Ernest, « Publicité, presse et vie moderne », *La Vie Intel-*
    lectuelle, 38 (1935), 25 October; pp. 227-248 and 10 November,
    pp. 403-427.
Piatier, André, « La publicité dans l'économie contemporaine »,
    Vendre, novembre, 1956, reprint, 8 pp.
Piettre, André, « Les fins humaines de l'économie », in *36ᵉ Semaine*
    Sociale de France, pp. 137-158.
— « Fondements, moyens et organes de la répartition du revenu
    national », in *39ᵉ Semaine Sociale de France,* pp. 181-194.
— « Les fins et les choix d'une politique d'expansion », in *43ᵉ Se-*
    maine Sociale de France, pp. 115-126.
— « Besoin et civilisation », in Lebret *et al. Economie et Civi-*
    lisation, tome 1, pp. 35-45.
Pirie, Margaret C. « Excerpts from an Address to the Fifth Annual
    Seminar of the American Marketing Association Toronto, Ja-
    nuary, 1958 », *Advertising Age,* April 21, 1958, pp. 86-90.
Pirou, Gaëtan, « La publicité et la théorie économique », *Melanges*
    dédiés a M. le Professeur Henri Truchy, Paris: Sirey, 1938;
    pp. 445-460.
Pope, Bayard F. « What Good is Advertising », *Advertising Agency*
    and Selling, May, 1952, reprint n. pag.
« What Advertising is... What it has Done... What it can do Now ».
    PI, May 15, 1953, reprint n. pag.
« Ad Ethics are Higher Today because Honest Ads Work Best »,
    PI. June 15, 1957, pp. 21-23; 46.
« The Challenge of Our Economy: How Advertising and Selling Can
    Speed Recovery Today » *PI.* May 16, 1958; pp. 23-70.

Potter, D. M. « Advertising: The Institution of Abundance », *Yale Review*, 43 (1953), September, no. 1, pp. 49-70.

Ray, Royal H. « Advertising and Economic Support, 1955-1975 », *Journalism Quarterly*, 32 (1955), Winter, no. 1, pp. 31-38.

Redlich, Fritz, « Reklame und Wechsellagenkreislauf », *Schmollers Jahrbuch*, 59 (1935), Erstes Heft, pp. 43-57.

Resor, Stanley « We can sell $ 600 Billion of Output », *U. S. News and World Report*, January 4, 1957; pp. 72-80.

Rice, Elmer, « The Supreme Freedom: Three Hundred Years after Milton », in R. M. Mac Iver, (ed.), *Great Expressions of Human Rights*, N. Y.: Harper and Brothers, 1950, pp. 105-125.

Roper, Elmo, « Women's Buying Habits », *Social Order*, 7 (1957), pp. 56-61.

Rothschild, K. W. « A Note on Advertising », *Economic Journal*, 52 (1942), pp. 112-120.

« The Advertising Business », *The Royal Bank of Canada Monthly Letter*, July, 1948; n. pag.

Sandage, C. H. « The Role of Advertising in Modern Society », *Journalism Quarterly*, 28 (1951), Winter, pp. 31-38.

Schneider, Erich, « Eine Theorie der Reklame », *Zeitschrift für Nationalökonomie*, 9 (1939), pp. 450-456.

Seiler, Walter, « How Advertising and Selling Drive our Fastpaced Economy », *PI.* October 21, 1955, pp. 36-42 (notes from reprint, n. pag.).

Seligman, D. « Amazing Advertising Business », *Fortune*, September, 1956; pp. 106-110.

— « How Much for Advertising », *Fortune*, December, 1956; pp. 123-126.

Schultz, William J. « Discretionary Spending: Key to Upturn », *P. I.* April 11, 1958; p. 35.

Siegfried, A., « Ce que j'ai appris de la vie sur la publicité ». *Journal de la Publicité*, mai, 1947, no. 32.

— « Philosophie de la publicité », *La Revue de Paris*, avril, 1953; pp. 3-15.

Slichter, Sumner H. « Curing the Recession », U. S. *News and World Report*, April 4, 1958; pp. 42-47.

Smith, Henry, « The Imputation of Advertising Costs », *Economic Journal*, 45 (1935), pp. 682-699.

— « Advertising Costs and Equilibrium », *Review of Economic Studies*, 2 (1934), pp. 62-65.

Snider, Joseph L. « Funds for Stability », *HBR.* 30 (1952), July-August, no. 4, pp. 86-96.

Stocking, C. A. « Advertising and Economic Theory », *American Economic Review*, 21 (1931), pp. 43-55.

Stridiron, J. G., « De financierung der reclame in crisis-tijden ». in *Reclame en de crisis, erste Nederlandsche Reclamecongres*, (Amsterdam: Genootschap voor Reclame, 1932), pp. 6-19.

Thommen, Andreas, « Wirtschaftswerbung und Reklame », *Bulletin des schweizerischen Zeitungsverlegerverbands*, März, 1958, pp. 3-18.

« Do Admen Keep Up with the Johnses », *Tide.* November 8, 1957, p. 27.

« The Myth of Madison Avenue », *Tide*. March 14, 1958; pp. 71-74.

« Advertising's Enigma: The Changing Consumer », *Tide*, March 14, 1958; pp. 21-31.

« Consumers- to Admen They're a Puzzlement », *Tide*, March 14, 1958; pp. 49-51.

« Autos: The Cellini of Chrome », *Time*, (Atlantic ed.) November 4, 1957; pp. 61-65.

(Press) *Time*, (Atlantic ed.) March 17, 1958, pp. 45-46.

(Business). *Time* (Atlantic ed.) March 24, 1958, pp. 58-59.

(Business). *Time* (Atlantic ed.) December 29, 1958, pp. 42.

« Auto Prestige: Conspicuous Consumption is Waning », *Time* (Atlantic ed.) March 31, 1958, p. 50.

United States Information Service, « Prestige, Personal Influence and Opinion », in Schramm, *Process and Effects of Mass Communications*. pp. 402-410.

Wagner, Louis C. « Advertising and the Business Cycle », *The Journal of Marketing*, 6 (1941) October, pp. 124-135.

Vaile, Roland S. « Use of Advertising during Depression », *HBR*. 5 (1927), pp. 323-330.

— « The Effects of Advertising on a Depression », *PI*. January 1, 1931, pp. 41-44.

— « Consumption, the End Result of Marketing », in *Annals*. 209 (1940), pp. 14-21.

— « Comment on Cyclic Policy and the Advertising Appropriation », *JM*. 16 (1951) July, no. 1, pp. 81-82.

Villaverde, Albert, J. « Publicidad y la Moral », *Razón y Fe*, 151 (1955), pp. 402-407.

Vlaemminck, J.-H. « Quelques incidences économique de l'effort publicitaire », *Annales de Sciences Economiques Appliquées*. 12 (1954), December, no. 5, pp. 447-494.

Vignoles, C. M. « The Civic Responsibilities of the Advertiser », *JAA*. 7 (1957), October no. 12, pp. 10-14.

Wallenberg, Marcus, « The High Cost of Money », *Fortune*, December, 1957; pp. 134-135.

Warton, Don, « Beware the Phoney Price-tag Bargin », *Reader's Digest*, December, 1958; pp. 40-42.

Weisinger, Mort, « They're Out to Get Your Money », *Reader's Digest*, October, 1957, pp. 189-191.

Whyte, William H. « The Web of Word of Mouth », *Fortune*, November, 1954, pp. 140 ff.

Wiebe, Gerhart D. « Mercandizing Commodities and Citizenship on Television », *POQ*. 15 (1951-52), Winter, no. 4; pp. 679-691.

Wilson, Francis G., « The Christian Conscience and Economic Growth, IV, No Alienation, No Failure », *Social Order*, 7 (1957), pp. 162-63.

Woolf, James D. « The More You Tell, The More You Sell », *Advertising Age*, February 10, 1958, p. 66.

Wright, David Mc Cord, « Associations, Morals and Growth », *Social Order*, 6 (1956), pp. 32-39.

— « The Christian Conscience and Economic Growth, VI, Faith is the Lost Factor », *Social Order*, 7 (1957), pp. 166-167.

Zeuthen, F., « Effect and Cost of Advertisement from a Theoretic Aspect », *Nordisk Tidsskrift for Teknisk Okonomi*, 1 (1935), pp. 62-72.

UNPUBLISHED MATERIALS AND MATERIALS
NOT AVAILABLE IN COMMERCE

American Association of Advertising Agencies, *29th Annual Meeting: Area 3, Ethics*, N. Y. 1947; 15 pp. mimeo.
— *30th Annual Meeting, Area of Ethics*, N. Y.: 1948; 12 pp.
— *31st Annual Meeting, Area of Ethics*, N. Y.: 1949; 20 pp.
— *32nd Annual Meetings, Area of Ethics*, N. Y.: 1950; 38 pp.
— *37th Annual Meeting, Group II*, N. Y.: 1955, 62 pp.
— *Interchange of Opinion on Objectional Advertising, 10th Anniversary Report, 1946-1956*, N. Y.: 1956; 13 pp.
Advertising Association (London) « Advertising, Expansion and Prosperity », *Notes For Speakers*, March 8, 1955, 13 pp.
— Advertising is Economical Communication, « *Notes for Speakers* », October 1954, 8 pp.
— « Advertising Pays for Itself », *Notes For Speakers*, no. 3, October 1954, 9 pp.
— « How Much Advertising is Economically Disputable? » *Notes for Speakers*, no. 11, December 1955, 11 pp.
— « Advertising, T. V. and Inflation », *Honest Answers to Awkward Questions*, Series 2, December 1955, 5 pp.
Bourgeois, Richard, *La publicité facteur du progrès économique et social.* Unpublished thesis: Institut supérieur commercial et consulaire, *Mons*, 1952-53, VII, 99 pp.
Brophy, Thomas D'Arcy, « The Role of Advertising in Our Economy », *Address to the Advertising Club of New Orleans*, June 5, 1956, 15 pp. mimeo.
Cone, Farifax M. *Advertising has a Bigger Job Ahead*, N. Y.: A.A.A.A., 1957; 31 pp. mimeo.
Duffy, Bernard C. « Some Examples of How Advertising has Increased the Standard of Living », in *Advertising to Raise the Standard of Living: Eight Addresses from the Fifth Annual Chicago Tribune Distribution and Advertising Forum*, May 18, 1954, pp. 24-27.
Gundell, Glen, « Advertising Must be Believable », in *Advertising to Raise the Standard of Living*, pp. 5-6. Mimeo. (*cf.* Duffy *supra*).
Henkel, Jost, *Die volkswirtschaftliche Bedeutung der Werbung*, Dissertation, Köln, 1934; 114 pp.
Johnson, Arno H. « The Job for Advertising in the Continuing Expansion of Our National Economy », in *37th Annual Meeting of the A.A.A.A. Group II*, N. Y.: 1955, pp. 1-28. mimeo.
Mortimer, Charles C. « Advertising an Integral Function of Business », *Highlights of a Speech at the Printers' Ink Annual Award Dinner*, February 13, 1957, n. pag.
Musewald, Alfred, *Die Reklame als volkswirtschaftliche Erscheinung*, Dissertation, Dortmund: Lücher, 1934, 96 pp.

Mc Keehan, William C. « If We as a People ... The Challenge to American Enterprise ». in *37th Annual Meeting of the A.A.A.A. Group II*, pp. 29-48. mimeo.

O'Brien, J. Chalmers, « Advertising's Job : To get People to Live it up », in *Advertising to Raise the Standard of Living*, pp. 11-12 (*cf. Duffy Supra*).

Partain, Lloyd E. « How Advertising Affects your Job », *Address to the Philadelphia Foreman's Club*, December 7, 1955, 8 pp. photocopy of manuscript.

Reed, Vergil D. « We Uncultured Americans », *Speech Given at 35th Annual Meeting of A.A.A.A.* White Sulphur Springs, West Virginia, April 24, 1953, 13 pp. Typescript.

Sänger, Oskar, *Werbung als dominanter Faktor des Absatzprozesses*, Dissertation, Freiburg im Breisgau, 1956, IV, 161, XII, pp. mimeo.

ADDITIONAL BIBLIOGRAPHY

Note : Since the completion of this thesis a considerable amount of material has appeared which will be useful for future students of the question. Though we have cited only a few of the pertinent articles, nearly every issue of both *Advertising Age* and *Printer's Ink* from November 1, 1959 on contains a large amount of material on the scandals which rocked the advertising world during the years 1959-1960.

BIBLIOGRAPHIES

Books for the Advertising and Marketing Man, Supplement N. Y. Advertising Federation of America, 1958; 16 pp.

A Short Bibliography of Marketing and Advertising Research, N. Y. Advertising Research Foundation, 1953; 28 pp.

Public Relations in Print, N. Y.: Public Relations Society of America: 1959; 7 pp.

Printers' Ink Articles on Results of Advertising, N. Y.: Printers' Ink, mimeo. (One of a series of P. I. bibliographies).

CODES AND COMMENTARIES

Interpretation of the A.A.A.A. Copy Code with respect to Television Commerciales, N. Y. A.A.A.A., 1960.

Self-Regulation in Advertising, N. Y. Association of National Advertisers, 1960; 68 pp.

Code of Ethics and Standards of Practice, N. Y.: International Advertising Association, 1955; 3 sections, mimeographed copy of preliminary work to be published in 1960.

The Television Code, Washington, D. C., The National Association of Broadcasters, 5th edition, 1959 with supplements.

Background Material : The Television Code of the N.A.B., 1958, 8 pp. mimeo.

BOOKS

Abelson, Herbert I, *Persuasion*: *How Opinion and Attitudes are Changed* N. Y. Springer Publishing Co, 1959; ix, 118 pp.

Bursk, Edward C., (ed.) *Business and Religion*, N. Y.: Harper and Brothers, 1959.

Dovring, Karin, *Road of Propaganda*: *The Semantics of Biased Communication*, N. Y.: Philosophical Library, 1959; 159 pp.

The Editors of Fortune, *Markets of the Sixties*, N. Y.: Harper and Bros. 1960; 266 pp.

Harris, Ralph and Arthur Seldon, *Advertising in a Free Society*, London: Institute of Economic Affairs, 1959; xiii, 213 pp.

Head, Sydney W., *Broadcasting in America*, Boston: Houghton Mifflin, 1956; 502 pp.

Hunter, Edward, *Brainwashing*, N. Y.: Farrar Straus and Cudahy, 1956.

Ross, Irwin, *The Image Merchants*, Garden City, N. Y.: Doubleday, 1959.

Steinberg, Charles S. *The Mass Communicators*, N. Y.: Harper Bros. 1958.

Taplin, Walter, *Advertising*: *A New Approach*, London: Hutchinson, 1960.

Tyler, Poyntz, (ed.) *Advertising in America*, N. Y.: Wilson, 1959.

PAMPHLETS

Finn, David, *Struggle for Ethics in Public Relations*, N. Y.: Ruder and Finn, 1959 (reprint from Harward Business Review).

— *The Social Consequences of Public Relations*, N. Y. Ruder and Finn, 1959.

Goldman, Eric F. *Broadcasting and Government Regulation*, Santa Barbara, Calif.: Center for the Study of Democratic Institutions, 1959.

Winick, Charles, *Taste and the Censor in Television*, N. Y.: Fund for the Republic, 1959.

ARTICLES

Garrett, Thomas M., « Publicità e progresso economico », *Aggiornamenti Sociali*, aprile 1960, pp. 221-230.

« A Program for Truth and Taste in Advertising », *Printers' Ink*, November 27, 1959, pp. 23-34; December 4, 1959; pp. 21-36; December 11, 1959, pp. 29-39; December 18, 1959, pp. 19-29.

UNPUBLISHED

Fisher, Thomas K, Statement before the subcommittee on communications and power of the House Committee on Interstate and Foreign Commerce, April 12, 1960, mimeo copy supplied by C.B.S.

Weil, Gilbert H., Legal Rules of the Road to Honest Advertising, mimeo copy from Association of National Advertisers, 1960.